*Perfect Days in*

# PRAGUE

www.marco-polo.com

# Contents

 **TOP 10**   4

**That Prague Feeling**   6

**9** **The Magazine**
- Magic & Mystery ■ The Tumultuous 20th Century
- Art Nouveau and Modern Architecture
- The Jewish Community ■ Defenestration
- A Musical Love Affair ■ The Best Beer in the World
- The Kafka Cult ■ Prague on Film

**35** **Finding Your Feet**
- First Two Hours
- Getting Around
- Accommodation
- Food and Drink
- Shopping
- Entertainment

**49** **Staré Město (Old Town)**
**Getting Your Bearings** ■ **The Perfect Day**
**TOP 10** ■ Karlův most ■ Staroměstské náměstí
**Don't Miss** ■ Kostel Panny Marie Před Týnem ■ Stavovské divadlo
**At Your Leisure** ■ More Places to Explore
**Where to...** ■ Eat and Drink ■ Shop ■ Go Out

**79** **Hradčany, Malá Strana and Beyond**
**Getting Your Bearings** ■ **Two Perfect Days**
**TOP 10** ■ Pražský hrad ■ Katedrála sv. Víta ■
Strahovský klášter ■ Zlatá ulička
**Don't Miss** ■ Zahrady ■ Malostranské náměstí
**At Your Leisure** ■ More Places to Explore
**Where to...** ■ Eat and Drink ■ Shop ■ Go Out

**117** **Josefov**
**Getting Your Bearings** ■ **The Perfect Day**
**TOP 10** ■ Starý židovský hřbitov
**Don't Miss** ■ Pinkasova synagoga ■ Staronová synagoga
**At Your Leisure** ■ More Places to Explore
**Where to...** ■ Eat and Drink ■ Shop ■ Go Out

## 139 New Town and Beyond
**Getting Your Bearings** ■ **The Perfect Day**
**TOP 10** ■ Vltava Embankment ■ Obecní dům
■ Václavské náměstí
**Don't Miss** ■ Muchově muzeu ■ Národní divadlo ■ Vyšehrad
**At Your Leisure** ■ More Places to Explore
**Where to...** ■ Eat and Drink ■ Shop ■ Go Out

## 169 Excursions
■ Kutná Hora
■ Mělník
■ Terezín

## 181 Walks
■ 1 On and Off the Royal Route
■ 2 Castle Hill
■ 3 Malá Strana

## Practicalities 193
■ Before You Go
■ When You are There
■ Useful Words and Phrases

## Street Atlas 201

## Street Index 211

## Index 215

## Picture Credits 218

## Credits 219

## 10 Reasons to Come Back Again 220

For chapters: See inside front cover

# TOP 10

**Not to be missed!**
**Our TOP 10 hits – from the absolute No. 1 to No. 10 –**
**help you plan your tour of the most important sights.**

### ⭐1 PRAŽSKÝ HRAD ➤ 84
The Hradčany dominates the horizon. Visible for miles around, this enclosed castle complex is the largest of its kind in the world.

### ⭐2 KARLŮV MOST ➤ 54
The Charles Bridge (pictured left), flanked by 30 statues of saints, ranks among the oldest bridges in Europe. Make time to walk across it, preferably more than once.

### ⭐3 KATEDRÁLA SV. VÍTA ➤ 90
One of the most magnificent examples of Gothic architecture towers 70m (230ft) over the city. Centuries in the making, this cathedral guards the mortal remains of Charles IV and St Václav (St Wenceslas).

### ⭐4 STAROMĚSTSKÉ NÁMĚSTÍ ➤ 58
Prague's Old Town Square boasts the famous Astronomical Clock, two imposing churches and impressive facades. This is the beating heart of the city.

### ⭐5 VLTAVA ➤ 144
A walk along the Vltava River from the National Theatre to the Dancing House provides a striking view of the glamorous Prague town houses – especially when the sun captures them in the right light.

### ⭐6 OBECNÍ DŮM ➤ 146
The Municipal House is the *Gesamtkunstwerk* of 30 artists and is regarded by many to be the most fascinating piece of Art Nouveau architecture in Prague. Take your time: there is plenty to admire!

### ⭐7 STRAHOVSKÝ KLÁŠTER ➤ 95
Though rather unprepossessing on the outside, the monastery contains not one but two of Europe's most beautiful libraries. The Philosophical Hall and the Theological Hall are worth a visit in their own right.

### ⭐8 ZLATÁ ULIČKA ➤ 98
Crouched in Golden Lane, the homes once inhabited by alchemists and poets look almost like doll's houses. Franz Kafka lived here for a while which is why this little street is so famous.

### ⭐9 STARÝ ŽIDOVSKÝ HŘBITOV ➤ 122
Around 100,000 people lay buried in the Old Jewish Cemetery. The stones on the graves are a sign of respect and love for the departed.

### ⭐10 VÁCLAVSKÉ NÁMĚSTÍ ➤ 148
Wenceslas Square is the city's main place of assembly and has seen many major demonstrations, mass rallies and attempted coups.

# THAT PRAGUE

**Experience the city's unique flair and find out what makes it tick. Just like the people of Prague.**

### LOOK DOWN OVER THE STARÉ MESTO

Just how small the Old Town really is can be best seen from a bird's-eye view high above the city. There are three ways to do this: from the east, from the **Powder Tower** (▶ 160), and from the west, from the **Old Town Bridge Tower** (▶ 55) as well as the **Old Town Hall Tower** (▶ 59), where from time to time visitors can also enjoy the performance of a trumpeter in historical dress.

### VISIT A COFFEE HOUSE

Prague has long since revived its legendary tradition of *Grand Cafés*. Guests once used to sit here for hours on end over a cup of coffee, studying the newspapers and magazines, and scribbling things down in their notebooks. No waiters charge up to a table with another menu or the bill unrequested. Highly recommended are: **Café Slavia** (▶ 162) or **Grand Café Orient** (▶ 76).

### CATCH A TRAM

Naturally, there are organised city tours that take in all the main highlights. Tram 22 does not do that, but from 32Kč you can travel right across the town with people who actually live in Prague. The tram starts off in the Vinohrady neighbourhood on the Náměstí Míru. Rumbling along the Národní Třída, it descends to the Vltava, the National Theatre and Café Slavia. Also en route: the Infant Jesus of Prague, the Church of St Nicholas, the Wallenstein Palace and Gardens as well as Strahov Monastery and Břevnov Monastery.

### TAKE A BOAT TRIP THROUGH PRAGUE

A wooden rowing boat offers a nice way to explore Prague from the "wild water" – the translation of *Vltava* – in a couple of hours. As you row along squinting in the bright sunshine, you are rewarded with a postcard panorama in 3D quality. If the physical exercise sounds too strenuous, there are steamer trips available leaving from the **Charles Bridge** (▶ 54) – choices ranging from small to large vessels, and with lunch or dinner aboard.

# FEELING

**View of the time-honoured Café Savoy**

# That Prague Feeling

Tip: the best trips include a trip along the **Devil's Channel** (▶ 107).

### DINE WITH STUDENTS

You will soon find yourself engrossed in a conversation when you go to the cafeteria at the Prague Art Academy. Lunch is inexpensive and you can chat to the students about everything ranging from art and politics to ice hockey and the new city hotspots. A choice of three different dishes is available on weekdays and the price is 70Kč. The entrance is on Malostranské Náměstí 13 (✚ 205 D3), opposite the Church of St Nicholas.

### DELVE INTO THE SPIGOT SCENE

They are loud, stink of cigarette smoke and in the taproom there are battered-looking wooden tables without tablecloths, and chairs without cushions. The *hospoda (pub)*, the *pivnice (beer halls)* and the *výčep (bar)* belong as much to Czech lifestyle as roast pork, dumplings and cabbage. Czech beer ranks among the best there is and remains by far the country's most popular drink. The most original beers are to be found in the small breweries such as Klášterní pivovar Strahov or Pivovarský Dům.

### GO TO AN ICE HOCKEY MATCH

Sports fans should try to catch an ice-hockey match. The supporters in the home country of six-time world champions and Olympic gold medallists of 1998 are both savvy and enthusiastic. In Prague there are two top *Extraliga* teams to choose from, Sparta and Slavia, plus the **O₂-Arena** (✚ 207 by F4), which holds up to 18,000 spectators and is the largest ice hockey hall in Europe.

### DANCE AND CHILL

The club and lounge scene in Prague forged strong ties with its western neighbours of Vienna and Munich long ago – and leading DJs often perform here. Yet the old haunts from student days, which have been around for decades, are also still going strong. Popular among these are the **Buddha Bar** (Jakubská 8, ✚ 206 B3) with its international sound and the **SaSaZu** (Bubenské nábřeží 306/13 ✚ 207 F5); at the weekend up to 2,500 people dance on several floors in the gigantic SaSaZu disco.

**Ice hockey fans will get their money's worth in Prague**

# The Magazin

| | |
|---|---|
| Magic & Mystery | 10 |
| The Tumultuous 20th Century | 14 |
| Art Nouveau and Modern Architecture | 18 |
| The Jewish Community | 21 |
| Defenestration | 24 |
| A Musical Love Affair | 26 |
| The Best Beer in the World | 30 |
| The Kafka Cult | 32 |
| Prague on Film | 34 |

The Magazine

# MAGIC & MYSTERY

Every great city has its myth – part truth, part imagination. Prague's myth is one of eternal magic and mystery. For centuries, the city was a haven for alchemists, astrologers, saints, martyrs and monsters.

### Rudolf II, Man of Wisdom and Woo-Woo

Five centuries ago, alchemy and astrology were regarded as hard sciences – as serious in their day as chemistry and astronomy are now. The man who brought to Prague this passion for turning base metals into gold and divining a man's fate from the stars was a young Habsburg emperor named Rudolf II.

**Sunset falls over the Church of St Francis, Old Town and Charles Bridge**

## The Magazine

Rudolf came here in 1576, at the age of 24, from the Habsburg court of Madrid. When he arrived, he spoke Spanish, German, Italian and Latin. He endeared himself to the people by also learning Czech. As an ardent patron of the arts, he accumulated in Prague one of Europe's finest collections of paintings. (Plundered during the Thirty Years War, almost all ended up in Stockholm, Dresden, Munich and Vienna.) But he also collected strange stuff, meticulously inventoried, like two nails from Noah's Ark, a magic gold-framed gallstone and a clump of the earth from which Adam was said to have been fashioned.

Philosophy and science were Rudolf's other passions. He discussed humanism with Italy's Giordano Bruno and the cosmos with Tycho Brahe from Denmark and Johannes Kepler from Germany. As court astronomers, Brahe completed a comprehensive study of the solar system and his disciple Kepler calculated the planets' elliptical orbits around the sun – both with astounding accuracy considering the telescope was not yet invented.

# The Magazine

**A view of the castle from Charles Bridge**

However, Rudolf also paid Brahe and Kepler to moonlight as alchemists and astrologers. They shared his belief in the fabled "Philosopher's Stone" that might bring gold and longevity, and in the influence of the stars on man's destiny. Also in town at the time was English mathematician John Dee, who dabbled in alchemy and performed magic tricks at Prague Castle. He fell in with fellow countryman Edward Kelley, a scoundrel who wasted no time on a day job in "serious" science. Together, they fleeced Rudolf and his courtiers until Dee was called home to read the stars for Elizabeth I, and Kelley, whose run-ins with the law had already cost him two ears and a leg, took poison rather than go back to jail.

As if to give alchemy a helping hand, Praguers to this day seem to want to stick the "golden" label on everything they can, starting with the city itself, long known as Zlatá Praha (Golden Prague). One of Prague's most venerable pubs is U Zlatého tygra (Golden Tiger). It vies for attention with the Golden Pear, Anchor, Star, Fox, Mouse and Serpent.

## The Golem

Another essential figure in Prague's magic aura is the golem. It wasn't enough for some followers of Rabbi Loew – a 16th-century contemporary of Rudolf's – that the rabbi was the great sage of the city's Jewish community. Despite Rabbi Loew's lifelong rejection of such esoteric nonsense, his followers sought to endow him with the mystic powers of a pious Frankenstein who infused human life into a statue of clay – known as the golem.

# The Magazine

**Prague's main artery: the Vltava in the twilight**

The word "golem" appears in the Bible (Psalms 139, verse 16) meaning "unshaped flesh" (in modern Hebrew "raw material"). Jewish mystics applied it to a creature whose legend dates back at least to the 12th century, when ritual gestures and Hebrew letters were combined to perform the miracle of bringing the statue to life. Rabbi Loew, said his followers, knew the combination, the *shem*, which he wrote on a scroll and put in the creature's mouth. Writer Franz Klutschak and later Gustav Meyrink, neither of them Jewish, depicted the golem as Loew's assistant. Neglected while Loew tends to his sick daughter, the golem runs amok until the rabbi performs an appropriate ritual to calm him down. Today, theatre troupes put on golem shows for tourists.

### GOING FOR BAROQUE
Many of the city's baroque monuments have been associated with mystic powers in the Catholics' 17th- and 18th-century campaign to revitalize the faith in Bohemia. In St Vitus Cathedral (▶ 94), the tomb of St John of Nepomuk was long proclaimed to contain the medieval martyr's still-pulsating tongue. Pilgrims continue to flock to the Loreta sanctuary's replica of the Virgin Mary's home (▶ 109).

In the Our Lady of Victory Church (▶ 107), thousands seek to have prayers answered and illnesses healed by the Infant Jesus of Prague (Pražské Jezulátko), whose statue is venerated here.

# The Magazine

# THE TUMULTUOUS 20th CENTURY

**It would take a graduate degree in history to understand the ups and downs of the 20th century here, but a little knowledge of recent history is necessary to fully grasp the city and its people.**

What began promisingly enough in 1918, with the declaration of an independent Czechoslovak state from the ruins of the Austro-Hungarian empire, ran into disaster two decades later with the Nazi occupation. The Germans stayed until their capitulation in 1945. But in 1948, Czech communists – backed by the Soviet Union – declared a coup. The dark years of communist occupation lasted four decades. It wasn't until the eve of the century's last decade – in 1989 – that the clock turned back full circle, with the country's independence again.

## First The Good News: 1918 and the First Republic

For 300 years, Bohemia had been a backwater of the Austro-Hungarian Empire. Even prosperous Prague was relegated to third place among the empire's cities – behind the capital Vienna, and Budapest.

The clamour for Czech independence began in the 19th century with the revival of the Czech language. Czech had been all but replaced by German under the Habsburgs, but the 1800s saw a reawakening of Czech literature, poetry and drama – and even the construction of a Czech-language theatre, the Národní divadlo (➤ 153) in 1881.

In 1914, the start of World War I saw the Czechs reluctantly enter the war on the side of Austria-Hungary and its ally, Germany. But already there were plans under way by the Czechs to use the war as a way of breaking free of the empire and leading politicians – such as future president Tomáš Masaryk – were dispatched to the United States to build support for an independent Czechoslovakia after the war.

Masaryk and his entourage successfully united America's large population of ethnic Czechs and Slovaks and the group won the crucial

# The Magazine

German troops rode into Prague unchallenged

support of American president Woodrow Wilson. In 1918, with the defeat of Germany, the Austro-Hungarian Empire imploded. With Wilson's backing and Masaryk's leadership, an independent Czechoslovakia was declared.

In retrospect, the years 1918–1938, the First Republic, are seen as that rarest of Golden Ages – a time of political and cultural rebirth and economic prosperity. While much of the world suffered after the stock market crash of 1929, and times were lean here too, Czechoslovakia clawed its way to be one of the world's 10 richest nations.

## World War II and the Nazi Occupation

However, life was never going to be easy for the new Czechoslovakia, sitting between Hitler's Germany and Stalin's Soviet Union. Hitler had never forgiven the Allied powers for disarming and dismembering the German Empire at the end of World War I and had made annexing the Czechs a priority in his quest to acquire territories in the east.

Hitler was able to occupy the country without a shot fired thanks to an agreement in Munich in September 1938. It was here that British Prime Minister Neville Chamberlain granted Hitler his wish to occupy the Czech border regions in exchange for a promise Hitler would go no further. Chamberlain thought he had achieved "peace for our time", but Hitler had no intention of stopping. Overmatched Czechoslovak soldiers held their fire as the Germans rode in on tanks in March 1939.

Czechs are often criticized for their seeming passivity during World War II. In fact, the war years here were no picnic. The Nazi governor of the Protectorate of Bohemia and Moravia, Reinhard Heydrich, was a vicious man who executed thousands of potential resisters, closed

# The Magazine

**Warsaw Pact tanks crushed the so-called Prague Spring**

schools of higher education and sent tens of thousands of Jews to the concentration camp at Terezín (Theresienstadt, ▶ 178).

The high point of the Czechs' anti-Nazi resistance came in May 1942 when a small group of Czech patriots, brought in from London, succeeded in assassinating Heydrich by bombing his motorcade. The resistance fighters were later found hiding in the church of SS Cyril and Methodius on Resslova Ulice and executed – the bullet scars from the shoot-out can still be seen ✚ 209 D4). German reprisals were horrific: thousands were executed, the villages of Lidice and Ležáky were wiped out and mass deportations took place.

The Czechs eventually rose up against their oppressors in the final days of the war in May 1945. By that time the Soviet Red Army had reached the outskirts of the city and the US Army was nearby, in the city of Plzeň. Around the area, you'll still see hundreds of plaques denoting where Prague citizens fell defending the city.

## From Hitler to Stalin

The end of World War II brought another period of brief respite to the city. But unlike during the First Republic, there would be no enduring democracy and precious little cultural rebirth.

By the cruel fate of the Yalta agreement, the new Czechoslovakia found itself on the other side of the Iron Curtain. The first free elections,

# The Magazine

in 1946, saw the Communists win a plurality of the votes among war-weary Czechs. In February 1948, with the backing of Stalin's Soviet Union, the Communists took power in a bloodless coup.

## The Prague Spring

Two decades of political repression followed. Then, during the "Prague Spring" of 1968, newly installed First Secretary of the KSČ Alexander Dubček famously promised "Socialism with a Human Face", encouraging many to believe that Communism really could be reformed from within. But the party's old guard turned to the Kremlin for support and in August the Soviet Union led an invasion of Warsaw Pact forces. As the tanks rolled into Prague, Dubček was flown to Moscow in handcuffs and eventually demoted. Under the new policy of "normalization" the hardliners returned Czechoslovakia to the Soviet orbit and, for the next 20 years, ran the country as a police state. But their days were numbered; the economies of Eastern Europe were stagnating and by the late-1980s even the Soviet leader, Mikhail Gorbachev, was coming to realize that political as well as economic change was inevitable.

> "It was a fairy-tale ending to a dramatic display of non-violent people power"

Looking back on 40 years of Communism it's hard to see it as anything other than an unmitigated disaster, and the modest advances in health care and literacy are overshadowed by the destruction of the economy and the environment, and by restrictions on travel and individual repression.

## Velvet Revolution

The year 1989 will always be remembered in history books as the year freedom came to Eastern Europe. In September, 4000 DDR citizens sought refuge in the West German embassy in Prague.

The Czechs were among the last to revolt – in the final weeks of November of that year. The Czech police made the mistake of halting a relatively small group of student protesters on 17 November at a point on Národní třída (National Avenue). News of the police action and rumours (later proved untrue) that one of the students had died managed to move nearly the entire population to revolt. Within days, Václavské náměstí (Wenceslas Square) was filled with thousands of ordinary citizens demanding that the Communists step down.

By the end of the year, the Communists had capitulated and a mild-mannered dissident-playwright named Václav Havel had been proclaimed president. It was a fairy-tale ending to a dramatic display of non-violent people power.

Today, Czechs look back on the Velvet Revolution as the moment when their country was reborn as a nation, and freed at last from foreign domination.

## The Magazine
# ART NOUVEAU
## AND MODERN ARCHITECTURE

**Prague's history is written in its buildings. Many visitors think the story begins and ends with Gothic, Renaissance and baroque, but there's much more. Some of Prague's most exciting architecture is from the late 19th and the early 20th century – in the "modern" styles of Art Nouveau, Cubism and Functionalism.**

By the early 19th century, historicism was taking hold in many parts of Europe. This architectural movement took its inspiration from past artistic styles, recreating them in combination with new ideas. Prague architects at the time took their cue from Vienna, where a doctrinaire version of classicism – neo-classicism – held sway. Prague today is filled with block after block of these plain but handsome 19th-century buildings. This neo-classicism later gave way to a mix of historical "neo" styles – a kind of 19th-century retro movement that saw the emergence of neo-Renaissance and, especially in Prague, neo-Gothic. Many, if not most, of the spires that dominate the Prague skyline date not from the 14th or 15th centuries but from the neo-Gothic frenzy of the last half of the 19th century.

### Art Nouveau Brings Fresh Air
The turn of the 20th century brought much-needed fresh air to the city's architecture. Art Nouveau, with its seductive curves imported from Paris and its sparer Viennese cousin – Secession – both made a major impact here. The Obecní dům (Municipal House, ➤ 146 is usually regarded as the finest example of this architectural period, but be sure to check out the Hotel Paříž around the corner at U Obecního Domu 1.

### Cubist Paintings You Can Walk Into
The early decades of the 20th century brought more experimentation in the form of Cubist architecture – a uniquely Czech phenomenon that prized playful geometric designs. The House of the Black Madonna (➤ 70), is considered the best example in the city centre, while just below Vyšehrad Castle there is a row of rare Cubist houses that form the greatest concentration of this style anywhere in the world (➤ 157).

**Art Nouveau stained glass in the cafe of the Municipal House**

# The Magazine

# The Magazine

**Ramble through a history book of European architecture: Karlova Street**

## Stripping Away the Decoration

In the 1920s and early 1930s a new minimalist, functionalist aesthetic took hold, inspired by the Bauhaus school in Germany. Functionalism was all the rage, as young architects worked to strip away any unnecessary design. Most of the functionalist buildings in Prague took the form of private villas on the outskirts of town. One of the best of these, the Vila Müller (Nad Hradním vodojemem 14, Prague 6; www.mullerovavila.cz) by Adolf Loos, is open to the public. The Bat'a shoe store at Václavské náměstí 6 is a good example of functionalism in a downtown setting.

## Communist Kitsch

At the end of World War II and through to the mid-1980s, Prague experienced a building boom. In the early decades of communism, local architects took pains to emulate what was happening in the Soviet Union, where "Socialist Realism" was the official line. The best Socialist Realist building is the former Hotel International – now the Crowne Plaza hotel (Koulová 15, Prague 6). Communist style evolved in the 1960s and 1970s, inspired in part by the Brussels 1958 World Expo. Two department stores in central Prague, Kotva (Náměstí Republiky 8) and Tesco (Národní třída 26), are good examples of 1970s Brutalist design. The immense Žižkov TV tower (➤ 164) is way out of proportion to the setting and the city and a pure example of 1980s communist kitsch.

**The Magazine**

# THE JEWISH community

**Although Prague's Jewish community may now number just a few hundred, Jewish people have been a vibrant part of the city for more than a millennium and form an inseparable part of the city's fabric.**

Early written records of the Jewish presence here date to around AD965, when diaries from a Spanish traveller report them selling tin, furs and slaves. The earliest Jewish inhabitants settled in Malá Strana at the foot of Prague Castle. They later accompanied Vratislav II across the river when he moved to a new castle at Vyšehrad and crossed back again when the court returned to Hradčany. Between times, they traded wheat, wool, cattle and horses for silks, jewels, gold, wine and Oriental spices. Business was good.

## Early Pogroms

The First Crusade (1095) put a stop to the good times. The early Christian crusaders were violently anti-Semitic and their pogroms eventually spread to Prague. To escape the plunder, forced baptism and killing, the Jews tried to leave town. The rulers replied by confiscating their property.

In the 13th century, the Jews resettled on the right bank of the Vltava in the area now called Josefov – which a papal decree turned into a ghetto in the late Middle Ages (it still contains the most important sights associated with Prague's Jewish history).

Down through the centuries, the monarchs alternately protected and plundered Jewish property according to the needs of the royal treasury. In the worst of the medieval pogroms, in 1389, mobs urged on by fanatical priests massacred more than 3,000 Jewish men,

**Emblem of the Josefov Staronová synagoga**

# The Magazine

women and children. In the next century, Hussite reformist street battles against the Catholic establishment habitually ended with a raid on the Jewish Quarter. The Hussites' fights for religious freedom had not overcome the centuries-old anti-Semitism of the people.

## Peace and Prosperity

But there were peaceful and prosperous times as well. The last half of the 16th century and the early 17th century ushered in an era of achievement for the Jewish community. Emperor Rudolf II sought to forge close ties with the Jews. Practically all of his cherished goldsmiths were Jewish. Two men stand out: Mordechai Maisel and Rabbi Loew. Maisel was financier to the emperor and mayor of the Jews, who personally paid to pave streets and build housing, a hospital, schools, synagogues and the Jewish Town Hall. Loew was the community's outstanding spiritual leader and a scholar of unbending integrity who scorned the occultist mysticism and magic that later myth-makers associated with his name (▶ 12). Both are buried in the Old Jewish Cemetery (▶ 122).

## Beginning of the End

In the late 18th century, the character of the Jewish ghetto began to change. In 1781, Emperor Joseph II issued the Edict of Tolerance, which would eventually allow Prague's Jews to leave the ghetto and live where they wanted. As incomes rose in the 19th century, many Jewish families

**Ancient gravestones in the old Jewish cemetery in Prague**

## The Magazine

sought to make their fortunes elsewhere in the city or around the Austro-Hungarian Empire. By the end of the century, the Jewish Ghetto had become a "ghetto" in the modern sense of the word – it was squalid, poor and crime-ridden.

In an early example of an urban redevelopment – and not anti-Semitism – Prague city authorities chose to raze the ghetto, leaving only a handful of synagogues, the Old Jewish Cemetery and the Jewish Town Hall – essentially what remains today. In place of the former ghetto, developers built the beautiful Art Nouveau and Secession-style town houses you see today – hence the irony of the former Jewish Ghetto being one of the most prosperous-looking neighbourhoods in the city.

Horror befell Prague's Jews in the 20th century with the Nazi occupation. Though not many Jews were living in Josefov at that time, Jews from around the city were rounded up and transported to the concentration camp at Terezín (▶ 178). Many were later transferred to Auschwitz to be executed. Some 45,000 Prague Jews were eventually deported to the camps. After the war, only a few thousand were left to continue the 10 centuries of Jewish history here.

In one of history's supreme ironies, Hitler had planned to form a museum to the "extinct race of the Jews" in Prague and had much of the plundered Jewish property and religious artefacts from around Central Europe transported here. The Prague Jewish Museum's holdings are vast – largely and tragically due to Hitler's diabolical vision.

**Chandeliers illuminate the altar in the Staronová synagoga**

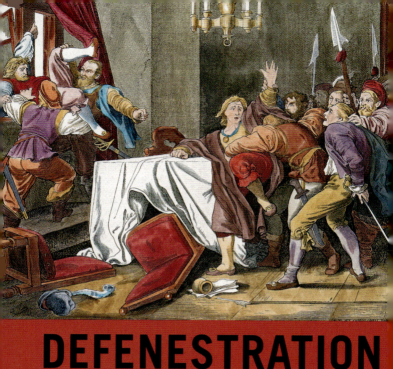

# DEFENESTRATION

**Being thrown or jumping out of a window has for centuries been a peculiarly Prague way of dying. Defenestration has launched riots and pogroms and even sparked a war.**

The prototype began on a Sunday morning in July 1419, following a sermon by fiery Protestant preacher Jan Želivský. Anti-Catholic feeling was still running high four years after Reformist Protestant leader Jan Hus was burned at the stake as a heretic by a Catholic Church Council.

## Pikes and Lances

Catholics and Hussites, at the time, were engaged in a violent doctrinal battle over Communion rites. A major tenet of the Hussite creed was to give Communion to all believers, not just the clergy. Following Hus's execution by order of the Council of Constance 1415, Catholic priests had expropriated Hussite churches and "purified" them by scrubbing down altars "profaned" by the disputed communion practices. For Želivský, it was time to take action. He led his congregation to Nové Město's town hall. Breaking into the council chamber, the Hussites seized the intractable

**Above: Bohemian protestants throw royal officials from the palace windows**

mayor and a dozen aldermen and hurled them out of the window. Those not impaled on the crowd's pikes and lances were clubbed to death. The rebels then ransacked Catholic churches and rampaged through the Jewish Quarter.

## Onto the Dunghill

The most famous (second) Defenestration earned its capital "D" on 23 May 1618, a day of farce that ended in horror. Two radical Protestants, preacher Václav Budova and Count Matthias Thurn, were enraged by the Bohemian King Ferdinand II's refusal to end what the men saw as pro-Catholic discrimination. The two men led a group of Protestant parliamentarians to the castle's Bohemian Chancellery to confront Catholic governors Vilém Slavata and Jaroslav Borzita of Martinice. Cutting short all efforts to talk, Thurn and his men grabbed the two governors – along with an unlucky secretary – and threw them out of the window.

For a change, the victims had a safe landing: on a pile of horse dung, said Protestants; on the Virgin Mary's cloak, said Catholics. Less amusing were the raids on the Jewish Quarter and monasteries in which monks were killed. Worse still, the violence escalated into a revolt that sparked the Thirty Years War.

## Pushed or Jumped?

A third tragic Defenestration occurred in more recent times – though it's unclear whether the victim jumped or was pushed. In March 1948, just two weeks after the Communist coup d'etat, foreign minister Jan Masaryk (son of the founding President) fell to his death from a window in the Černín palace. Masaryk was the only non-Communist in the government at the time and was said to be despondent over the coup. His friends maintained he would not have taken his own life.

**An obelisk commemorating the Defenestration**

## The Magazine

# A musical LOVE AFFAIR

From the world premiere of arguably Mozart's greatest opera to a president who was friends with rock stars like Frank Zappa and the Rolling Stones, Prague has always loved music. Everywhere you go there are fliers for classical concerts, chamber music, jazz sessions, rock and techno.

### *Figaro* Here, *Don Giovanni* There

Not until the Czechs' nationalist movement got into top gear in the 19th century did their own great classical composers, Bedřich Smetana and Antonín Dvořák, make their mark on the European scene. Before them, Wolfgang Amadeus Mozart could have told them what terrific taste Prague had in things musical. In 1786, Vienna had given his *Marriage of Figaro* premiere at best a lukewarm reception. It closed after just nine performances. The Prague production later the same year got rave reviews. Wolfgang was brought to town for four weeks in January 1787 and found, as he wrote in a letter: "The talk here is about nothing but *Figaro*. Nothing is played, sung or whistled but *Figaro*." At a ball he attended, he observed with delight that the music had been pirated for quadrilles and waltzes. He conducted the opera himself and presented a new orchestral work, now known as the *Prague Symphony*.

Before he left, Mozart was commissioned to write the possibly most ambitious of all his operas, *Don Giovanni*. He came back nine months later to complete it, invited by pianist František Dušek to work at his Villa Bertramka. Typically, he completed the overture one day before its world premiere. On 29 October, 1787, at what is now the Stavovské divadlo (Estates Theatre, ▶ 65), Wolfgang of course arrived late to conduct the orchestra. The reception by the public and press was rapturous. Again, the Viennese reaction was cooler, but, as Mozart told

# The Magazine

**This piano once belonged to Antonín Dvořák**

his friends: *"Meine Prager verstehen mich"* ("My Prague people understand me").

Four years later, just three days after his death and burial in an anonymous grave in Vienna, hundreds of his admirers in Prague attended a memorial service at the Church of St Nicholas (▶ 105) in Malá Strana, where he had himself played the organ. It seems appropriate that Miloš Forman shot his Oscar-winning film *Amadeus* not in Vienna but in the streets of Prague.

## Bedřich Smetana and Antonín Dvořák

Music has always played a patriotic role in Czech life. Prague's two main opera houses make the point. "Národ sobě" ("The Nation For Itself") is written in gold over the arch of the Národní divadlo (National Theatre, ▶ 153) while the facade of the Stavovské divadlo (Estates Theatre, ▶ 65) proclaims "*Patriae et Musis*" ("To Fatherland and the Muses").

Not that composer Bedřich Smetana (1824–84) needed any prompting. His most overtly patriotic opera, *Libuše*, solemnly portraying the nation's

# The Magazine

**A chamber music concert in the Mozart Museum in Villa Bertramka**

legendary foundation by a mythic princess, premiered at the opening of the new National Theatre in 1881 (▶156). His best-known works, the romantic opera *Prodaná nevěsta (The Bartered Bride)* and symphonic poem *Má vlast (My Country)*, are joyous paeans to the Czech landscape and country life. See ▶66 for details of the Smetana Museum.

The gloriously melodic Antonín Dvořák (1841–1904) was the first Czech composer to gain an international reputation. Though less explicitly nationalist than Smetana's work, his music never lost its unmistakably fresh Czech quality. His *New World Symphony*, which he wrote in 1893 while directing the Conservatory of Music in New York, may show gospel and other American influences, but Prague music-lovers point to its equally strong Bohemian folk themes. These are even more apparent in Dvořák's *Slavonic Dances* and his opera *Rusalka*. To find out more about the composer visit the Dvořák Museum in Vila Amerika (Ke Karlovu 20, Prague 2, Nové Město, tel: 224 918 013; www.nm.cz, open Oct–Mar Tue–Sun 10–1:30, 2–5; Apr–Sep Tue, Wed, Fri–Sun 10–1:30, 2–5; Thu 11–3:30; 4–7. Metro I.P. Pavlova; tram 4, 10, 16, 22; 50Kč).

# The Magazine

**WHERE TO HEAR MUSIC**
Apart from the places mentioned in this article, you can also hear live music from a wide range of genres at:
- **AghaRTA** – reliable venue for live jazz (▶78; www.agharta.cz).
- **Jazz Boat** – enjoy the view of the river while listening to sets by leading Czech musicians over dinner (more information from www.jazzboat.cz or tel: 731 183 180).
- **Liechtenstein Palace** – home to the Prague Chamber Ensemble (▶104. Tickets tel: 603 296 327).
- **Lobkovický Palace** – daily lunchtime (1pm) concerts in superb baroque surroundings (▶106).
- **Klementinum Mirror Chapel** – regular organ concerts and recitals (▶67; Jan–March 5pm, April–Oct 6pm;. For schedules and ticket reservations www.klementinum.com).
- **Municipal House** – Symphony concerts take place in the Smetana Hall (▶147), but there are also jazz nights in the American Bar (tel: 222 002 101 or www.obecnidum.cz).
- **Rock Café** – Czech rock bands and solo artists perform regularly at this well-established club, often with free admission (Narodní 20, tel: 224 933 947 or www.rockcafe.cz ).
- **St Lawrence Church** – chamber recitals are given in the restored 10th century chapel (Hellichova 18, Malá Strana – tickets at the door (tel: 776 223 232).
- **Spanish Synagogue** – concerts on Jewish themes, everything from Gershwin to selections from Klezmer and Jewish folklore music (▶133; for schedules and ticket information see www.jewishmuseum.cz).

## Walking on the Wild Side

Not the least of President Václav Havel's early appeal to his free-spirited supporters was his taste for jazz and rock. In the leaden years of Communist rule, this music was part of the dissidents' culture. They liked in particular Frank Zappa's blend of rock, rhythm and blues. In 1968, when the Prague Spring revolt was crushed by Soviet tanks, they heard his 1967 album titled *Absolutely Free*. And 23 years later, Zappa played at a concert in Prague Castle, celebrating the departure of Soviet forces. Other guests at the castle were Lou Reed and Mick Jagger, brought there by one of Václav Havel's top advisers, and the Czech rock star Michael Kocáb.

In the years since the Velvet Revolution, the Czech music scene has developed and fragmented in much the same way as in Western Europe and the US, with major sub-genres clustered around the familiar poles of rap, hip hop, pop, rock, R&B and techno. There's even been a softening of attitudes toward Communist-era "oldies" – and 1970s crooners like Karel Gott and Helena Vondráčková enjoy enduring popularity. And that's the great thing about music here: There's a club and a scene for just about whatever style of music you are looking for.

The Magazine

# The BEST BEER in the world

**The rich flavour and deep amber colour of Czech beer are, Czechs insist, unique, despite the many attempts to copy them.**

### How It Started
The Bohemian brewers were fermenting malt, water and hops to produce "liquid bread" more than 1,000 years ago. Their rulers, too, took a keen interest – Charles IV forbade the export of local hops while Rudolf II even bought the Krušovice brewery to ensure a steady supply to one of his private estates. By the 19th century there were more than 60 independent breweries in Prague alone. Today, many have been swallowed up by international conglomerates but Czechs are discerning drinkers and standards remain high.

### Cream of the Crop
Pilsner Urquell (Plzeňský Prazdroj in Czech) has been produced in the industrial town of Plzeň, southwest of Prague, since 1842. It is made with top quality Saaz hops and the famously soft local water – a key ingredient. Its most famous rival is Budweiser Budvar. This mild, sweet-

**PUB TALK**

| | |
|---|---|
| *Pivo, prosím* | a beer, please |
| *Velké pivo* | large beer (0.5l) |
| *Malé pivo* | small beer (0.3l) |
| *Světlé* | light |
| *Tmavé* | dark |
| *Na zdravy* | cheers! |
| *Zaplatime, prosím* | We'd like to pay, please |

# The Magazine

### FAMOUS PIVNICES

- U Fleků (➤ 166). A pub with a 500-year history, a beer museum (guided tour reservations: www.ufleku.cz or tel 224 934 019/20) and its own dark beer. Ask for Flek.
- U Medvídků (➤ 75). Another famous pub, where the beer is served from high-pressure steel tanks to maximize flavour.
- Potrefená husa (➤ 136). A pub chain serving three types of beer produced by the Prague brewery, Staropramen, including the dark, sweetish Granát.

**Above: U Fleků offers rustic flair; Left: Old beer poster in Plzeň**

- Pivovarský dům ("Brewery House"; ➤ 166). This microbrewery offers beers with exotic flavours like banana, sour cherry and coffee.
- Kláštení pivovar on the grounds of Strahov Monastery (➤ 95, 114). St Norbert dark beer is sold from the brewery.

ish brew hails from the southern town of České Budějovice and is unrelated to American "Bud". If you see the goat emblem on a pub sign, you're set to sample the popular light and tangy bitter, Velkopopovický kozel. Drunk in draughts as long as its name, it's made by the Velké Popovice brewery located to the southeast of Prague.

## What to Expect

Many of Prague's oldest and best known pubs (*pivnice*) have been given a makeover to appeal to tourists. Most now serve food and some have designated non-smoking areas or at least tables. In summer, beer gardens are popular – one of the best is in Letenské Sady (Letná Gardens), approached from the steps at the Čechův Bridge (tram 12, 17). The traditional *pivnice* serves several varieties of beer from the one brewery. Waiters come to you and keep a paper tally of what you are eating and drinking. When you're done, call one of them over or take the paper chit to the bar yourself. Czech customers expect refills to arrive at the table without asking – if you don't want that extra beer, hand the drink back. Incidentally, the percentage figures shown prominently on bottle labels (10, 12, etc) refer to the malt content, although beers with a higher figure tend to have slightly higher alcohol levels too.

**In the Franz Kafka Society of Prague bookshop**

# THE KAFKA CULT

**"Prague doesn't let go – this little mother has claws." Franz Kafka's love-hate relationship with the city of his birth is well attested but it left an indelible impression on one of the most influential writers of the twentieth century.**

### Close to home
Kafka was to spend much of the first half of his life within walking distance of Old Town Square. He was born in 1883 in a house on what is now náměstí Franze Kafky, and his father owned a haberdasher's shop at Staroměstské náměstí 8. He was educated at local schools and the Karolinum (► 70).

### Kafkaesque
After graduating from law school Franz went to work in an insurance office on Wenceslas Square (► 148). Though a conscientious employee, his fantastic imagination was ill-suited to the role of pen-pushing bureaucrat and he spent every spare moment working on the novels that would make him famous. In his writings Franz transfers his frustration with the humdrum world of the office to characters who are constantly thwarted by sinister

# The Magazine

Franz Kafka on Old Town Square c1922

authority figures. In *The Castle* the hero "K" is repeatedly refused access to a castle where he has been appointed to work as a minor official. Josef K, the protagonist of Kafka's best known novel, *The Trial*, is arrested and threatened with dire punishment, yet the charges he faces are never specified. The bewildering, not to say unfathomably menacing world Franz creates is so powerful that it has given the English language an adjective – 'Kafkaesque'.

### *Metamorphosis*
Kafka's short stories are for many his finest work. The most famous is *Metamorphosis*, about a fictitious person Gregor Samsa who wakes up one morning to discover he has turned into a giant insect and is ultimately rejected by his family. Since it was first published in 1915, this single idea has inspired stage adaptations, movies, animated films, an opera, an episode of *The Simpsons* and several video games.

## Cage in Search of a Bird
In the end Prague reluctantly let go its claws but the circumstances were tragic. In 1917 Franz was diagnosed with tuberculosis after suffering a massive haemorrhage. He retired from the civil service and spent the rest of his life in sanatoriums. He died in 1924. His grave in Prague's New Jewish cemetery is now a place of pilgrimage for lovers of literature the world over.

The exhibition at the Franz Kafka Museum (Muzeum Franze Kafky; ▶ 107) has a rather lugubrious tone but is still worth a visit, especially for Kafka fans. Exhibits include first editions by the novelist.

---

### FATHER FIGURE
Franz's relationship with his father (pictured right) was troubled, to say the least. His lasting memory of Hermann Kafka, a self-made man who began life as a travelling salesman, was of a tyrannical bully, bawling at the assistants in his shop. In his 1912 story *The Judgement*, a father turns on his son, covers him with insults and reproaches and eventually "sentences him to death" by drowning.

## The Magazine
# PRAGUE **ON FILM**

**From the left: Open staircase, National Museum; Charles Bridge; Malá Strana**

**If, when visiting Prague for the first time, you feel that you've seen the Charles Bridge, the Rudolfinum or the Strahov monastery somewhere before, the chances are you're right.**

### Leading Role
It was the émigré Czech director, Miloš Forman who gave the ailing Barrandov Studios a new lease of life with the making of *Amadeus* in 1984. His movie, based on the life of the great Austrian composer and filmed on location in the Estates Theatre, was to pave the way for many more international movies including *Mission Impossible, Oliver Twist, The Chronicles of Narnia, The Bourne Identity, The Omen* and *Casino Royale.* Prague not only stars as itself but regularly stands in for other major cities.

### Pulling Power
What attracts film-makers to the city? The stunning locations aside, it's a question of hard-nosed economics. Competitive labour and production costs, tax incentives and other inducements can mean savings of up to 40 per cent over shooting a movie in other European or American cities. Other pluses include some of the best studio facilities in Europe, the professional savvy of Czech production crews and the fact that many movie stars find Prague a fun place to be in off camera as well as on.

### Find Out More
Pick up the English-language brochure and map *Lights! Camera! Action!* issued by the Czech Film Commission and available free of charge from tourist information offices. It plots nearly 50 locations featured in the movies mentioned above and many more besides. Also check out the websites www.filmcommission.cz and www.barrandov.cz.

# Finding Your Feet

| | |
|---|---|
| First Two Hours | 36 |
| Getting Around | 37 |
| Accommodation | 40 |
| Food and Drink | 44 |
| Shopping | 46 |
| Entertainment | 47 |

Finding Your Feet

# First Two Hours

## Arriving by Air
- **Ruzyně Airport** (tel: 220 111 888; www.csl.cz/en) ATM cash dispensers, exchange facilities, car-rental and hotel-booking agencies and free WiFi connection available 24/7 from both terminals.

## Getting into Town
The airport is nearly 20km (12mi) northwest of the city centre, and whether you choose taxi, express minibus or a combination of bus and underground train, expect between 30 and 50 minutes to get to your hotel.
- **Taxis** Reputable companies with English-speaking operators include **AAA** (tel: 222 333 222) and **Airport Cars** (tel: 220 113 892). Beware the silver Mercedes taxis at the kerbs, they have a reputation for overcharging. A ride into the centre should cost around 600Kč. Insist that the driver run the meter and tell the driver you will need a receipt.
- **Čedaz** white **mini-buses** are parked outside the arrivals hall and operate 7:30am–7pm. Tickets from the Čedaz information desk in the arrivals hall cost 150Kč. The bus will take a party of up to four directly to their hotel in Prague for ca. 500Kč. Parties of 5–8 people cost ca. 1000Kč.
- **Insider Tip**: The best way to get into the centre of town is to take a **City bus** or the **Metro** (underground). Exit the arrivals hall and locate bus 119. Buy a 32Kč ticket (coins required) from the yellow ticket machine; you will need two tickets if you are carrying a lot of luggage. The bus ends at Dejvická Metro station, transfer to the A-line (green) on the same ticket for the city centre.

## Arriving by Train
- **Hlavní nádraží**, Wilsonova Boulevard, is Prague's main railway station for the overnight train from London – via Brussels and Cologne (information: tel: 221 111 122; www.cdrail.cz). International trains also arrive at **Nádraží Holešovice** – but watch out for unscrupulous taxi drivers.
- **Hlavní nádraží** has restaurants, food kiosks, ATM cash-dispensers, exchange facilities, a tourist information office and hotel-booking agency, plus a 24-hour left-luggage office. It is only a few minutes' walk from **Václavské náměstí**. Its Metro stations, Můstek and Muzeum, are on the A-line (green).

## Arriving by Bus
- **Florenc**, Křižikova Boulevard, is the main bus station for international buses, on the east side of town.
- It has few amenities apart from a 24-hour left-luggage office, but the adjacent **Florenc B- and C-line Metro station** takes you quickly into the city centre. For bus and train timetables visit: www.idos.cz

## Tourist Information Offices
- The **PIS** (Pražska informační služba – Prague Information Office, www.pis.cz/en) has information on attractions, opening times, a ticket agency and English-speaking personal guides, as well as free maps of the city centre and public transport routes. Listed below are the main offices:
- **Staroměstská radnice (Old Town Hall)**, Staroměstské náměstí 1, tel: 224 372 423, 224 373 162, open daily 9–7
- **Staré Město (Old Town)**, Rytířská 31, tel: 224 372 423, 224 373 162; daily 10–6
- **Ruzyně Airport** Terminal 2, tel: 224 247 223, open daily 8am–8:30pm

# Getting Around

## Getting Your Bearings
The Vltava River divides the city into two distinct areas. On the right bank, **Staroměstské náměstí** (Old Town Square) is the hub. On the left bank, commonly known as Mala Straná (literally "Little Side"), **Malostranské náměstí** (Malá Strana Square) is the centre of the action, leading up to Pražský hrad (Prague Castle).Restaurant Prices

> **The Major Neighbourhoods**
> - **Staré Město (Old Town)** is the right bank's historic quarter, taking in the river bend east of Karlův most (Charles Bridge). It is bounded by Národní Street, Na přikopě, náměstí Republiky and Revoluční.
> - **Josefov**, once the separate Jewish neighbourhood, is now the Old Town's northern section, running from Staroměstské náměstí (Old Town Square) to the Vltava River.
> - **Hradčany** is the left bank hilltop area immediately around Pražský hrad (Prague Castle).
> - **Malá Strana** runs along the left bank, below Prague Castle, taking in Kampa Island at the foot of Charles Bridge and surrounding the parkland and gardens of Petřín Hill.
> - **Nové Město (New Town)** lies on the right bank, east of Revoluční to Wilsonova, and south of Národní Street to Vnislavova.
> - **Vyšehrad** is the castle district south of Vnislavova.
> - **Vinohrády**, **Karlín** and **Žižkov** are residential neighbourhoods east of Wilsonova.
> - **Smíchov** is an up-and-coming neighbourhood south of Malá Strana's Holečkova Street.
> - **Letná** and **Holešovice** are left-bank commercial and residential neighbourhoods east of Hradčany.

# Getting Around

**The best way to visit the sights in each of Prague's historic centres is on foot. For trips between and around neighbourhoods, use the excellent tram system, and the underground Metro, which is inexpensive, fast and reliable. There is an English-language website, www.dp-praha.cz, for detailed information on Dopravní podnik (Public Transport Company). Take taxis only when you really need door-to-door service.**

## Metro
The fast and clean system of three colour-coded underground lines covers the city's main areas, intersecting at stations in the centre (Museum, Můstek and Florenc – ▶ map on inside back cover).
- **Trains run** 5am–midnight, with a train every two or three minutes during rush hour and four to ten minutes off-peak. The platform's clock tells how many minutes have passed since the last train.
- The **A-line**, coded green, links the city centre and Malá Strana. Key stations are Můstek, Muzeum, Václavské náměstí (Wenceslas Square), Staroměstská and Malostranská.

## Finding Your Feet

- The **B-line**, coded yellow, runs between the northeast and southwest suburbs via Florenc, náměstí Republiky, Můstek and Národní třída.
- The **C-line**, coded red, runs from Holešovice in the north through the city centre via Florenc, Muzeum and south to Vyšehrad Castle.
- **Useful signs** to look out for include *výstup* (exit) and *přestup* (transfer).

## Trams

The network of electric trams is the most enjoyable way of zipping around town, with the added bonus of being able to sightsee on the way.

- Tram **times** are 4:30am–midnight, with trams running every six to eight minutes during peak hours, and every six to 15 minutes outside these hours. **Timetables** at tram stops show the departure time from that stop.
- There is a **night service** running midnight–4:30am. Nine trams, numbered 51 to 59, cover the left- and right-bank neighbourhoods, and run about every 30 minutes. All pass through Lazarská in the city centre.
- The best **sightseeing** tram is No 22, from Vinohrady through Nové Město across die Moldau to Malá Strana and the Hradčany district.
- There is also a **nostalgia ride** in the old-fashioned No 91 tram running from Náměstí Republiky via major right- and left-bank sights to Výstaviste, 40 minutes each way.

## Buses

- Essentially a service for outlying **suburbs**, few buses come into the city centre.
- **Times** are about 4:30am–midnight, with **night buses** (numbers 501–504, 601–604) running hourly from midnight to 5am.

## Tickets

- Tickets must be purchased **before** boarding a tram, train or bus. On **trams** and the **Metro**, punch the ticket to validate it, in electronic machines at the entrance to the Metro platforms or inside the tram.
- You can **buy** tickets at Metro stations, travel agencies, newsstands *(traffika)*, *tabac*, department stores and many hotels.
- **Single tickets** can be bought from automatic machines, but they offer a variety of types of ticket (all of which are explained on the machine) and may require a moment's study before you put your money in.
- A **transfer ticket** (32Kč per adult, 16Kč per child) is valid on unlimited tram and Metro changes for 90 minutes from the time of punching.
- A **discounted ticket** (24Kč per adult, 10Kč per child) is valid for 30 minutes on the Metro for five stations and 1 tram.
- **Multi-day tickets**, the simplest solution, provide unlimited travel for an extended period and are validated just once, when first used. These cost 110Kč for 24 hours, 310Kč for three days and 510Kč for five days.
- **Children** under six years and pet animals, which must be muzzled or in a carrying case, travel free.

---

### Prague Card

The Prague Card (www.praguecitycard.com) is a **tourist pass,** which is valid for two, three or four days and provides free admission to more than 40 Prague memorial sites and museums (adults: 880Kč, 990Kč or 1200Kč; children/students 580Kč, 690Kč or 850Kč). Buy the cards at any Prague Information Service office (➤36).

# Getting Around

## Taxis

All licensed cabs in Prague are strictly regulated and must conform to the following legal requirements

- **Licensed cabs** are painted yellow, have a roof lamp and official taxi sign.
- **Receipts** can be printed out from the taxi meter on request: "*Prosím, dejte mi potvrzení*" ("Please give me a receipt").
- The **registration number, company name and price list** must be displayed on both front doors and must conform to the information on the meter.
- **Taxi meters** must be running.
- At the completion of a journey the driver must provide a **printed receipt**.
- Customers are advised to order a taxi through a **non-stop dispatching office**; alternatively, to hire a cab from an **official stand** with the yellow 'Taxi Fair Place' sign (for a list, visit the Prague Information Service, ➤36).
- There is a **boarding fee** of 40Kč, after which **the fare** within the downtown area is calculated at 28Kč per kilometre. A 10-minute ride should cost around 90Kč–120Kč, including taxes. There is a 6Kč **waiting charge** which includes time spent in traffic holdups. While drivers are not obliged to accept payment in foreign currency, they must post the fact prominently in the cab.
- Reliable taxi companies offering a 24-hour service include:
**AAA** ☎ 222 333 222
**Halotaxi** ☎ 241 444 441
**City Taxi** ☎ 257 257 257
**Profitaxi** ☎ 261 314 151

## Driving

Your car is best saved for an excursion out of town. Driving within Prague can be horrendous for the uninitiated. Here are some of the rules.

- Drive on the **right**. **Headlights** are compulsory year-round.
- **Seat belts** front and rear are compulsory in and outside town.
- There is zero tolerance for **alcohol**.
- **Trams** have priority at all times.
- **Speed limits** are 50kph (31mph) in town, 90kph (56mph) on country roads (reduced to 30kph/19mph preceding railway level-crossings) and 130kph (81mph) on motorways.
- **Children** smaller than 150cm (4ft 11in) and weighing less than 36kg (79lbs) must sit in a child seat.
- **Pedestrians** have right of way at crossings.
- The use of **mobile phones** while driving is strictly prohibited.

## Car Rental

- You must have an **EU or international driving licence**.
- You must be **over 21**.
- **Payment** must be guaranteed by an international credit card.
- All **major international companies** are represented in Prague, but the local companies are usually much cheaper (Compact cars are available from 30 euros per day). You could try one of the following:
**Dvořák Rent-a-Car** ☎ 542 211 334; www.dvorakrentacar.cz
**AA Auto** ☎ 227 027 182; aa-auto-cz.czechtrade.us
**CS Czechocar** ☎ 261 222 079; www.czechocar.cz
**Vecar** ☎ 224 314 361; www.vecar.info

## Finding Your Feet

# Accommodation

Old Patrician houses will entice you with their romantic rooms, and magnificent suites await you behind art deco facades. However, the quality of the accommodation can also be far from dreamlike: in some hotels you will be kept awake by the noise of the traffic, and in others the fans sound like you are sitting in a gale – the Prague hotel scene is extremely dynamic.

## Types of Accommodation

Few cities can match Prague's historic **small hotels and pensions** for sheer aesthetic appeal. They offer historic charm and authenticity, usually occupying houses dating from the Middle Ages, 17th and 18th centuries and elaborate 19th-century wedding-cake houses.

An **unhosted apartment** can be an economical and very pleasant alternative to a hotel – many are located in attractive old neighbourhoods. They offer an apartment solely for the use of the person who has booked it, normally equipped with either a full kitchen or a cooker and fridge. Some are fully furnished with TV, radio and so on, and others are more like simple hotel rooms, except with cooking facilities. The establishments in the higher price category in this book almost always provide the standard luxury amenities and service. In the other hotel accommodation, you may find that the beds are very narrow and do not have sprung mattresses.

Travellers with special requests or needs – air-conditioning, lifts or wheelchair access – try to get them answered prior to arrival.

## Where to Stay

Most visitors dream of staying in picturesque Staré Město (Old Town) or Malá Strana – but **you need to book well in advance** if you want to be guaranteed a room in either of these areas. There are far more rooms available in Nové Město (New Town), and the diverse inner suburbs like Vinohrády, Žižkov and Smíchov offer a wide choice of accommodation. Good public transport brings the city centre within relatively easy reach of most outlying districts.

## Prices

Room rates generally drop 20–50 per cent during the low season. At many hotels, prices also drop slightly in mid-summer. **Some smaller hotels give discounts for cash**. Reservation assistants don't always divulge their secrets unasked – so don't be shy! Room rates generally include taxes and breakfast, except in some luxury hotels.

## Booking

It is advisable to book your hotel in advance, as Prague has become increasingly popular. Peak season runs from April to October, or longer at some hotels, with the peak of the peak in May, June and September. The competition is fierce during major holidays, such as Easter and Christmas.

## Booking Agencies

If you arrive in the city without a place to stay and need assistance with planning your visit, these are excellent places to try.

- **DC Service** is a long-established agency. Use their website or call to find a suitable apartment, hotel or pension in the city or country. They can also arrange airport transfers, sightseeing tours, cultural tickets, and out-of-town excursions (tel: 224 816 346; www.visitprague.cz).

# Accommodation

- **E-travel** is another experienced, full-service accommodation and booking agency; tel: 800 872 835; www.travel.cz.
- **PIS** (Pražska informačni služba – Prague Information Office, ➤ 36) is the city's official tourism and accommodation agency; tel: 221 714 714; www.prague.eu/en.

## Places to Stay
Here is a selective list of some of the city's best lodgings, in alphabetical order. A handful of standard names in the hotel industry also have branches in Prague, among them Kempinski, Hilton, Marriott, Radisson and InterContinental.

> **Accommodation Prices**
> for the least expensive double room per night in high season, including taxes.
> **£** under 3,000Kč   **££** 3,000Kč–6,000Kč   **£££** over 6,000Kč

### Angelo £
Very modern establishment not far from the underground and great value for money.
🏠 208 A3  ✉ Radlicka 1g, Smíchov  ☎ 234 801 111; www.vi-hotels.com/en/angelo-prague

### Aria £££
This melodious hotel used to be a theatre. Each of the four floors is dedicated to a different style of music: from opera to jazz. The rooms bear the names of renowned composers, such as Puccini, Dvořák, Bernstein, Mozart and Billie Holiday. Its pretty terrace affords a lovely view of the mountain.
🏠 205 D3  ✉ Tržiště 9, Malá Strana
☎ 225 334 111; www.ariahotel.net

### Betlem Club £
From the cellar breakfast room up through a warren of stairs and Gothic galleries to rooms furnished mostly in 1970s style, with brass and mirrors, this is an authentic, old Prague house which has been transformed into a funky, affordable small hotel. Betlémské náměstí (Bethlehem Square) oozes charm.
🏠 206 A2  ✉ Betlémské náměstí 9, Staré Město
☎ 222 221 574; www.betlemclub.cz

### Boscolo Carlo IV. £££
A magnificent building with a Classicist-style portal and a wonderful, snow-white stucco lobby. The interior décor offers a mixture of classic and modern elements. The hotel has a large indoor pool as well as a whirlpool, which is not a common occurrence in Prague hotels.
🏠 206 C2 BSenovazne Náměstí 13, Nové Město
☎ 224 593 111; www.prague.boscolohotels.com

### Corinthia ££
This modern glass tower has 539 rooms, one of the city's largest hotel pools, a spa and three restaurants. You will almost always be able to find a free room here. Don't forget to ask about their special offers either. ==Discounts of up to 50% are available in the low season.== **Insider Tip**
🏠 209 E1
✉ G2 Kongresová 1, Nusle, 14000 Praha 4
☎ 261 191 111; www.corinthia.com

### Domus Henrici ££
Tranquillity and elegance define the atmosphere at this hotel located between Strahov Monastery and the Loreto convent. Guests wake to church bells and birdsong drifts through the windows from nearby wooded Petřín Hill. The eight elegant rooms have whitewashed walls, modern luxuries and hand-carved furniture. The exceptional personal service ranges from organizing tickets to driving guests

# Finding Your Feet

to dinner across the river and even sourcing fine local wines.
➕ 204 C3  ✉ Loretanská 11, Hradčany
☎ 220 511 369; www.domus-henrici.com

## Dům U Velké Boty ££
This welcoming and well-run eight-room bed and breakfast (the name whimsically translates as House at the Big Boot) is overseen by Charlotte, husband Jan, and sons Jakub and Tomáš. From the painted armoires to hand-carved sleigh beds, all the furnishings in the large, bright bedrooms are lovingly restored antiques. The hotel faces a quiet square in Malá Strana across from the German Embassy and is just a few steps from Nerudova Street, which leads up to the castle. There are five double rooms and two suites, and a family suite with two connected rooms. There are few modern amenities – the rooms lack televisions – but in such a perfect location, why stay inside?
➕ 204 C3  ✉ Vlašská 30, Malá Strana
☎ 257 532 088; www.dumuvelkeboty.cz
Ⓜ Malostranská

## Four Seasons £££
The five-star establishment offers its guests a postcard panorama that includes a sensational view of the Charles Bridge, Petřin observation tower, Strahov Monastery, St Nicholas Church and St Vitus Cathedral. With 141 room and 20 suites, it is the largest hotel in the Old Town. The furnishings are luxurious, the service impeccable.
➕ 205 F2  ✉ Veleslavínova 2a, Staré Město
☎ 221 427 777; www.fourseasons.com

## Hotel Anna £
A member of the Small Charming Hotels group, the 24 rooms here are spacious with comfortable beds, elegant writing desks, large windows and pictures of the old city of Prague on the walls.  There are wine bars and quiet pubs nearby, and three blocks away, a gorgeous, wooded park has replaced the old vineyards.
➕ 210 B3  ✉ Budecská 17, Vinohrady
☎ 222 513 111; www.hotelanna.cz
Ⓜ Náměstí Míru

## Hotel Černý Slon ££
Tucked in the shadow of the spires of Tyn Church, off Staroměstské náměstí, this cosy hotel is in a 14th-century building on UNESCO's protected list. Everything has been modernized inside, but the architecture has remained Gothic. The 16 rooms are decorated in a charming, simple style with antique furniture and lace curtains. Original ceiling beams and fresh flowers throughout make this hotel feel more like a home. There's a fine wine bar in the cellar, and a restaurant, which serves traditional Czech dishes with courtyard seating near the church.
➕ 206 B3  ✉ Týnská 1, Staré Město
☎ 222 321 521; www.hotelcernyslon.cz

## Hotel Daliborka ££
In a green area on the edge of town, slightly off the beaten track, this beautiful Art Nouveau building has 21 rooms, all furnished in appropriate style. It takes about 20 minutes with a taxi to the centre of town.
➕ 209 by E1  ✉ K Nóvemu dvoru 124/54, Lhotka, 14200 14000 Praha 4
☎ 261 711 307; www.daliborka.cz

## Hotel Standard ££
The hotel's two penthouse suites boast a view of the Vltava and of Prague Castle (➤ 84). This attractive seven-floor building is one of a long series of similarly beautiful buildings lining the banks of the Vltava. Although the eleven double rooms do not offer particularly spectacular view, the prices are fair. Each room has air-conditioning and a minibar, and there is a restaurant that serves Czech dishes.
➕ 208 C2  ✉ Rašinovo nábřeží 38, Nové Město
☎ 224 916 060; www.standard.cz

## Accommodation

### Hotel U Šuterů £
This simple and pleasing pension, on a small side street just off Václavské náměstí, is located above a great traditional Czech restaurant of the same name. The building dates back to the 14th century, and many rooms retain the original period architecture. There are ten bedrooms with private bathrooms, a mini-bar, direct-dial telephone and satellite TV. This convenient hotel is often full, so book early.
✚ 209 E5 ✉ Palackého 4, Nové Město
☎ 224 948 235; www.usuteru.cz Ⓜ Můstek

### ICON Hotel ££
This new high-tech boutique hotel boasts amenities like in-room iPods and Skype connections. Swish Swedish beds and a great Nové Město location. Deals sometimes are available via the hotel's website.
✚ 209 E5 ✉ V Jámě 6, Nové Město
☎ 221 634 100; www.iconhotel.cz Ⓜ Můstek

### The Mark Luxury Hotel £££
Before the first guests arrived here, this historic 17th-century town house was home to the city's high-ranking officials, such as leading court judges. These days, as a five star hotel, it offers every imaginable comfort including a breakfast buffet that is out of this world. In summer, the wonderful interior courtyard-cum-garden is an oasis for lunch, dinner or an aperitif.
✚ 206 C2 ✉ Hybernska 12, Staré Město
☎ 226 226 111; http://en.themark.cz

### Le Palais ££
Located in Vinohrady, this palatial residence was completely remodelled in the style of the Belle Époque between 1888 and 1897 for Antonin Chmel, the leading producer of Prague ham at the time. The remarkable frescoes in some of the suites are by the well-known Bohemian painter Ludek Marold, who once lived on the top floor. In the centre but still quiet with few walk-in customers, Le Palais offers very fair prices, thanks to its flexible pricing system. Great breakfast terrace.
✚ 209 F2 ✉ U Zvonarky 1, Vinohrady
☎ 234 634 111; www.lepalaishotel.eu/

### Mandarin Oriental £££
The five star hotel in a former 14th-century monastery has even played host to the Dalai Lama. The MO offers impeccable service, and its restaurants are also top notch compared with other hotel restaurants. The spa is actually located in the former monastery chapel.
✚ 205 D2 ✉ Nebovidská 1, Malá Strana
☎ 233 088 888;
www.mandarinoriental.com/prague/

### Palace ££
An evergreen on any list of Prague's best places to stay, this Art Nouveau-style hotel, dating from 1909, offers great comfort without being ostentatious. Most of the 114 rooms and 10 suites have king-size beds and internet access. Several floors are reserved for non-smokers. The cool, quiet lobby makes a pleasant spot for a brief escape from Nové Město's liveliness. You can have a drink here with piano accompaniment in the afternoons and evenings. <mark>Children under 12 stay free in their parents' room.</mark> The restaurant is in "English-club style" with an expensive Continental and international menu.
✚ 206 C2 ✉ Panská 12, Nové Město
☎ 224 093 111; www.palacehotel.cz

### Romantik Hotel U Raka ££
This charming farmhouse-style hotel offers a taste of the countryside in the heart of the city. If you're lucky enough to reserve one of its half-dozen rooms, all furnished simply and elegantly, you'll also get to enjoy open fires, pretty courtyard gardens and even a small gallery featuring work by the owners.
✚ 204 B4 ✉ Černínská 10 Hradčany
☎ 220 511 100; www.romantikhotel-uraka.cz

## Finding Your Feet

### Sax ££
Even with just 22 rooms, this designer hotel qualifies as a sizeable place in its diminutive hillside neighbourhood below Pražský hrad (Prague Castle, ►84). The atrium is lined with three floors of rooms. Rooms are furnished in the styles of the 1950s, 60s or 70s and some are decorated in the vibrant colours popular in those decades. Unashamedly urban, the Sax blows a different tune from many other Malá Strana hotels. There's no restaurant, but a breakfast room is available.

🗺 204 C3 ✉ Jánský vršek 3 (at Břetislavova), Malá Strana ☎ 257 531 268; www.sax.cz

### U Dvou Zlatých Klíčů £
The location of "At the Two Golden Keys" couldn't be more convenient: two minutes' walk from Narodní třídá Metro station and the No 22 tram stop for Prague Castle, and within comfortable walking distance of the Old Town, Wenceslas Square and the National Theatre. The rooms are plainly furnished but generously-sized and have satellite TV and WiFi access while at the reception there's free internet and a ticket reservation service.

🗺 205 F1 ✉ Spálená ulice 98/31, Nové Město ☎ 224 932 010; www.udvouzlatychklicu.cz

# Food and Drink

**Dining out in Prague is still a hit or miss affair. While standards are rising, too many restaurants still rely on the tried and true formula of pushing out mediocre meals to the masses of tourists. In general, avoid restaurants on the main tourist thoroughfares in the Old Town and Malá Strana and instead follow the recommendations here and in local sources like the English-language newspaper *The Prague Post*.**

The restaurant situation is in a constant state of flux, with new places opening weekly to great fanfare only to close down in a year or two after the vogue has moved on. Surprisingly, **traditional Czech food can be hard to find**. Most of the newer restaurants focus on international cooking and more exotic cuisines. Lunch is usually the best time to sample Czech food, as many pubs and restaurants will offer a daily set menu focusing on a local speciality like goulash or roast pork. Vegetarian restaurants are still thin on the ground but most menus include at least a couple of vegetarian options.

## Czech Cuisine
Czechs like to say that their best cooks stay at home. If you're not lucky enough to be invited into a Czech home, however, you can still taste decent local cuisine despite the plethora of other dining options.

- **Lunch** is customarily the main meal. A typical one might include *polévka* (soup), often an onion or garlic broth. *Kulajda* (dense, tangy potato and mushroom soup) is a South Bohemian speciality.

- For the **main course**, *vepřové* (pork) features strongly – everyone eagerly anticipates the annual pig slaughter and subsequent feast. At inexpensive restaurants pork dishes are generally more appetizing than *hovězí* (beef). Meat courses are typically accompanied by *knedlíky* (fluffy bread dumplings) or *hranolky* (french fries). Fish is less popular, but as a traditional Bohemian food, especially in the autumn, it appears on menus even in humble establishments – try *pstruh* (pond-raised trout), *štika* (pike) or *úhoř* (eel) and at Christmas *kapr* (carp).

# Food and Drink

- **Vegetables** are becoming more available as the city becomes cosmopolitan. A standard Czech meal may include just some *zelí* (sauerkraut) or *obloha* (picked vegetables). *Šopsky salát* (salad) is typically cucumber, tomato and red pepper with a slightly sweet vinegar dressing.

- Traditional **desserts** are *palačinky* (crêpes), filled with chocolate syrup, fruit or ice cream, and *ovocné knedlíky* (fruit dumplings), which are substantial enough to be served as a main course.

- **Beer** *(pivo)* is, of course, the main accompaniment. Lager beer was invented in the Bohemian town of Plzeň (Pilsen in German, thus Pilsner). The quality and price of beer in Prague are not surpassed even when compared with other beer-brewing centres such as Munich, Brussels or Dublin.

- Czech **wine** is worth trying as well. Under communism, mechanized viniculture devastated the old Moravian and Bohemian wine industry. But in recent years the country has begun producing drinkable varietals. The best reds *(červené)* include Frankovka and Svatovavřinecké; whites *(bílé)* to try are Rýnský ryzlink (Riesling), Tramín Červený and Veltlínské zelené.

## *Restaurace, Hostinec* or *Vinárna?*

Restaurant, pub or wine bar? The sign outside may not completely disclose what's inside.

- Many establishments use the word ***restaurace***, but more resemble a pub: the beer's draught, cold and thirst-quenching, while the food serves as more of an accompaniment, although there may be an extensive menu.
- The ***hostinec*** is a pub or inn where some kind of hot food is served.
- The locals at the neighbourhood ***pivnice*** (beer hall) may look askance at strangers, but generally turn out to be friendly enough. If there are no free tables, ask to share: "*Je tu volno?*" ("Is this place free?").
- ***Vinárna*** literally "a place for wine" includes stand-up counters for a quick drink, dimly lit cellar wine bars and some of the city's finest restaurants.

## Coffee Culture

A city guide published in 1913 listed no fewer than 27 "grand cafes". Four remain in business, reminders of a vanished Czech-German-Jewish cultural mélange that nurtured such cafe regulars as Bedřich Smetana, Franz Kafka and Albert Einstein. These are the Café Slavia (▶162), Café Louvre (▶166), the cafe in Obecní dům (▶147) and the Grand Cafe Orient (▶76). The culture, and the coffee houses, vanished during the Cold War. The situation grew so dire that in the early 1990s a good cup of coffee was as rare in the city as an authenticated sighting of Kafka, who died in 1924. Yet the city yearned for the return of literary cafes, musical cafes, all-night cafes. And so a new generation is reviving something of the hothouse atmosphere of those vanished cafes.

For a more mellow refreshment stop, the **tearoom** *(čavojna)* may be just your cup. The wide-eyed tea zealots who run these places travel the world to find the most aromatic varieties and learn the secrets of proper brewing, whether in Japan, Nepal, Vietnam or Zimbabwe. What's more, most tearooms are non-smoking zones.

## A Survival Guide to Dining in Prague

- During peak season you should **reserve** whenever possible. Otherwise go at 11am or 6pm for an early lunch or dinner. Most inexpensive places, and many in the upper price brackets, stay open all day and nearly always have free places in late afternoon.

## Finding Your Feet

- **Casually presentable dress** suffices nearly everywhere, but you should ask about dress guidelines when making reservations at the chicest places.
- In smaller places the menu may only be available in Czech, but larger establishments should have English and German menus as well. **Useful words** are *jídelní lístek* (menu); *denní nabídka* (daily specials), served at less expensive restaurants; *polévky* (soups); *jídla na objednávku* (main dishes cooked to order).
- **Service has improved greatly**. You can count on prompt, efficient, knowledgeable and friendly service in most restaurants. As with everything else in Prague, you need patience to savour the experience to the full. Service is almost never included in the bill, except in the case of large groups. At the more expensive establishments, **tip** around 10 to 15 per cent. In pubs and inexpensive restaurants, give a small tip, usually by adding a few crowns to round up the total.
- Major **credit cards** are accepted at most of the restaurants listed in this guide (these should be indicated on the door). Many inexpensive restaurants, pubs and cafes only accept cash.
- **VAT is usually included** in the bill.

### Bests...
...**Asian:** NOI (➤ 112)
...**cafe:** Kavárna Slavia (➤ 76)
...**historic interior:** Pálffy Palác (➤ 112)
...**Italian:** Cotto Crudo (➤ 72)
...**kosher:** King Solomon (➤ 135)
...**pizza:** Pizza Nuova (➤ 74)
...**riverside fish restaurant:** Rybářský klub (➤ 113)
...**tearoom:** Dobrá Čajovna (➤ 166)
...**terrace:** Hergetova Cihelná (➤ 112)
...**view:** Terasa U Zlaté studně (➤ 113)

> **Restaurant Prices**
> Expect to pay per person for a meal, including drinks, tax and service:
> £ under 500Kč      ££ 500Kč–1,000Kč      £££ over 1,000Kč

# Shopping

Souvenir stands line the pedestrian zones of Old Town Square, Karlova, the Charles Bridge and Malá Strana. These are fine for small gifts like coffee mugs, T-shirts and key chains. You'll have to look a little harder, though, for goods of higher quality. Pařížská in Josefov is the place for ultra-high-end luxury names like Hermès and Louis Vuitton. Na příkopě in Nové Město is Prague's "high street", with trendy fashion shops like Mango, H&M and Zara. The area around the Obecní dům is a good place to start for antiques and antiquarian bookshops.

## Czech Specialities
- There are three main **traditional Bohemian and Moravian** products: crystal and glass, porcelain, and marionettes. It is hard to go wrong, as value for money is excellent. Simply styled glassware and porcelain can be quite inexpensive and very attractive. At the higher end of the market, brands such as Moser are world famous – but don't expect to find bargains.

# Entertainment

- Other **popular buys** are garnet jewellery, crafts, shoes and leather goods, and locally made spirits – especially the herbal liqueur, Becherovka.
- Prague is also a **bargain basement** for good deals on domestic products like women's fashions, classical CDs and musical instruments.
- Due to 50 years of isolation during the Cold War, the market in **antiques and fine art** has huge growth potential and canny shoppers can find good deals, but also items of dubious authenticity. Reputable dealers will provide the necessary customs documentation.

## Where to Shop

- In general **Nové Město** (New Town) offers the largest stores.
- **Staré Město** (Old Town) and **Josefov** (Old Jewish Quarter) have boutiques, souvenir stalls and lots of chic international fashion and accessory stores.
- In **Malá Strana** and around **Pražský hrad** (Prague Castle), it is best to let yourself wander among the tiny shops.

## Markets

- You can't miss the crowded **Havelská street market** in Staré Město (Old Town), with crafts, toys and clothes alongside fruit and vegetables. It runs every day from 10am to 7pm.
- **Staroměstské náměstí** (Old Town Square) returns to its roots at Easter and Christmas, when it fills with booths offering traditional crafts, grilled sausages, Prager Schinken and hot mulled wine.
- Throughout the city there are *tržnice,* little courtyard markets, selling fresh produce, inexpensive clothing, shoes and many other products. *(Insider Tip)*

## Service

Whereas in the past you'd have faced a long counter manned by humourless matrons who, if you could communicate with them at all, would grudgingly hand over the goods, the norm today is an open-plan shop with English-speaking staff.

## Opening Times

- Downtown shops and department stores often stay open until 7 or later (Monn–Fri), and close a couple of hours earlier on Sat and Sun.
- Elsewhere most shops keep to traditional hours of 9–6 (Mon–Fri) and 9–1 on Sat, closed on Sun. Many of the Vietnamese-run mini-markets, off-licences and greengrocer's are open until midnight, others around the clock, every day of the year.

# Entertainment

**Beloved by opera fans and admirers, Prague offers a surprisingly broad range of performing arts to cater for all tastes.**

## Information and Bookings

- You can buy **tickets** to all kinds of events at a number of ticket agencies, major hotels, the city tourist information office (PIS), and travel agents.
- Tickets to **major performances** are scarce on the day of the show, but it's worth stopping off at the box office if there's an opera or symphony you particularly want to catch. Opera tickets are easiest to come by in winter.

## Finding Your Feet

- **Bohemia Ticket International**, Na příkopě 16, Nové Město; tel: 224 215 031; www.ticketsbti.cz, sells leftover Státní opera (State Opera House) tickets at half-price on the day of the performance.
- For tickets for the **Prague Spring Festival**, contact www.festival.cz; visit the **PIS** Prague Information Office (➤ 36) or **Ticketpro**, Klimentská 1515/22, tel: 234 704 234; www.ticketpro.cz).

### Further Information
Check the Night and Day section of the English-language *Prague Post* (www.praguepost.com), which is published on Wednesdays, and Prague TV website (www.prague.tv) for weekly listings and reviews.

## Opera and Classical Music
- The city has three **opera houses** – Stavovské divadlo (Estates Theatre, ➤ 65), Národní divadlo (National Theatre, ➤ 153) and Státní opera Praha (Prague State Opera, ➤ 168).
- **Ticket prices** for opera are high.
- The **Czech Philharmonic** and **Prague Symphony** orchestras offer world-class music performed in stunning surroundings. The Czech Philharmonic plays in the Rudolfinum (➤ 130) and the Prague Symphony Orchestra in the Obecní dům (Municipal House) ➤ 146.

## Theatre and Dance
Leaving aside the thriving Czech-language dramatic theatre, there's still plenty to choose from.
- **Blacklight theatre**, a local invention, entertains the crowds nightly at a variety of venues with its blend of mime, clowning and lighting effects using UV light. You can find out about tickets to these shows from **Ticketpro**; tel: 234 704 234; www.ticketpro.cz
- **Non-verbal theatre and dance** play regularly to knowledgeable audiences. Top-flight performers appear at **Archa** (➤ 168) and in festivals such as **Tanec Praha** every June (➤ below).

## Pop and Jazz
- Top jazz musicians, among others, put their skills to the test at the Prague clubs in the city centre. **Jazz** has a long tradition in the city. Check with the *Prague Post* for what's on, or look at individual club websites.
- Check in the *Prague Post* for local **rock**, **blues** and **folk** concerts.
- **World music** is also popular in the city. Check with PIS for what's on.

## Festivals
For more detailed listings see the individual chapters.
- The venerable **Prague Spring Music Festival** brings the best classical performers to the city every year from mid-May to early June (www.festival.cz).
- The **Prague Autumn Festival** does the same in September, albeit at a slightly lower level (www.pragueautumn.cz in Czech).
- June brings the **Prague Writers' Festival** where major English-language and other writers give readings and hold discussions (www.pwf.cz).
- In June there is the **United Islands of Prague world-music festival** (www.unitedislands.cz) and the **Tanec Praha** celebration of **contemporary dance** (www.tanecpraha.cz).
- The top two **film festivals** are March's FebioFest (www.febiofest.cz) and One World international human rights documentary film festival (www.jedensvet.cz).

# Staré Město
# (Old Town)

| | |
|---|---|
| Getting Your Bearings | 50 |
| The Perfect Day | 52 |
| TOP 10 | 54 |
| Don't Miss | 62 |
| At Your Leisure | 66 |
| Where to… | 72 |

 **Little Treats**

### You Must Try Chlebičky
These open-faced sandwiches are a popular snack. Try them at Jan Paukert in **Národní** (no. 17, not far from Charles Bridge, ➤ 55).

### Enjoy a Vintage Car Tour of the Old Town
The one-hour tours that start in the **Old Square** (➤ 59; www.3veterani.cz) are not only popular with car enthusiasts.

### A Treasure Trove with a Difference
The Česká Spořitelna in Rytířská 29, not far from the **Stavovské divadlo** (Estates Theatre (➤ 65), is not just a bank branch, it is an Art Nouveau gem.

## Staré Město (Old Town)

# Getting Your Bearings

**Staré Město (Old Town), a World Heritage Site since 1992, is Prague's historic hub. This was the "Royal Route" kings took to their coronation because they knew it was here that they would draw the biggest crowds. Today ancient and modern mix well here, cyber-cafes buzzing and beeping in medieval vaulted cellars.**

Staré Město sits in a bend of the Vltava River. It extends from the monumental Charles Bridge via Old Town Square, site of the majestic Old Town Hall and its ever-popular astronomical clock, and east to the end of Celetná Street. North of Celetná is the historic twin-spired Týn Church and its courtyard, the Ungelt. Its southern section embraces a maze of cobblestoned lanes and alleyways that are so dense that trams have to go around, not across, the neighbourhood.

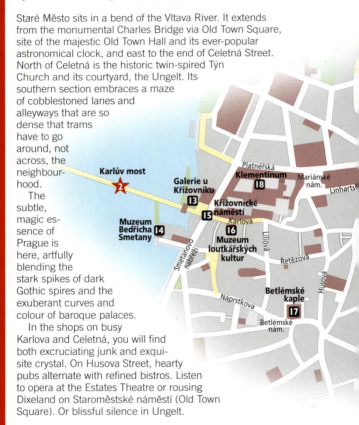

The subtle, magic essence of Prague is here, artfully blending the stark spikes of dark Gothic spires and the exuberant curves and colour of baroque palaces.

In the shops on busy Karlova and Celetná, you will find both excruciating junk and exquisite crystal. On Husova Street, hearty pubs alternate with refined bistros. Listen to opera at the Estates Theatre or rousing Dixeland on Staroměstské náměstí (Old Town Square). Or blissful silence in Ungelt.

## TOP 10

- Karlův most (Charles Bridge) ➤ 54
- Staroměstské náměstí (Old Town Square) ➤ 58

## Don't Miss

- ⓫ Kostel Panny Marie Před Týnem ➤ 62
- ⓬ Stavovské divadlo (Estates Theatre) ➤ 65

50

# Getting Your Bearings

## At Your Leisure

- ⓭ Galerie u Křižovniku ➤ 66
- ⓮ Muzeum Bedřicha Smetany (Smetana Museum) ➤ 66
- ⓯ Křižovnické náměstí (Kreuzherrenplatz) ➤ 67
- ⓰ Muzeum loutkářských kultur (Puppet Museum) ➤ 67
- ⓱ Betlémské kaple ➤ 67
- ⓲ Klementinum ➤ 67
- ⓳ Svatého Mikuláš (St Nicholas) ➤ 68
- ⓴ Dům U Zlatého prstenů (House of the Golden Ring) ➤ 69
- ㉑ Svatého Jakub (St James) ➤ 69
- ㉒ Celetná ➤ 70
- ㉓ Karolinum ➤ 70

**Looking past the Old Town Hall to the spires of Týn Church**

## Staré Město (Old Town)

# The Perfect Day

*Perfect Days in...*

A walk through the Staré Město is one of the highlights of a visit to Prague. Make sure you reserve lots of time for the tour – you won't regret it! Follow our itinerary and you will not miss any of the top sights. For more information see the main entries (➤ 54–71).

## ⊙ 9:00am
Make an early start to avoid the mob that will descend on ★**Karlův most** (Charles Bridge, ➤ 54), Prague's most popular landmark. Its 31 statues make this more than just another bridge. Save the climb up the Old Town Gate Tower for sunset, take in the river scene and then head off east on Karlova Street alongside the **18 Klementinum** (➤ 67), passing **15 Křižovnické náměstí** (➤ 67) en route.

## ⊙ 10:00am
Time for a coffee on ★**Staroměstské náměstí** (Old Town Square, ➤ 58). Choose the cafe for the view you want – of the town hall, the church, the palaces or the **Jan Hus Monument** (left, ➤ 60), before strolling over for a closer look. This would be a good time to pick up information and maps at the Old Town Hall tourist office. Look around the **19 Svatého Mikuláš** (St Nicholas Church, ➤ 68) and cross the square to the passage between the Stone Bell House and the Týn School.

## ⊙ 11:30am
It's interesting to compare the **11 Týn Church** (➤ 62)

# The Perfect Day

with St Nicholas. There is plenty to see here, inside and out, before you stroll to ⓫ **Týn Courtyard** (➤ 63) and explore its craft shops and art galleries. It was here that foreign merchants used to pay customs, or "Ungelt", which is how this complex of buildings earned its name. Or visit the Prague City Museum at the ⓴ **Dům U zlatého prstenu** (House of the Golden Ring, ➤ 69).

## 🕐 1:00pm
Hungry? Take a short detour to **Pizzeria Rugantino** for – many would say – Prague's best pizza (➤ 74).

## 🕐 2:30pm
Try some window-shopping or serious bargain-hunting on ㉒ **Celetná ulice** (➤ 70).

## 🕐 4:00pm
Back to Staroměstské náměstí (Old Town Square) to the second floor of the Grand Café Praha, a surprisingly charming place right opposite the **Astronomical Clock** (➤ 59), where you can enjoy the local coffee and cakes.

## 🕐 5:30pm
Operas start early in Prague, so either shower and relax back at the hotel or go over to Ovocný trh for a pub snack at **Kogo** (➤ 65) before the show.

## 🕐 7:00pm
End the day in style with an opera at the ⓬ **Stavovské divadlo** (Estates Theatre, below, ➤ 65), the best way to see this magnificent house.

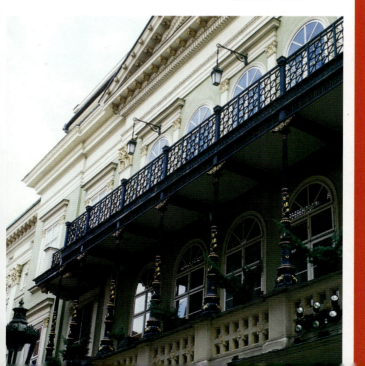

Staré Město (Old Town)

# ⭐2 Karlův most (Charles Bridge)

**The bridge and the famous statues on its parapets are the stuff the city's dreams are made of. Not all the statues are masterpieces but together they form a bewitching parade between the two historic halves of the city. By day, the thoroughfare is thronged with people strolling past stalls of souvenirs, art and near-art, to and from Prague Castle on the hill.**

Up until the 19th century, this was Prague's only bridge across the Vltava River. Indeed, for 500 years it was known just as the Stone Bridge until 1870, when it was finally named after its original builder Charles IV, Holy Roman emperor and king of Bohemia. Royal processions carried kings across to be crowned or buried in Pražský hrad (Prague Castle, ➤84). Knights galloped across in jousting tournaments. Merchants met here to do business. Criminals and "heretics" were hanged or decapitated here. German SS troops paraded in 1939, followed by Communist militia in the coup d'état of 1948. On a more upbeat note, jazz and rock musicians have succeeded the medieval minstrels to sing here for their supper. Karlův most's magic hour is midnight.

### In the Beginning
Winter floods of the fast-flowing Vltava River wrought havoc with the Charles Bridge's predecessors. The earliest

**Blessed by its saints, Karlův most is enchanting at any time of day**

# Karlův most (Charles Bridge)

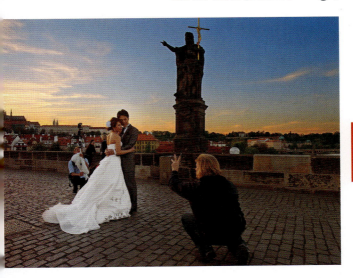

**Posing for the photographer: Wedding photo on Charles Bridge**

recorded bridge, noted when the body of Bohemia's patron saint Václav (Wenceslas) was carried over in the tenth century to be buried at Prague Castle, was a flimsy wooden affair often swept away. A stone bridge, built by King Vladislav I in 1170 and named after his wife Judith, was also regularly breached by floods.

Charles IV, crowned Emperor in 1355, found the bridge in ruins and had architect **Peter Parléř** design a new one while working on St Vitus Cathedral (▶90). After his elaborate vaulting for the church's nave and choir, the master builder had little trouble with the 16 arches for the bridge. Built just to the south of the old one, the new bridge, 516m (1,690ft) long and 10m (33ft) wide, uses some of the old pier foundations, resulting in an S-curve from one bank to the other.

## Staré Město (Old Town) Bridge Tower

With its chisel-blade roof and golden globes, corner turrets and battlemented gallery, this superb tower gate has a silhouette that is both formidable and elegant. Originally endowed with a portcullis lowered to ward off attackers, it served as a firewall against enemy assaults

### HEADS
The morning after an Austrian Catholic army had executed 27 Protestant leaders in 1621 during the Thirty Years War, 12 of their severed heads were displayed on the Staré Město Bridge Tower. They stayed there for 10 years until a Protestant army of Saxons seized the city long enough to take them down and give them a decent burial in Týn Church (▶62).

# Staré Město (Old Town)

**Detail of the statue of St John of Nepomuk (patron saint of bridges) with his five star halo**

## THE STATUES AND SCULPTURES

1. Madonna and St Bernard
2. St Ivo
3. Madonna, St Dominic and St Thomas Aquinas
4. St Barbara, St Margaret and St Elizabeth
5. Bronze Crucifixion
6. Pieta
7. St Anne with the Madonna and Child
8. St Joseph
9. St Cyril, St Methodius and three allegorical figures
10. St Francis Xavier
11. St John the Baptist
12. St Christopher
13. St Wenceslas, St Norbert and St Sigismund
14. St Francis Borgia
15. St John of Nepomuk (above)
16. St Ludmilla and St Wenceslas
17. St Anthony of Padua
18. St Francis in ecstasy
19. St Jude Thaddaeus
20. St Vincent Ferrer and St Procopius
21. Bruncvik (Roland Column)
22. St Augustine
23. St Nicholas of Tolentino
24. St Cajetan
25. St Luitgard
26. St Philip Benitius
27. St Adalbert
28. St Vitus
29. St John of Matha, St Felix of Valois and Blessed Ivan
30. Jesus, St Cosmas and St Damian
31. St Wenceslas

### THE TOP TEN

Of the bridge's 31 statues and sculptures, the following deserve a longer look (numbers refer to their position on the plan below):

- **St Ivo (2)** by Matyáš Bernard Braun shows the lawyers' patron saint with a blindfolded Justice.
- The group of saints **Barbara (4)** – patron of silver miners, with **Margaret** and **Elizabeth** – is a joint work of the great Brokoff family workshop.
- Jesuit missionary **Francis Xavier (10)**, with Chinese, Indian and Arab converts, is generally considered Ferdinand Maximilian Brokoff's masterpiece.
- Most famous of the sculptures, the bronze **John of Nepomuk (15)**, also by Brokoff, stands at the centre of the bridge from where the archbishop's corpse was thrown into the river 300 years before.
- **St Ludmila (16)**, grandmother of St Wenceslas, was Bohemia's first martyr, depicted here holding the veil that was used to strangle her.
- **St Jude Thaddaeus (19)** by Jan Meyer shows the apostle with the cudgel of his martyrdom.
- The Augustinians had Jan Bedřich Kohl sculpt **St Augustine (22)** upholding the flaming heart of his order.
- **St Nicholas of Tolentino (23)** distributes bread to the poor.
- Quintessence of the baroque statues is Matyáš Braun's Cistercian nun, **St Luitgard (25),** about to act out her vision of kissing the wounds of Jesus.
- The university medical faculty commissioned Jan Mayer's **Cosmas and Damian (30)**, patron saints of physicians, brothers flanking Jesus.

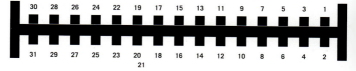

**Malá Strana Bridge Tower**                **Staré Město Bridge Tower**

# Karlův most (Charles Bridge)

> **INSIDER INFO**
>
> Go early morning or late afternoon to climb to the top of the **Staré Město (Old Town) Bridge Tower**, built at the end of the 14th century. The viewing gallery, on the first floor, provides a wonderful view of Prague Castle and Staré Město.

on Prague Castle or the city. Most notably in 1648, at the very end of the Thirty Years War, the tower withstood the Swedes' artillery in their last assault on the city. On the tower's eastern facade over the Gothic arch, the statue of St Vitus is flanked by the enthroned figures of a tired-looking Charles IV on the left and his son Václav IV on the right. Beneath them is a row of 10 Bohemian coats of arms. Standing in the upper windows are the patron saints Adalbert and Sigismund.

### The Statues

The bridge had only a wooden crucifix until the Jesuits launched the series of sacred sculptures now gracing the parapets. The first statue, erected in 1683, was of St John of Nepomuk (Jan Nepomucký), a Czech martyr promoted by the Church as a popular counterpart to the national hero – and Protestant – Jan Hus.

By 1714, inspired by the Bernini statues on Rome's Ponte Sant'Angelo, Czech baroque sculptors produced some 25 statues for the bridge. Respectable copies, and six new statues, were added in the 19th and 20th centuries. Some of the baroque originals, mostly in weather-beaten sandstone, can be seen in the dungeons of Vyšehrad Castle (➤ 157).

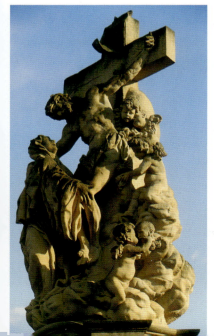

St Luitgard's statue by Matthias Braun

### TAKING A BREAK

Less than two blocks from the bridge is the **Café Rincon** (Na Zabradli 1, Staré Město; daily noon–2am; tel: 222 222 173) with picture windows and outdoor seating providing a **stunning view of the river and castle** to go with the salads, sandwiches, coffee and cakes on offer.

*Insider Tip*

---

✚ 205 E3 ✉ Staré Město, Praha 1
☎ 224 220 569
🕐 Staré Město Bridge Tower:
Apr–Sep daily 10am–10pm;
March, Oct until 8; Nov–Feb until 6
🚊 Tram 17, 18
🎫 Bridge Tower: 90Kč

Staré Město (Old Town)

# ⭐ 4 Staroměstské náměstí (Old Town Square)

**This colourful, bustling square is undoubtedly the centre not only of the Old Town (Staré Město) but of the whole city. Historically, it has been a magnet for all sections of the population. A town hall, merchants' mansions, princes' palaces and two majestic churches – St Nicholas (➤ 68) and Týn (➤ 62) – look down on the massive modern monument to the nation's reformist hero, Jan Hus.**

The square began in the 11th century as the city's marketplace, both for local peasants and for merchants from all over Europe. It was known then simply as Velké náměstí (Great Square) and acquired its current name only in 1895. Vestiges of the era's Romanesque houses can be seen in the vaulted basements of today's largely baroque mansions.

The centre of trade was the obvious place for the town hall, formed by knocking together adjacent houses. The square was the best address in town. The wealthiest citizens – import and export merchants, bankers and business representatives for the Kutná Hora silver mines (➤ 170) – built mansions. The royal family and nobles put up palaces here, which were much more comfortable than their damp and draughty castle.

*Old Town Square – the beating heart not only of the Old Town but of all of Prague*

58

## Staroměstské náměstí (Old Town Square)

**The Town Hall clock tells you more about the stars than the time of day**

Besides buying and selling at the market, people gathered here to throw rotten eggs at rascals in the pillory, cheer champions in tournaments, kings at their coronations, and executioners decapitating the monarchs' enemies.

### Staroměstské radnice (Old Town Hall)

The present largely Gothic edifice on the west side of the square represents a conglomeration of several houses acquired over the centuries, starting with a house for the town scribe in 1296. The belfry, 66m (216ft) high, was built in 1364, incorporating 17 years later the municipal chapel, with its distinctive oriel window.

Only a fragment remains from a northern neo-Gothic wing bombarded by the Germans in 1945. The main entrance is through the south side's 15th-century portal. Civic weddings and art exhibitions are held here, and there are 45-minute guided tours of the chapel and the council chamber where Bohemian kings were elected, until the arrival of the Habsburgs. The tower is worth the climb (or use the lift) for the rooftop view. (The tourist information office is at the rear, ➤ 36.)

> **DEATH IN THE MORNING**
>
> Old Town Square's most spectacular public execution took place on 21 June, 1621, near the start of the Thirty Years War. Eight months after the Catholics' victory at Bílá Hora (White Mountain), Prague's imperial governor had 27 Protestant leaders condemned to death. At 5am, cannons boomed out to summon people to the spectacle. With drums rolling and trumpets blaring to drown out any last words of protest, the executioner cut off the heads, each with one blow, of 24 nobles and knights. For them, decapitation was a "privilege" of rank. Three commoners were hanged. Today, this traumatic moment in Prague history is marked by 27 white crosses set in the paving on the east side of the town hall.

# Staré Město (Old Town)

## Astronomical Clock
Set against the belfry, the Town Hall's top tourist attraction draws its crowds when fanciful characters are set in motion every hour, on the hour, 9–9. The clock was built in 1410 not so much to tell the precise time (of no great interest in those less hurried days) as to show the state of the universe, the position and movement of the stars and planets – and their astrological impact on daily life. The hour's last chime starts a procession in the upper windows of the 12 Apostles, copies of 18th-century woodcarvings destroyed in 1945.

Flanking the 24-hour clock, the skeleton of Death tolls his bell and shows by an hourglass that time is up for his Turkish neighbour, who is meant to embody Lust, and the figures of Vanity and Usury opposite, all shaking their heads in disbelief. The windows shut, a cock crows and the show is over. Below the clock, the revolving calendar dial's 12 rustic scenes were painted in the 19th century by Josef Mánes.

## Monument to Jan Hus
Revered more as a patriotic symbol than an artistic masterpiece, the ponderous monument facing Týn Church celebrates Jan Hus, the hero of Czech religious reformism (1370–1415). Sculptor Ladislav Šaloun completed it in 1915 for the 500th anniversary of Hus being burned at the stake, charged with heresy.

A conservative opponent of church corruption, Hus stands among his militant disciples, the humbled Protestants later forced to emigrate, and a mother and child symbolizing national renewal. The Nazis covered it in swastikas, and in 1968, during the Soviet invasion, Prague students draped it in black cloth. On the monument's base are Hus's famous words: *Pravda vitězí* (Truth prevails).

## The Square's Houses
The mansions, palaces and merchants' houses on the square are fine examples of the city's civic architecture, many with characteristic rib-vaulted arcades – their arched ceilings supported by stone ribs crossing at a diagonal – that prove a blessing in the rainy days.

On the west side of the square at right angles to the town hall, the **Dům U minuty** (The Minute House) is renowned for its splendid Renaissance *sgraffito* friezes of knights, princes and allegorical figures. It has served variously as the town pharmacy, home to Franz Kafka and municipal offices.

On the south side at No 20, **Dům U zlatého jednorožce** (House of the Golden Unicorn), once Smetana's music school, has an 18th-century facade, Gothic portal and vaulting, and a 13th-century Romanesque basement that at one time formed its ground floor.

On the east side, the grand, 18th-century rococo **Palác Goltz-Kinských** (Goltz-Kinský Palace) was designed by

# Staroměstské náměstí (Old Town Square)

**The focal point of the Old Town Square is the monument to Jan Hus, one of the country's leading national figures**

Kilián Ignác Dienzenhofer, who also built the Church of St Nicholas across the square (➤ 68). In the 19th century it housed the German Gymnasium (high school) and the haberdashery store of Franz Kafka's father Hermann. A permanent exhibition on antique and oriental art opened in spring 2010.

Set back to the right of the palace, in fine stylistic counterpoint, is the four-square Gothic **Dům U kamenného zvonu** (House of the Stone Bell). A baroque facade was removed in 1970 to reveal its 14th-century honey-coloured limestone and graceful mullioned windows. The goldsmith's mansion is now a modern art gallery.

### TAKING A BREAK
There are plenty of open-air cafes on the square; or for a light lunch, follow the street Dlouhá that leads off the square, bearing left on the street Kozí until you come to **Bakeshop Praha** (Kozí 1, Staré Město).

🞤 206 B3 ☎ Old Town Hall general information: 236 002 629; tours in English 236 002 562; Dům U kamenného zvonu (Stone Bell) 222 327 851
🕐 Old Town Hall: Mon 11–10; Tue–Sun 9–10; Stone Bell: Tue–Sun 10–8
Ⓜ Staroměstská 🚌 17, 18
💰 Old Town Hall Tower: 100Kč; Stone Bell: 120Kč

## INSIDER INFO

- Closed to traffic, the square is now a popular spot for **people-watching** from the open-air cafes.
- Avoid the square's mob scene for the noontime "show" at the Astronomical Clock.

Staré Město (Old Town)

# ⓫ Kostel Panny Marie Před Týnem
# (Týn Church & Týn Courtyard)

**With their dramatic clusters of spires, the two towers make the venerable Týn Church one of the Old Town's most striking landmarks. This important church of the Hussite reform movement rises behind the graceful white Venetian-style gables of the former Týn School on the east side of Old Town Square.**

### The Treasures of Týn Church
After taking in the silhouette from across Old Town Square, take the narrow Týnská ulička between the House of the Stone Bell and the Týn School to get to the church – its full name meaning Church of Our Lady Before Týn (Chrám Matky Boží před Týnem).

# Kostel Panny Marie Před Týnem (Týn Church & Courtyard)

*Botanicus, selling organic products, is in Ungelt, behind the church*

Its north portal has a splendid Gothic pediment of *The Passion of Christ* (1390), sculpted by Peter Parléř. Inside, the slender nave's baroque ceiling was built after a fire in 1689, but the aisles' original Gothic vaulting has survived. Notice the fine 15th-century **stone pulpit** and, on the main altar, Karel Škréta's *Assumption of the Virgin Mary* (1649). Just right of the presbytery steps is the russet marble **tomb of Tycho Brahe** (1546–1601), renowned court astronomer to Rudolf II (➤ 10).

*Opposite: There's a defiant air to the spires of Týn Church, testament to the Czechs' early history of religious reform*

## Týn Courtyard (Ungelt)

The courtyard behind the church is where German merchants met from the 12th to the 18th centuries to find lodgings, do business and pay customs duty (*Ungelt* in medieval German – which gave it its name). It has been tastefully refurbished. Warehouses and customs offices have been converted into shops, art galleries and studios, cafes, restaurants and an elegant hotel. Along the north side is the **Granovský palác** (1560), a handsome Renaissance mansion built over earlier Romanesque dwellings.

## Strife-Torn Týn

The church has borne witness to much of the blood and thunder of Prague's religious conflicts. The German merchants built a chapel here in the 1100s. As trade expanded, they began a bigger church in 1365. Work stopped during the insurrection that followed the burning of Jan Hus (➤ 60) – roof timber was diverted for gallows to hang Hussite rebels. Many German merchants prudently left town and the rebels' successors completed the church as a counterpart to the cathedral of St Vitus (➤ 90).

The Hussites' champion, Bohemian-born King Jiři z Poděbrad (George of Poděbrady), pointedly went to Mass at Týn Church after his coronation in 1458. The statue of this last king of Bohemia was placed in the gable overlooking Old Town Square. In

> **TYCHO'S NOSE JOB**
> Astro-alchemist Tycho Brahe was attracted to gold. He lost a bit of his nose in a duel and had a new part made up in gold and silver. When his tomb was opened in 1901 the costly appendage had gone.

# Staré Město (Old Town)

**THE FATEFUL BATTLE**

For many Czechs, 8 November, 1620, stands out as a day of infamy on a par with the invasion of Warsaw Pact troops in 1968 or the communist takeover in 1948. Early in the Thirty Years War, the Catholic victory over the Protestants at Bílá Hora (White Mountain) sealed the fate of Bohemian nationalism for 300 years. On a hilltop in the western outskirts of modern Prague, Czech Protestant leaders gathered 21,000 mercenaries from Moravia, Germany, Austria and Hungary to fight the Habsburgs' Catholic army, commanded by Maximilian of Bavaria. The numerical superiority – 28,000 – of his German, Spanish and French soldiers (including philosopher René Descartes) was offset by their uphill fight. However, the Protestants' Hungarian troops fled at the first assault, little more than a probe, and the Bohemian force collapsed. Its leaders were unable to rouse the citizens of Prague to resist and Maximilian entered the city without firing a shot. The Protestant aristocracy and intelligentsia were – often literally – decapitated, with 36,000 families and all non-Catholic clergy driven to emigrate. Bohemia was annexed to the Habsburg Empire until 1918.

1623, after the Catholic victory at Bílá Hora, Jesuit students tore down the statue and chalice, later replaced by the present effigy of the Virgin Mary, with the gold of the chalice melted down for her sceptre, crown and halo.

**The handsome Granovský palác overlooks Ungelt Square**

### TAKING A BREAK

Enjoy an excellent, if expensive, fish dinner at **Riby trh** in the Ungelt, or join other visitors at Ungelt's sports cafe in the northwest corner for satellite sports and beer.

✚ 206 B3 ✉ Church: Staroměstské náměstí; Ungelt: Týnský dvůr
🕐 Tue–Sat 10–1, 3–5  🚇 Staroměstská  ✋ Free

Stavovské divadlo (Estates Theatre)

# ⑫ Stavovské divadlo (Estates Theatre)

**Historically Prague's most important theatre, offering Mozart some of his greatest operatic triumphs (► 26), the Stavovské divadlo has been restored to the neo-classical splendour of its 19th-century heyday.**

The lofty facade presents a fittingly theatrical backdrop at the west end of Ovocný trh (fruit market). The portico, with two pairs of Corinthian columns, is thrust gently into the square by two gracefully curving wings. Crowning the columns is the inscription *Patriae et Musis* (To Fatherland and the Muses). The elegant blue-walled interior has five tiers of boxes in a U shape around the orchestra stalls.

### "Where Is My Home?"

Theatre has always been vital to the Czech national identity, but, apart from Mozart's Italian operas, *The Marriage of Figaro* and *Don Giovanni*, and a couple of Czech plays, the repertoire was entirely German, and remained so until 1920, when Czech nationalists drove out German directors to the cry of "The Stavovské for the nation!" After World War II, Communists reclaimed its Czech identity, naming it after Josef Kajetán Tyl, composer of the national anthem *Kde domov můj?* (*Where Is My Home?*). Today, the Stavovské is triumphantly cosmopolitan. Czechs tend to take their opera seriously and dress accordingly. Evening dress is not a must but it's worth making an effort.

### TAKING A BREAK

For a meal or drink before the show, try **Kogo** (Havelská 27, Staré Město) for great steaks, pasta and pizza.

The restored 19th-century facade of the Estates Theatre

🕂 206 B2  ✉ Ovocný trh 1
☎ 224 902 322; www.estatestheatre.cz
🕐 Performances 7 or 7:30pm  Ⓜ Můstek

Staré Město (Old Town)

# At Your Leisure

Bedřich Smetana sits with his back to the Vltava River, which features in his symphonic poem *Ma Vlast*

### 13 Galerie u Křižovníku

Next door to the church of sv František on Knights of the Cross Square is the entrance to a former medieval hospital, now home to a commercial art gallery and an exhibition on the Judith Bridge, the medieval successor to the Charles Bridge, built around 1170 before succumbing to a flood in 1342. On the ground floor, apart from the paintings you can see a model of the bridge, a garishly painted artificial grotto complete with baroque stalactites (part of the original decoration), and religious objects from the church's treasury, some dating back to the 16th century. Take a few musty steps below ground and you'll be surprised to discover a surviving span of the Judith Bridge as well as the original water stairs. The price of admission includes a coffee and a glass of "Elixir of St John Nepomuk" served by friendly young women in colourful medieval dress. The gallery is only a short walk from the pier for departing river cruises.

✚ 205 F3 ✉ Křižovnicke náměstí 3
☎ 236 033 680 ⏰ Tue–Sun 10–5
Ⓜ Staroměstská 🚋 Trams 17, 18

### 14 Muzeum Bedřicha Smetany (Smetana Museum)

The riverside Smetana Museum devoted to the most patriotic of Czech composers (➤ 27) Bedřich Smetana (1824–84), is housed in a remarkably ornate neo-Renaissance building. The small collection of memorabilia – his spectacles, furniture from his home, garnet necklaces he bought for his wife, his musical scores – provides only a modest peek into the great man's life. **You'll get a better idea of him from the occasional recitals of his chamber music that take place here.**

*Inside Tip*

✚ 205 F2
✉ Novotného lávka
☎ 222 220 082;
www.nm.cz
⏰ Wed–Mon
10–noon; 12:30–5
🚋 17, 18  💰 120Kč

66

# At Your Leisure

## GETTING LOST AROUND HUSOVA TŘÍDA

South of Karlova Street's all too modern tourist traps, the medieval Prague of labyrin-thine lanes, cobbled alleys, vaulted passages and cul-de-sacs comes into its own. It is perfectly safe, even desirable, to lose your way here, particularly at night, the best time to go, when the crowds have disappeared and only you and the fabled ghosts walk the streets. You can always scamper back to the safe haven of restaurants and taverns on Husova Street running through the middle of the maze. Daytime visitors may stumble on such landmarks as the venerable Romanesque **dům Pánů z Kunštátu a Poděbrad**, on Řetězová, now a small museum commemorating the Hussite hero George of Poděbrady, who lived there until he was crowned King of Bohemia in 1458 (➤ 63; Řetězová 3, open May–Sep daily 11–11; 50Kč); and the 14th-century Gothic **Church of St Giles** (sv Jiljí, Husova třída), remodelled on baroque lines in 1733 with fine trompe-l'oeil ceiling frescoes inside.

*Insider Tip*

### 15 Křižovnické náměstí

The "Knights of the Cross Square" is a forecourt to Charles Bridge, and people arrange to meet at the foot of the 19th-century **statue of Charles IV**, the king who built the bridge.

On the north side of the square, Kostel sv Františka z Assisi is the baroque **church of the Czech knights**, once gatekeepers to the bridge. Its imposing dome was modelled after that of St Peter's in Rome. See the interior's fine purple marble columns and the cupola's ceiling fresco of *The Last Judgement* by Václav Vavřinec.

Incorporated into the Klementinum on Karlova Street, the Jesuit **Church of San Salvator** (Kostela Nejsvětějšího Salvátora) has an Italian-style Renaissance facade and an elaborate baroque interior.

205 F2  Staroměstská  17, 18

### 16 Muzeum loutkářských kultur (Puppet Museum)

Tucked away among Karlova Street's kitschy souvenir shops is this oasis of genuine folk art. The puppet museum displays, in Gothic-vaulted cellars, beautifully carved and costumed puppets mostly from the 19th and early 20th centuries, but inspired by a Czech tradition dating back to the Middle Ages. There are also puppets from Asia, Africa and other European countries, with many on sale at the museum shop. All the displays are static, and unfortunately there aren't any puppet demonstrations. (For puppet shows ➤ 78.) Their website, www.puppetart.com, is worth a look.

205 F2  Karlova 12  224 241 103
Museum: Tue–Sun 9–6
Staroměstská  17, 18  60Kč

### 17 Betlémská kaple (Bethlehem Chapel)

The Bethlehem Chapel is a reconstruction of a major shrine to Czech national history, the chapel in which Jan Hus (➤ 22) preached his Reformist brand of Christianity in the early 1400s. Built 1391–94 and totally destroyed in the 18th century, the chapel, with its distinctive roof of twin wooden gables, was resurrected in 1950 in a post-war campaign to restore Czech self-esteem. Every detail of the structure has been meticulously reproduced from the original. Displayed inside is part of a permanent exhibit of the revered chapel's history.

205 F2  Betlémské náměstí 4
Apr–Oct Tue–Sun 10–6;
Nov–Mar Tue–Sun 10–5:30
Národní třída  6, 9, 18, 22  75Kč

### 18 Klementinum

More than 30 houses, three churches, 10 courtyards and

# Staré Město (Old Town)

> **CAUGHT IN THE ACT**
> Less subtle than the Church of sv Jakub's treasures, but a great crowd-pleaser, are the remains of a human forearm (best seen with binoculars) suspended high up on the west wall. The story goes that it was chopped off a thief who got his hand stuck while trying to steal the Madonna's jewels at the high altar – 400 years ago.

several gardens were demolished to make way for the sprawling complex of the former Jesuit college. Extending east from Křižovnická along Karlova over to Mariánské náměstí, the Klementinum's formidable combination of Renaissance, baroque and neo-classical styles covers an area second only to Prague Castle.

Founded by the Jesuits in 1556 to counter the Hussite influence, it now houses the National Library. Besides special exhibitions of library manuscripts, two architectural gems are open to the public: the 18th-century **Zrcadlová kaple (Chapel of Mirrors)** during chamber music recitals, and the ==splendid **Baroque Library Hall** (1727) on guided tours.== *Inside Tip* The **Astronomical Tower**, at the very heart of the complex, has been recording the weather since 1775.

✚ 205 F3 ✉ Karlova 1 (entrance next to church of St Clement)
☎ Reservations (advised) 606 100 293; www.klementinum.com
🎧 Guided tour only, taking in Baroque Library Hall, Mirror Chapel and Astronomical Tower Jan–Mar daily 10–4, Apr, Oct 10–5, Nov–Dec 10–4. Tours take 50 mins and leave every hour on the hour (every half hour at peak times)
Ⓜ Staroměstská 💰 220Kč

## 🄳 Svatého Mikuláš (St Nicholas)

German merchants established the first church of St Nicholas on Old Town Square in the 12th century, using it as a community centre until the Old Town Hall was built. In 1620, Benedictine monks took it over and subsequently replaced it with the present church. The monastery was closed in 1787 and the church used as a warehouse until 1920. The church is little used today except as a ==venue for better-than-average church concerts.== *Insider Tip*

It was built in 1735 by Kilián Ignác Dienzenhofer, whose father Kryštof had designed the St Nicholas Church of Malá Strana (▶ 105). Because of houses once hemming in the church on three sides (removed by slum clearance in the 1890s), the architect gave the main twin-towered facade a southern rather than more conventional western exposure.

The decoration of the lofty interior includes frescoes by the

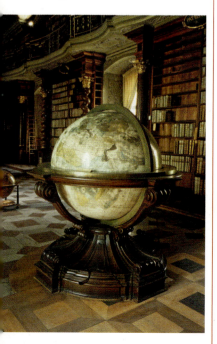

**An antique globe in the Baroque Library Hall in the Klementinum**

# At Your Leisure

*After 100 years as a warehouse, the Church of St Nicholas is a leading venue for church concerts*

Austrian-Czech artist Johann Lucas Kracker. St Nicholas and St Benedict adorn the arch of the cupola. The painting of the Virgin Mary on the altar is 20th century.

🞡 206 A3 ✉ Staroměstské náměstí
☎ 224 190 991 Ⓜ Staroměstská

## ⓴ Dům U zlatého prstenu (House of the Golden Ring)

The Prague City Gallery (also known by its old name Dům U zlatého prstenu, from the Golden Ring emblem it once had) has premises all over town and uses this fine 13th-century mansion for its collections of Czech 20th-century art. Presented on three floors in constantly changing exhibitions, the collections include symbolists (Bílek and Švabinsky), Cubists (Filla and the aptly named Kubišta), Realists (Čapek, Zrzavý) and surrealists (Teige, Štyrský) and more recent conceptual artists. Shows of avant garde contemporary works are held in the Gothic-vaulted cellars.

🞡 206 B3 ✉ Ungelt, Tynská 6
☎ 224 827 022; www.ghmp.cz
🕐 Tue–Sun 10–6
Ⓜ Náměstí Republiky 🚋 5, 8, 14 💰 120Kč

## ㉑ Svatého Jakub (St James)

The impact of this 14th-century church, tucked away east of Ungelt, is wonderfully rich and subtle. Total reconstruction in exuberant baroque style after a fire in 1689 does not conceal the church's fundamentally Gothic character. The subdued light, lofty and narrow nave and extended choir make a delicate counterpoint to the elaborate sculpture and effusive paintings of the altars.

# Staré Město (Old Town)

Its acoustics make it an ideal venue for concerts and organ recitals. Reiner's impressive **Martyrdom of St James** adorns the main altar, but the church's undoubted outstanding masterpiece, in the north aisle, is the **tomb of Count Mitrovice** (1714) designed by the great Austrian baroque architect Johann Bernhard Fischer von Erlach and carved by the Prague sculptor Ferdinand Maximilian Brokof.
✚ 206 B3  ✉ Malá Štupartská 6
☎ 604 208 490
🚇 Náměstí Republiky  🚋 5, 8, 14

### 22 Celetná
One of Old Town's most elegant shopping streets is an ancient thoroughfare, once the main medieval trade route between Old Town Square and eastern Europe via the Prašná brána (Powder Tower, ➤ 160). It was once the beginning of the *Králova Cesta* (Royal Route) for kings' coronation processions to Prague Castle.

The colourful baroque facades on originally Romanesque and Gothic houses have been beautifully restored, often with a handsome *pavlač* (balconied courtyard). On the south side of the street, at No 22, look out for the **U Supa** (At the Vulture), a pub installed in one of the street's finest houses. On the north side of the street, in a historic house is a theatre, Divadlo v Celetné.

On the corner of Ovocný trh, breaking but not clashing with the prevailing baroque style, the **House of the Black Madonna** (Dům U černé Matky boží, 1912 – Museum of Czech Cubist Art) is a powerful statement of Czech Cubist architecture by Josef Gočar. It was built in 1912, originally as a department store. It still contains

**An example of the beautiful detailing to be found on the buildings of Celetná street**

> **THE PRIEST AND THE WHORE**
> Prague is famous for its ghosts and Celetná has two. Coming out of one of the street's many covered passages, a lady of the night bumped into a priest and thought she would try her luck with him. The outraged priest hit her on the head with his cross, and she fell dead at his feet. Horrified at what he had done, he died of a stroke. The lady can still be seen pursuing her holy killer, most frequently after the pubs close.

the **Grand Café Orient** (➤ 76) with its Cubist interior. The Museum of Czech Cubism that used to be housed here has in the meantime moved to the National Gallery.
✚ 206 B2

### 23 Karolinum
The red brick university building running along the north side of the Stavovské divadlo is reserved now for graduation ceremonies.

# At Your Leisure

**Only the Karolinum's Gothic chapel window survived World War II**

After destruction by the Nazis in 1945, only a stone oriel window of the Gothic chapel remains from the original Karolinum founded here by Charles IV in 1348. It was the oldest German university – Vienna and Heidelberg followed later in 1365 and 1386. Like the town's churches and theatres, the university provided yet another focus for rivalries between the Czech- and German-speaking communities. In 1882, the university formally divided its teaching into separate and parallel faculties. At the end of World War II, the German faculty was closed.

✚ 206 B2
✉ Ovocný trh 3  Ⓜ Můstek

## Staré Město (Old Town)

# Where to...
# Eat and Drink

**Prices**
Expect to pay per person for a meal, including drinks, tax and service:
**£** under 500Kč    **££** 500Kč–1,000Kč    **£££** over 1,000Kč

## RESTAURANTS

### Cotto Crudo £££
Prague's first-ever Michelin star went to the house restaurant of the Four Seasons Hotel. Allegro set the standards in the capital. And Cotto Crudo is a worthy successor. The overall theme is Italian and Mediterranean. In nice weather, try to get a table on the terrace. Reservations are recommended.
🏠 205 F3  ✉ Veleslavínova 2a
☎ 221 426 880; www.fourseasons.com
🕐 Daily 11:30–10:30  Ⓜ Staroměstská

### Ambiente Brasileiro ££
**Insider Tip**
==If you would like to eat top-quality meat then you should go to the Old Town Hall.== There you will find a *Rodizio* – a Brazilian-style steakhouse serving various kinds of quality meat on a skewer. The restaurant may be located in a vaulted cellar in Prague, but it is almost as good as those in Rio de Janeiro.
🏠 206 B3 BU Radnice 13, Staré Město
☎ 224 234 474; www.ambi.cz
🕐 Daily 11:30–midnight  Ⓜ Staroměstská

### Brasserie La Provence ££/£££
The owners of this popular restaurant have done their homework, and it shows. This is an authentic Parisian brasserie, that is – in every sense: from the old silvered mirrors and red leather booths to the stencilled "*huitres*" and "*vins*" on the front doors. The emphasis is on fresh seafood, but there are also plenty of French favourites like rabbit, roast chicken and quiche on offer. Half the fun here is gazing about the sparkling *belle-époque* room, or out the massive windows that encase this lovely corner restaurant.
🏠 206 B3  ✉ Štupartská 9
☎ 296 826 155; www.kampagroup.cz
🕐 Daily 11am–midnight  Ⓜ Náměstí Republiky

### Da Nico Wine Bar and Restaurant ££
The Czech-Italian owner of this intimate new wine bar-restaurant takes his cooking seriously, and the pleasure of his guests even more so. Don't be surprised to see him wander out of the kitchen to ask how you liked the risotto or squid-ink pasta, and then bring you something new to taste. The atmosphere is warm and welcoming. This is the kind of place where a meal may last all night, and end up with the chef sitting in the dining room, passing a bottle of grappa around the room.
🏠 206 B3  ✉ Dlouhá 21
☎ 222 311 807; www.danico.cz
🕐 Daily 11–11  Ⓜ Náměstí Republiky

### Le Degustation £££
This is the top end of the Czech Ambiente chain of very good restaurants. It's a kind of concept restaurant – the concept being seven- to eight-course set meals that unfold slowly throughout the evening. In other words, it's no place for light appetites or quick bites. The quality is excellent and you can choose from a traditional Bohemian set menu or something more Continental and contemporary.

# Where to...

206 B3 ✉ Haštalská 18
☎ 222 311 234; la degustation.cz
🕐 Daily 6pm–midnight
Ⓜ Náměstí Republiky

## Dubliner Irish Pub £

The great fish & chips taste best on a Champions League evening; the games are shown on twelve screens.

206 B3 ✉ Týn 1, Staré Město
☎ 224 895 4 04; www.aulddubliner.cz
🕐 Sun–Wed 11am–1am, Thu–Sat 11am–3am
Ⓜ Staroměstská

## La Finestra £££

Trattoria atmosphere, super pasta, and good fish which is shown to the guests at the table before it is prepared. The restaurant is one of the centre's hot spots.

206 A3 ✉ Platnéřská 13, Staré Město
☎ 222 325 222; www.lafinestra.cz
🕐 Daily 5pm–midnight  Ⓜ Staroměstská

## Indian Jewel ££

Indian Jewel has been earning plaudits for its Mughal cooking ever since it opened its doors in 2009. While tandoori grills are to the fore, curries and kebabs are also available and there is a small but appetizing selection of vegetarian dishes. Outdoor seating is available on the terrace with views of the fabulous Ungelt courtyard.

206 B3 ✉ Týn 6
☎ 222 310 156; www.indianjewel.cz
🕐 Daily 11–11  Ⓜ Staroměstská

## Klub Architektů £

Young people pack into this stone-vaulted space beneath the Bethlehem Chapel (➤ 67). The menu offers Czech comfort food: *smažený sýr* (fried cheese), *smažený celer* (fried celery), and *zapečený kuřecí steak s broskví a sýrem* (chicken topped with melted cheese and peaches).

206 A2 ✉ Betlémské náměstí 5a
☎ 602 250 082; www.klubarchitektu.com
🕐 Daily 11:30am–midnight
Ⓜ Staroměstská

## Kolkovna £

Yes, it's in all the other guidebooks and, yes, it's as touristy as can be. But if you want a sure-fire, can't miss, relatively cheap and good night out in a Czech restaurant, this is the place. ==The Pilsner Urquell on tap is some of the freshest in town,== **Insider Tip** and you can't beat the roast pork, *gulas*, dumplings, duck and just about everything else Czech that comes out of the kitchen. In the meantime, there is a chain of four restaurants in the city.

206 B2 ✉ Na Příkopě 10
☎ 277 008 880; www.kolkovna.cz
🕐 Daily 11am–midnight  Ⓜ Můstek

## Mlynec £££

This is a place for a special meal, so make a reservation and prepare to be pampered. The chef is the only one in the country to have received the Michelin "Bibendum" distinction not once, but three times. Why not try the tasting menu and something from the extensive wine selection with its fine choice of vintage and Grand Cru wines.

205 F2 ✉ Novotného lávka 9
☎ 277 000 777; www.mlynec.cz
🕐 Mon–Sun noon–3, 5:30–11
Ⓜ Staroměstská

## NoStress ££

Occupying a corner like some grand sailing ship of old, NoStress is a French-Thai fusion restaurant with a chic interior design gallery tucked into the back. The Belgian chef sends out a variety of hot and cold appetizers, and main dishes such as grilled duck breast with plums and fried potatoes, Thai spicy shrimp soup and codfish curry with jasmine rice. Desserts, such as the orange and chocolate mousse opera cake, are sublime. There is a laidback lounge if you just want a drink.

206 B3 ✉ Dušní 10 (entrance at V Kolkovně 9) ☎ 222 317 007; www.nostress.cz
🕐 Daily 10am–midnight  Ⓜ Staroměstská

# Staré Město (Old Town)

### Pizza Nuova ££
Like Le Degustation, another member of the Ambiente family, but this one is at the lower end of the food chain: pizza and pasta. There are good reasons to come here – the terrific pizza, the all-you-can-eat antipasto buffet that is very good value for money and an 👶 indoor playground for kids and a tolerant waiting staff – a godsend if you're with small children.

✚ 206 C3 ✉ Revoluční 1
☎ 221 803 308; www.ambi.cz
🕒 Daily 11:30–11:30
🚇 Náměstí Republiky

### Pizzeria Rugantino £
Decent pizza was a rarity in Prague until the changes of 1989. The wood-oven pizzas and salads are excellent in this busy place, which is popular with everyone from backpackers to local celebrities – a good choice for lunchtime or dinner.

✚ 206 B3 ✉ Dušni 4 (also at Klimentská 40)
☎ 222 318 172; www.rugantino.cz
🕒 Mon–Sat 11–11, Sun noon–11
🚇 Staroměstská

### Rybí trh ££/£££
Unlike the city's older riverside seafood restaurants, Rybí trh ("The Fish Market") lies inland amid the recently gentrified confines of the Týn courtyard (▶63). A huge selection of seafood is available, some of it swimming in the aquaria scattered around. There are two sparsely decorated dining rooms at the courtyard level and also a brick-arched cellar below.

✚ 206 B3 ✉ Týnský Dvůr 5
☎ 224 895 447; www.rybitrh.cz
🕒 Daily 11am–midnight
🚇 Náměstí Republiky

### V Zátiší £££
Winning so much praise and so many awards hasn't spoiled Zátiší, which still seems like an island amid a sea of touristy restaurants. The interior here is low-key elegance, the welcome is unstuffy and hospitable. There's nothing faddish about the cooking – just skilfully prepared European fare with enough Czech touches to remind you that, after all, you're in Prague's Old Town. You will find quite a few fish dishes on the menu and everything served is totally fresh. If you want local cuisine, try the Bohemian roast goose in honey-lavender sauce. Chocoholics rave over the *čokoládová pěna* (chocolate mousse) so make sure you leave room for dessert.

✚ 206 A2
✉ Liliová 1 (at Betlémské náměstí)
☎ 222 221 155; www.vzatisi.cz
🕒 Daily noon–3, 5:30–11

## INNS, PUBS AND BARS

### Bar and Books
With its red walls, soft leather banquettes and mellow mood music this classy cocktail lounge in the Týn courtyard is ==the perfect setting for an evening of gentle relaxation.== If a vodka martini made according to James Bond creator Ian Fleming's original recipe does not appeal, there's a fine selection of wines and spirits on offer, as well as Cuban cigars.

✚ 206 B3 ✉ Týnská 19
☎ 224 815 122; www.barandbooks.cz/tynska
🕒 Daily 5pm–4am

### Chateau Rouge
This is a raucous bar catering mainly to expats and their new Czech friends. There's a music club downstairs that's open until the wee hours. Most of the action, though, takes place at the street-level main bar. If you like drinking, noise and commotion, this won't disappoint.

✚ 206 B3 ✉ Jakubská 2
☎ 222 316 328; www.chateaurouge.cz
🕒 Daily noon–3am

# Where to...

## U Medvídků
A famous beer hall where the taps dispense a river of mild Budvar from South Bohemia (➤ 30). Accompanying the beer is a well-prepared menu of Czech specialities to soak it all up.
✚ 205 F2 ✉ Na Perštýně 7
☎ 224 211 916; www.umedvidku.cz
🕓 Mon–Sat 11–11, Sun noon–10

## U Vejvodů
A former smoky, ancient pub has emerged from reconstruction as a skylit Pilsner palace where visitors won't feel intimidated and locals appreciate the affordable prices.
✚ 206 A2 ✉ Jilská 4
☎ 224 219 999; www.restauraceuvejvodu.cz
🕓 Mon–Thu 10am–3am, Fri, Sat 10am–4am, Sun 10am–2am

## U Zlatého tygra
One of the last remaining traditional Czech pubs in the Old Town – traditional in the sense that there's absolutely no effort made to attract tourists. Each day at 3pm, the regulars line up and take their tables. You're welcome to line up too and sit if and where there's a spot. Excellent beer and passable Czech food complete the picture.
✚ 206 A2 ✉ Husova 17
☎ 222 221 111; www.uzlatehotygra.cz
🕓 Daily 3pm–11pm

### CAFÉS AND TEAROOMS

The resurgence of Prague's cafe scene (➤ 45) is nowhere more visible than in Staré Město, where delightful coffee houses and tearooms are dotted about in the winding lanes.

## Bakeshop Praha
This establishment is more a bakery than a coffee shop, but they do serve great coffee and there are chairs on hand to relax with a cup, as well as a slice of home-made cake, a brownie or a chocolate chip cookie. Bakeshop Praha is also a good spot to grab take-out salads and sandwiches for a picnic lunch later.
✚ 206 B3 ✉ Kozí 1
☎ 222 316 823; www.bakeshop.cz
🕓 Daily 7–7

## Cafe Konvikt
Popular with a young, trendy crowd, this inexpensive gathering place has a lofty room with views out to one of Staré Město's newly renovated courtyards. Just a few dishes and snacks are on the menu, including some nice vegetarian dishes and good desserts, such as *bábovka* (chocolate cake).
✚ 205 C3 ✉ Bartolomějská 11
☎ 224 232 427
🕓 Daily 11–midnight

## Café de Paris
If Obecní dům's (➤ 146) huge cafe is full on a summer's afternoon, you can often find a seat at this small, equally genuine Art Nouveau coffee house across the street. Light, international dishes are available, such as pasta, Caesar salad and bagel sandwiches.
✚ 206 C3
✉ Hotel Paříž, U Obecního domu 1
☎ 222 195 195; www.hotel-paris.cz
🕓 Daily 8am–midnight

## Choco Café
A great place for a break in your busy sightseeing schedule. **Insider Tip**
Choco Café serves bruschetta, sandwiches, salads, cakes, coffee and iced teas, but their star offering is hot chocolate with chilli and ginger, good on a winter's day.
✚ 206 A2 ✉ Liliová 4
☎ 222 222 519; www.choco-cafe.cz
🕓 Mon–Fri 10–9, Sat, Sun 10–8

## Culinaria
A combination coffee shop and deli, with Prague's smartest sandwich counter filled with

## Staré Město (Old Town)

delicacies such as beef Wellington and grilled salmon to take away. An espresso bar on the premises serves very good coffee, as well as juices and smoothies.
- 206 A2
- Skořepka 9
- 224 231 01; www.culinaria.cz
- Mon–Sat 10–7, Sun 5–noon

### Grand Cafe Orient
Czech designers have gone to great pains to recreate the early 20th-century interior of this cafe on the first floor of the House of the Black Madonna (▶ 70). Cakes, sandwiches and other light snacks are served.
- 206 B2
- Ovocný trh 19
- 224 224 240; www.grandcafeorient.cz
- Mon–Fri 9am–10pm, Sat, Sun 10am–10pm

### Grand Cafe Praha
An exclusive cafe situated on the first floor of the Grand Hotel. The choice of cakes is almost bewildering. In the summer, the garden offers a spectacular view of the Astronomical Clock..
- 206 B2
- Staroměstské náměstí 22
- 221 632 522; www.grandcafe.cz
- Daily 7am–10pm

### Kavárna Slavia
This cafe has welcomed just about every notable Prague writer, musician and actor over the past century. You can order the fabled artist's tipple, absinthe, here (it's distilled in the Czech Republic). Otherwise there are coffees, wine, beer and light meals to choose from, including a *toasty* (toast topped with meats). The best thing to do is to drop in for a drink, admire the marble and steel interior and just soak up the atmosphere.
- 205 F1
- Smetanova nábřeží 2 (at Národní třída)
- 224 218 493; www.cafeslavia.cz
- Daily 9am–11pm

# Where to...
# Shop

Staré Město has Prague's greatest concentration of boutiques. The main trick here is to get off the heavily touristed promenades and seek out the smaller side streets and alleyways.

### OLD TOWN SQUARE

For centuries the irregular cobbled plaza of Staroměstské náměstí (Old Town Square) has formed the social and commercial heart of the city, but you'll find more shopping opportunities along the streets that fan out from the square.

### Fashion
Pařížká is really the centre for high fashion in Prague, and Nové Město – particularly along Na příkopě – is best for high street fashion. Nevertheless, there are some decent clothing and fashion shops in the Old Town. Start first at the Obecní dům. Here you'll find the high-end Italian purse and leather goods maker **Coccinelle** (Náměstí Republiky 5, also at Železná 22; tel: 222 002 340). Small boutiques dot the streets behind the Obecní dům.

### Books, Prints and Maps
There are some excellent bookshops in the Old Town that also sell English books. **Anagram Books** in the Ungelt courtyard (tel: 224 895 737; www.anagram.cz) specializes in art, philosophy and history, but has a decent literature section too.

**Big Ben Bookshop** at Malá Štupartská 5 (tel: 224 826 565; www.bigbenbookshop.com), has a great selection of mysteries, thrillers and airport reads.

# Where to...

Prague is filled with second-hand bookstores (in Czech: *antikvariát*), that usually also offer lithographs, posters, maps, old magazines, and just about everything else.

### General and Gifts
The Palladium Shopping Centre at Náměstí Republiky (tel: 225 770 250) has several gift shops, as well as boutiques, drug stores, bars and restaurants – and it's open seven days a week.

On Celetná street, off Staroměstské náměstí, **Cristallino** (No 12, tel: 224 223 027; www.cristallino.cz) and **Celetná Crystal** (No 15, tel: 224 223 073) sell crystal, glassware, garnets and jewellery.

**Artěl**, at Celetná 29 (entrance on Rybná, tel: 271 732 161; www.artelglass.com), offers reproduction glassware from the 1920s and 30s, as well as odd but eye-catching books and jewellery.

**Botanicus** (tel: 234 767 446; www.botanicus.cz) in the Ungelt courtyard, has items made, grown or bottled on an organic farm outside Prague: candles, soaps, oils and vinegars.

Next door is **Obchod Marionety Truhlář** (www.marionety.com) which sells fantastic hand-carved wooden puppets.

There's a fascinating curiosity shop, **Bric à Brac** (tel: 222 326 484) in two buildings; one at Týnská 7 and the other behind it in a courtyard.

There are two shops worth seeking out on Dlouhá: **Studio Šperk** (No. 19, tel: 224 815 161) sells beautiful garnet jewellery in contemporary settings.

**Bohemia Granat Jewellery** (No 28, tel: 222 315 612) has Bohemian garnet jewellery at factory prices.

**Art Decoratif** (tel: 222 002 350) in the Obecní dům complex sells exquisite reproduction Art Nouveau lamps, jewellery and accessories.

## TOWARDS KARLŮV MOST

Don't neglect the area south and west of Old Town Square. The central axis here is highly touristy Karlova. For a bargain or something more authentic head for the streets behind Karlova and between Old Town Square and Národní třída – such as Michalská or Na Perštýně.

### Antiques
**Alma Mahler Antiques** (Valentínská 7, tel: 222 325 865) has everything from bric-a-brac to antiques, as well as a wine bar.

**Art Deco Galerie** (Michalská 21, tel: 224 223 076), as the name implies, sells Czech early modern reproductions and some original pieces.

For the very nicest antiques, try the local branch of the Austrian auction house **Dorotheum**. Watch with astonishment as contemporary works by artists such as Enrico Castellani collect phenomenal prices. (Ovocný trh 2, tel: 224 222 001; www.dorotheum.cz).

### Books, Prints and Maps
The area just beyond Betlémské náměstí, along the street Betlémská, has a string of antiquarian bookshops and small art galleries. Great sources of rare lithographs, maps and poster art.

### General and Gifts
**Manufaktura**, at Melantrichová 17 (tel: 221 632 480), not far from Old Town Square, has lovely Czech-made ceramics, kitchen items, ornaments and home decor items.

==There is a market along the Havelska offering a wide selection of souvenirs== (daily 10–7); you will also find traditional shops behind the stalls, which are well worth exploring.

Insider Tip

## Staré Město (Old Town)

# Where to... Go Out

Jazz in an 800-year-old cellar, a chamber concert amid the luscious statuary of a baroque church, opera "sung" by lifelike marionettes... Staré Město's entertainment is in keeping with its medieval streets and historic architecture.

### THEATRE

### Divadlo Na Zábradlí
The tiny stage at this influential playhouse ("Theatre on the Balustrade") earned its fame not only for Václav Havel's dramatic works in the 1960s, but also for ground-breaking interpretations of classic and modern drama. Performances are in Czech.

✚ 205 F2 ✉ Anenské náměstí 5, Staré Město
☎ 222 868 868; www.nazabradli.cz

### National Marionette Theatre (Národní divadlo marionet)
This entertainment for adults and children alike wins kudos for keeping alive the venerable Czech art of puppet opera. *Don Giovanni* has played here since 1991. Younger kids will enjoy it too but may get fidgety by the third act.

✚ 206 A3 ✉ Žatecká 1, Staré Město
☎ 224 819 322; www.mozart.cz

### MUSIC

### AghaRTA
High-quality contemporary jazz and fusion in an 800-year old Gothic cellar. Shows start at 9pm, but get there by 8pm to get a seat.

✚ 206 B2 ✉ Železná 16, Staré Město
☎ 222 211 275; www.agharta.cz

### Buddha Bar
Lounge music in cool Buddha-Bar style surroundings. Tasty Asian dishes are served in the adjoining restaurant.

✚ 206 B3 ✉ Jakubská 8, Staré Město
☎ 221 776 300;
www.buddhabarhotelprague.com

### Klementinum
The lavish 18th-century Chapel of Mirrors is the setting for some memorable chamber music.

✚ 206 A2
✉ Karlova (next to church of St Clement)
☎ 222 220 879; www.klementinum.com

### Roxy
This arts centre provides performance space for top DJs and stars of world music.

✚ 206 B3 ✉ Dlouhá 33, Staré Město
☎ 224 826 296; www.roxy.cz

### Stavovské divadlo
Buy a ticket for a performance at the Estates Theatre (➤ 65) – the oldest theatre building in Prague – and marvel at the hall where Mozart conducted the first performance of *Don Giovanni*.

The excellent **Národní divadlo** (National Theatre) opera company (➤ 153) does a couple of Mozart's (as well as Czech and other international) operas in repertory. The box office is across from the back of the theatre in the Kolowrat Palace.

✚ 206 B2
✉ Ovocny trh 6 (box office), Staré Město
☎ 224 901 448; www.narodni-divadlo.cz

---

**BLACKLIGHT THEATRES**

Although the most well-known blacklight theatre, **Laterna Magika** (➤ 48, 168) is in the New Town, there are some good performances available in the Old Town as well:

**Ta Fantastika** (Karlova 8, Staré Město; tel: 222 221 366; www.tafantastika.cz)

**Divaldo Image** (Pařížská 4, Staré Město; tel: 222 314 458; www.imagetheatre.cz)

# Hradčany, Malá Strana and Beyond

| | |
|---|---|
| Getting Your Bearings | 80 |
| Two Perfect Days | 82 |
| TOP 10 | 84 |
| Don't Miss | 101 |
| At Your Leisure | 106 |
| Where to… | 111 |

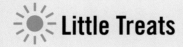

## Little Treats

### Spine-tingling Recitations
It is like being right in the midst of *The Castle* or *The Trial* – the deep voices in the **Franz Kafka Museum** (➤ 107) give you goose bumps.

### Latin America in Prague
The Christ child at **St Maria de Victoria** (➤ 107) draws in South Americans like a magnet; Spanish is often the dominant language here.

### Paris in Prague
What on earth is the Eiffel Tower doing in Prague? And wasn't it taller at one stage? You can ask these questions on the **Petřín hill** (➤ 110).

## Hradčany, Malá Strana and Beyond

# Getting Your Bearings

**Dominating the Vltava river's left bank is the sprawling castle complex and great Gothic cathedral within its walls. Baroque mansions and palaces, many with beautiful gardens, are now embassies, museums, pubs and smart restaurants. Beyond them, bourgeois and working-class neighbourhoods testify to the city's golden as well as less glittering periods.**

Hradčany is Prague Castle's neighbourhood. Made a township in the 16th century, it covers the monumental precinct within the castle walls and surrounding gardens, as well as the palaces to the west around Castle Square (Hradčanské náměstí).

Malá Strana (literally "Little Side", as opposed to the bigger right-bank districts) is the old aristocratic district running south of the castle, including the island of Kampa. Its largely unspoiled 18th-century architecture brought Miloš Forman back to his home town to shoot the film *Amadeus*, his life story of Mozart, in an urban landscape more "Viennese" than Vienna itself. Further south, Smíchov is a rather ungainly neighbourhood with the saving grace of the Mozart Museum (albeit currently closed to the public for an unspecified period).

North and east of the castle are the districts of Bubeneč, Letná and Holešovice, with a modern art museum, a couple of rare relics of the Communist era, and the Metronome (with great views).

# Getting Your Bearings

## TOP 10
- ★ Pražský hrad
  (Prague Castle) ➤ 84
- ★ Katedrála sv Víta
  (St Vitus Cathedral) ➤ 90
- ★ Strahovský klášter
  (Strahov Monastery) ➤ 95
- ★ Zlatá ulička
  (Golden Lane) ➤ 98

## Don't Miss
- ㉔ Zahrady
  (Castle Gardens) ➤ 101
- ㉕ Malostranské náměstí
  (Malá Strana Square) ➤ 104

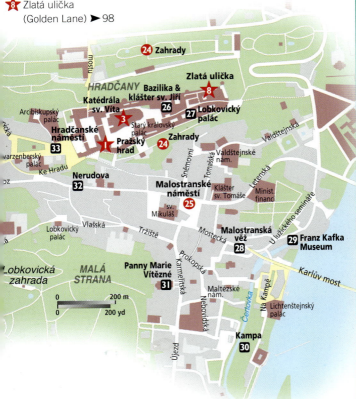

## At Your Leisure
- ㉖ Bazilika & klášter sv Jiří
  (St George Basilica & Convent) ➤ 106
- ㉗ Lobkovický palác ➤ 106
- ㉘ Malostranské věž
  (Malá Strana Bridge Towers) ➤ 106
- ㉙ Franz Kafka Museum ➤ 107
- ㉚ Kampa Island ➤ 107
- ㉛ Panny Marie Vítězné ➤ 107
- ㉜ Nerudova ➤ 108
- ㉝ Hradčanské náměstí ➤ 108
- ㉞ Loreta ➤ 109
- ㉟ Trojský zámek (Villa Troja) ➤ 109
- ㊱ Veletržní palác ➤ 110
- ㊲ Petřín ➤ 110

## Hradčany, Malá Strana and Beyond

# Two Perfect Days

Pražský Hrad (Prague Castle) alone offers sights galore for half a day or more. Ideally, you should reserve two days for the Hradčany and the Malá Strana. If you follow our itinerary, you will not miss any of the highlights. For more information see the main entries (➤ 84–110).

## Day One

### Morning
Steel yourself for a long but thoroughly absorbing exploration of ★ **Prague Castle** (➤ 84). One admission price gets you in to most of the main sights, including the Old Royal Palace, ★ **St Vitus Cathedral**, ➤ 90), **㉖ St George's Basilica** (➤ 106), and the ★ **Golden Lane** (➤ 98). You can rent an audio headphone from the ticket office, which provides information about Czech history. Leave at least 2 to 3 hours for the tour. For lunch, there's a restaurant at the Lobkowicz Palace within the castle complex (Jiřská 3, tel: 602 595 998), or for something more substantial, try **Cowboy's** (Nerudova 40, tel: 296 826 107), below the castle's main gates along the walk to Malá Strana.

### Afternoon
After lunch, take in the obligatory changing of the guard (at the top of the hour) at the main gates of Prague Castle. After that, follow the winding streets and steps down to Malá Strana along historic Nerudova street until you reach **㉕ Malá Strana Square** (➤ 104). The main sight here is the highly ornate, baroque St Nicholas Church (sv Mikuláše, ➤ 105). From Malostranské náměstí follow Mostecká street down toward the Charles Bridge, taking the stairs to the right just at the start of the bridge down to **㉚ Kampa Island** (➤ 107). Spend the rest of the day relaxing in Kampa Park, with its riverside view of the Old Town and Charles Bridge.

# Day Two

### Morning

This could be called the "parks and gardens tour"; be sure to wear some good walking shoes, because the cobbled streets can be very tiring. Start at the Malostranská Metro station (Line A, green line). Follow Valdštejnská street to No 12, the entry to a series of lovely 24 **terraced gardens**, the gardens below Prague Castle (Zahrady pod Pražským hradem; ➤ 192), all bearing the names of aristocratic families that once owned them.

Continue along Valdštejnská until you reach Valdštejnské náměstí (Wallenstein Square) and the palace of famed Habsburg general Albrecht von Waldstein (Wallenstein) and its lovely Renaissance garden. Walk through Malostranské náměstí and along Karmelítská street to the Vrtba Garden at No 25. After this, find one of dozens of places around for lunch. For something quick and easy, try **U malého glena** at Karmelitská 23, tel: 257 531 717.

### Afternoon

From 25 **Malostranské náměstí**, catch the No 22 tram for a scenic ride up to Prague Castle. Depart at the Pohořelec stop to visit the two beautiful libraries of the 7 **Strahov Monastery** (above, ➤ 95). From here, follow the signs along a little path – first paved and then dirt – that takes you across the top of the meadow to the mini Eiffel Tower on 37 **Petřín hill** (➤ 104). This is one of the most scenic walks in the city. End the day by visiting Petřin observation tower and have a drink or early dinner at romantic **Nebozízek restaurant** (Petřínské Sady 411, tel: 257 315 329), with the glitter of the city seemingly at your feet.

## Hradčany, Malá Strana and Beyond

# ★ Pražský hrad (Prague Castle)

**The romantic hilltop silhouette beckons wherever you go. Beyond the cool neo-classical facades rise the Gothic spires of St Vitus Cathedral (➤ 90). To wander through the courtyards and palace halls of Prague Castle is to revisit the theatre of Prague's history.**

The *hrad*, as the castle is commonly known, has remained the traditional symbol of state power. Kings were crowned here and presidents sworn in. From a first-floor window, Hitler proclaimed the Protectorate of Bohemia and Moravia in 1939. Communist Party bosses kept the people out while President Václav Havel threw open the doors: in 1990 he organised a huge party to celebrate independence at which beer flowed freely.

The first fortress, built in 870 by Duke Bořivoj, was little more than a massive log cabin. Defences of giant wooden beams, earthworks and natural ravines for moats were replaced by stone ramparts in the 11th century. Soběslav I's Romanesque castle of 1135 survives as the "basement" of the largely Gothic and Renaissance Starý královský palác (Old Royal Palace). In 1598, the *hrad* formally assumed its status as Prague's third township (after Old Town and New Town), embracing palaces, churches, chapels, gardens (➤ 101), aristocratic mansions, even artisans' cottages and workshops in the famous Zlatá ulička (Golden Lane, ➤ 98). Abandoned in the Thirty Years War (1618–48), it was given its neo-classical facelift by Empress Maria Theresa in the mid-18th century.

### First and Second Courtyards

Flanking the main entrance are copies of Ignaz Platzer's two *Conquering Giants* designed in 1768. At the rear of the first courtyard is the **Matyášova brána** (Matthias Gate), a triumphal arch of 1614 now incorporated in the 18th-century neo-classical structure. In the second courtyard to the right is the **Presidential Palace**, with off-limits offices and residential quarters.

To the left are the **Španělský sál** (Spanish Hall) and **Rudolfova galerie** (Rudolf Gallery), 17th-century halls renovated with great neo-rococo pomp for the aborted coronation of Franz-Josef as King of Bohemia. They open to the public for Prague Spring concerts (➤ 48), otherwise only for official state occasions.

*Prague Castle reigns supreme over the Vltava River's left bank*

### CHANGING OF THE GUARD

If the ceremony of the platoon "guarding" the castle seems faintly comic, it's not wholly unintentional. After Habsburg formality and the grey ritual of the Communists, President Havel gave the show some humour and life: the sentries' blue uniforms, tailored by the Oscar-winning costume designer for *Amadeus,* and a new fanfare for the big noon parade composed by rock musician Michal Kocáb.

# Hradčany, Malá Strana and Beyond

### MALÁ STRANA GARDENS
The baroque terraced palace gardens on the hillside sloping down from Prague Castle have been beautifully restored. With their ornate balustrades, fountains, loggias and arcades, they offer delightful walks and views over Malá Strana and across the Vltava River. They are also magical settings in summer for open-air concerts. Most spectacular is the strictly geometric **Valdštejnská zahrada**, garden of the Waldstein Palace, with a masterly 17th-century loggia by Giovanni Pieroni, bronze statues by Adriaen de Vries (copies; the originals were looted by the Swedes in 1648) and a posse of peacocks in the aviary (Entrance: Valdštejnská 12; April–Oct daily 9–7). The palace itself is open only for occasional concerts. More intimate but just as attractive are the three adjacent **Kolovratská, Ledeburská** and **Pálffyovská** gardens.

### Obrazárna Pražského hradu (Prague Castle Picture Gallery)
On the second courtyard's north side, the gallery exhibits a remnant of the castle's once great art collection of Rudolf and Ferdinand II. Among surviving gems are works by Veronese, Tintoretto, Rubens, Cranach and Holbein. Temporary exhibitions are held in the adjacent **Císařská konírna** (Imperial Stables).

### Starý královský palác (Old Royal Palace)
The third courtyard leads directly to the Old Royal Palace, home of Bohemia's kings from the 12th to 16th centuries. Begin your tour with the fabulous "Story of Prague Castle" exhibition which occupies the Gothic floor of the palace. Among the stone and woodcarvings, embroidered vestments and burial clothes, glass and pottery exhibits are the helmet and coat of mail belonging to St Wenceslas. For children there is a **Castle Game** and other interactive programmes to accompany the exhibition.

**A spiral staircase in the Old Royal Palace**

The main feature of the palace is the bare but magnificently star-rib-vaulted **Vladislav Hall** (Vladislavský sál). Completed in 1502, the flamboyant Gothic hall provided a grand setting for the kings' election (by their peers) and, since 1918, the swearing-in of presidents. It was also used for banquets and jousting tournaments, with horses cantering up the ramp of the **Rider's Staircase** on the north side. East of the hall, a spiral staircase leads to a terrace overlooking the city. In the southwest corner, stairs lead down to the Ludvík Wing and the Bohemian Chancellery from where the king's governors were defenestrated in 1618 (➤ 24). Two obelisks in the garden moat below mark the spot where they fell.

# Pražský hrad (Prague Castle)

Vladislav Hall, big enough for jousting tournaments

### TAKING A BREAK

The (usually) quietest of many reasonably priced open-air cafes within the castle grounds is tucked away in the north-west corner's **Garden on the Bastion** (**Zahrada na baště**) to the left of the main entrance as you come in.

---

✚ 205 D4   ✉ Hradčanské náměstí, Praha 1
☎ Prague Castle information centre: tel: 224 373 368; www.hrad.cz
🕒 Castle grounds: April–Oct daily 5am–midnight, Nov–Mar 6am–11pm, ticketed areas April–Oct daily 9–6, Nov–Mar 9–4
Ⓜ Malostranská   🚋 22 to Pražsky hrad
🎫 Grounds: free; combined ticket (buildings/museum): 350Kč

## INSIDER INFO

- For those who are reasonably fit, two beautiful paths lead to Prague Castle. For great **views** of the castle above and city below, take **Zámecké schody** (New Castle Staircase) to the front gate, which you can reach from the **Malostranské náměstí** via Zámecká und Thunovská. From Malostranská Metro station, **Staré zámecké schody** (Old Castle Staircase) is a **steep climb** to the rear entrance.
- Changing of the Guard and access to the castle grounds, streets, gardens, plus cathedral nave (➤ 91) are **free**. The Information Office in the third courtyard opposite the cathedral sells tickets for the cathedral chancel, ambulatory and crypt, Starý královský palác (Old Royal Palace), Basilica of sv Jiří (St George Basilica, ➤ 106), Zlatá ulička (Golden Lane, ➤ 98) and the Daliborka Tower. A combined ticket for most of the places of interest at Prague Castle costs 350Kč/175Kč concessions and is valid for two days. English-language audioguides cost an extra 250Kč.
- **Separate tickets** are necessary for exhibitions at the Burggalerie, Imperial Stables, St George Convent (➤ 106), Lobkovický palace (➤ 100) and Hraček Museum (Toy Museum). The **family ticket** costs 700Kč

## Hradčany, Malá Strana and Beyond

# Residence of the Bohemian Kings

**The Old Royal Palace was a seat of power until the 16th century. Its focal point is the imposing Vladislav Hall (Vladislavský sál) which is 62m (203ft) long, 16m (52ft) wide und 13m (43ft) high.**

❶ **Western facade:** After the modifications carried out to the castle under Empress Maria Theresa, the western facade of the Old Royal Palace was adapted to blend in with the buildings in the Third Courtyard.

❷ **Entrance:** Visitors enter through the west wing with its late Gothic and Renaissance architecture and pass the Baroque Eagle Fountain, to which Jože Plečnik (1872 to 1957) made a number of improvements.

❸ **Rider's Staircase:** The Rider's Staircase was conceived specially for the knights on horseback who took part in the jousting tournaments in Vladislav Hall.

❹ **Diet**: Vladislav II commissioned the Bohemian architect Benedikt Ried (ca 1454–1534) with the renovation of the palace, and he also drew the plans for the assembly hall. After a fire destroyed the Late Gothic rib-vaulted ceiling, it became the job of Bonifaz Wohlmut to renew it from 1559–1563. Apparently some of the government officials tended to put pleasure before their court duties. Thus during the reign of Frederick of Palatinate, a certain Mr von Roupow issued the following warning: "Wait a while Sires and beware lest you squander your home during dinner."

❺ **Rooms of the New Municipal Files**: New municipal files were the ledgers in which officials wrote down the results of parliament discussions. These records had the status of a law.

❻ **Vladislav Hall:** At the time, this hall, which was also designed by Benedikt Ried, was the largest vaulted secular building in all of Central Europe. The skilfully conceived star-ribbed vault transfers the pressure load to powerful supporting columns two floors below.

❼ **Observation Terrace:** The terrace offers a wonderful view over the rooftops to the Malá Strana and Vltava.

# Pražský hrad (Prague Castle)

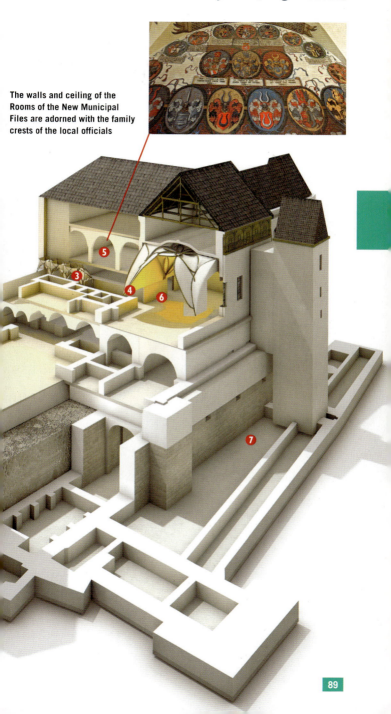

The walls and ceiling of the Rooms of the New Municipal Files are adorned with the family crests of the local officials

Hradčany, Malá Strana and Beyond

# ⭐3 Katedrála sv Víta
## (St Vitus Cathedral)

This magnificent Gothic cathedral lends drama to the profile of Prague Castle. As the "parish church" of Bohemian kings and Habsburg emperors, it is the guardian of sacred treasures that were symbols of political struggles. Their architects, from France, Germany and Austria, have created a setting of appropriately regal grandeur. The present church was more than 600 years in the making, and master builders completing the work after World War II were strikingly faithful to the original designs of the 14th century.

### The Long Haul

Work on the cathedral began in 1344, after Charles IV talked the pope, exiled in Avignon, into granting Prague the status of archdiocese and lending him his architect, Mathieu d'Arras. Mathieu died eight years later, but laid down a distinctively French ground plan derived from his work on Narbonne Cathedral. Immediately, German prodigy Peter Parléř, aged 23 when he began, came in to give the church its bold Late Flamboyant Gothic character, carried on by his sons until construction was halted by the Hussite troubles of 1420. Successors added incongruous Renaissance and baroque touches until 19th- and 20th-century builders returned to the original plans to complete the church in its Late Gothic form. The church

The cathedral's steeples display a mixture of styles – Gothic, Renaissance and baroque

# Katedrála sv Víta (St Vitus Cathedral)

Detail of Alphonse Mucha's Art Nouveau stained-glass window

was officially finished in 1929 for the 1,000th anniversary of the death of St Václav (Wenceslas), the nation's patron saint, but work continued for another 20 years.

### Exterior
The body of the church is like a huge inverted vessel with flying buttresses and steeply sloping diamond-patterned roof. On the **western facade**, with its three bronze doors, are slender towers flanking a broad rose window over the central portal. Before going inside, pass through to the castle's third courtyard to see the cathedral's spectacular south side. Here, Parléř's great Gothic **South Tower**, 96m (315ft), is spoiled only at a distance by its baroque onion-bulb dome added in 1770.

To the right of the tower, the German's splendid **Zlatá brána** (Golden Gate, 1367), originally the main entrance, is decorated with a Venetian mosaic depicting *The Last Judgement*. Notice, too, the open stone tracery of a spiral staircase on the gate's right wall. With elegant flying buttresses on five polygonal chapels, the **chancel** at the rear is the admirable, very French legacy of Mathieu d'Arras.

### Interior
There is a striking lofty spaciousness to the nave, colourfully illuminated by the modern stained-glass windows (Parléř had specified clear glass). Fans of Art Nouveau painter **Alphonse Mucha** (➤ 152) will want to see his 1931 window of *Cyril and Methodius* (Greek Christian missionaries to Bohemia) in the third chapel on the north wall.

The cathedral's most cherished treasure is Parléř's opulently decorated **Chapel of sv Václav** (St Wenceslas) off the south transept. Charles IV wanted this glorification of the country's patron saint to strengthen his fragile hold on the Bohemian crown. Over the site of the saint's grave, he had Parléř design a square gilded chapel bejewelled with jasper, amethyst and blue chalcedony to evoke the New Jerusalem of the Book of Revelations: "four-square – pure gold, like unto clear glass". The wall paintings depict episodes from St Václav's life (➤ 141–143) above scenes of Jesus Christ's Passion.

==To visit the chapels and ambulatory in the **chancel**, you need the Prague Castle combined ticket.== It's worth it.

Insider Tip

Hradčany, Malá Strana and Beyond

# Gothic Masterpiece

**Although the foundation stone was laid in 1344, it took until the beginning of the 20th century for St Vitus Cathedral to be completed. The architectural highlights are in large part thanks to the work of Peter Parler from Schwäbisch Gmünd, who was put in charge of the building work at the tender age of 23.**

❶ **West Facade:** The west end wall is dominated by an imposing rose window that measures over 10m (32ft) across.

❷ **Wooden Reliefs:** A two-part wooden relief by Kaspar Bechteler in the ambulatory depicts the *Flight of the Winter King, Frederick of Palatinate* from Prague after the defeat at the Battle of White Mountain. It offers a broad view of the city before 1635 that reveals many interesting details which are well worth seeing.

❸ **Tomb of Count Leopold Schlick:** The marble tomb of Field Marshal Count Leopold Schlick is the work of Franz Maximilian Kaňka (1674–1766), based on the design by architect Josef Emanuel Fischer von Erlach.

❹ **St Wenceslas Chapel:** The chapel is the cathedral's gem. The ribbed vault by Peter Parler crowns the square-shaped floor plan. It is here that the relics of the saint are kept. The interior of the chapel is spectacular. The walls are decorated with over 1300 semi-precious stones. Paintings show the Passion of Christ, and a further cycle by the Master of the Litoměřice Altarpiece depicts 31 scenes from the life of St Wenceslas.

❺ **Golden Gate:** The wall above the portal connecting the tower with the south transept bears a mosaic of the Last Judgement; Jesus Christ sits enthroned in the centre surrounded by a mandorla.

❻ **Southern Porch:** The three pointed arches of the Golden Gate open up into the southern porch, one of the most beautiful parts of the cathedral. Peter Parler cleverly designed the Gothic ribs of the vault so that they look almost as though they are floating.

# Katedrála sv Víta (St Vitus Cathedral)

**Gargoyle on the Gothic facade of St Vitus Cathedral**

Parléř's intricate patterns of ridge vaulting here revolutionized Gothic design in Central Europe. In the ambulatory on the southeast corner, the extravagant baroque solid silver **Tomb of St John of Nepomuk** (1736) was part of the Jesuits' effort to counter the popular fervour aroused by the Chapel of sv Václav. On the tomb, one of the winged angels is pointing to what was once thought to be the saint's severed tongue.

South of the choir, the **Vladislavoratorium**, an elaborate design by Benedikt Ried, was built in 1490 for King Vladislav Jagiello and linked by a covered passage to his bedroom in the Old Royal Palace (➤ 86).

The stained glass window in the chancel was designed by Max Svabinsky and added in 1934

### TAKING A BREAK

There's an **outdoor cafe** in the courtyard at the rear of the church, serving simple snacks and drinks.

---

✠ 205 D4  ✉ Pražský hrad (Prague Castle)
🕐 Apr–Oct Mon–Sat 9–5, Sun noon–5; Nov–Mar Mon–Sat 9–4, Sun noon–4
Ⓜ Malostranská  🚋 22
🎫 Ambulatory, chancel, crypt: 300Kč; combined ticket with Prague Castle: 350Kč; nave, Chapel of sv Václav: free

## INSIDER INFO

- Allow 1 hour for queuing to enter the Cathedral. To avoid queuing altogether, rent the audio guide. Queues tend to be shorter in the afternoons.
- Off the north aisle, the **Old Sacristy** is an absolute masterpiece of Peter Parléř's gravity-defying Gothic vaulting.

# Strahovský klášter (Strahov Monastery)

**Not one but two of the most beautiful libraries in Europe make this monastery stand out among Prague's great baroque monuments. Vladislav II had the monastery built in 1140, prompted by Moravian Bishop of Olomouc, Jindřich Zdík, and as testimony of its status as a scholarly institution, the libraries saved the monastery from dissolution by Emperor Joseph II in 1783. It was closed under the Communists, but monks are back in residence now and have revived the abbey church, refectories and gardens.**

Vladislav II located the monastery on the road to Pražský hrad (Prague Castle) so that it doubled as a useful defensive outpost. It served the Premonstratensian order, whose founder, St Norbert (1080–1134), placed study of the scriptures at the centre of monastic life.

At the entrance on the western edge of Hradčany, **St Norbert's statue** stands over the baroque gates (1742). Just inside the entrance, the small, late Renaissance parish **Church of St Roch** (1612) is a gallery for temporary exhibitions of religious art.

**Facade of the abbey church Virgin Mary of the Assumption**

# Hradčany, Malá Strana and Beyond

Across the courtyard is the 12th-century abbey-church, **Nanebezvetí Panny Marie** (Virgin Mary of the Assumption) transformed into its present baroque form in 1744. Vividly restored frescoes recount the life of St Norbert. Mozart played the organ here in 1787, creating his *Fantasy in G Minor*.

### The Libraries

Upstairs, the first and bigger of the two libraries is the **Philosophical Hall** (Filosofický sál). It was built to house the collections – scientific and religious – of the Louka monastery library in Moravia, closed by Joseph II around 1785. Indeed its construction was dictated by the dimensions of Louka's magnificently carved floor-to-ceiling walnut bookcases. The ceiling frescoes (1794) by Austria's Franz Anton Maulbertsch are an allegorical tribute to humanity's *Quest For Truth*. Further examples of the quest for truth are displayed in the glass cabinets: ancient insects, dessicated marine life – turtles, lobsters and crabs – and two whale penises exhibited in a narwhal horn.

The older, low-ceilinged **Theological Hall** (Teologický sál) was built in 1671 to replace the library destroyed by the Swedish army during the Thirty Years' War. Looking down on the lecterns and globes of the world are Friar Siard Nosecký's frescoes proclaiming the superiority of divine wisdom over the wisdom of rational study.

The monastery's oldest and greatest treasure is the bejewelled 9th-century *Strahov Gospel* from the German School of Trier, its Latin text in gold lettering exhibited in a glass case in the corridor.

The bejewelled cover to the monastery's 9th-century New Testament

## TAKING A BREAK

Return to the monastery courtyard for a hearty meal at the Klášterní pivovar restaurant and brewery (▶ 114).

Detail of the fresco decorating the ceiling of the former abbot's dining room

✚ 204 A3  ✉ Strahovské nádvoří 1/132, Praha 1
☎ 233 107 752; www.strahovskyklaster.cz
⊙ Libraries: daily 9–noon, 12:30–5  🚌 22 Pohořelec  💰 40Kč

## INSIDER INFO

A door in the monastery's east wall leads to **Strahovská zahrada**, Strahov's gardens and orchards at the northern end of Petřín Hill (▶ 104). From here there is a fine panoramic view of the city.

## Hradčany, Malá Strana and Beyond

# ⭐ 8 Zlatá ulička
# (Golden Lane)

**This legendary little street of alchemists, archers, paupers, peddlers and poets squatting in its tiny houses is best seen not bathed in broad daylight but shrouded in the night's dim lamplight and shadow. The souvenir vendors have gone and your imagination is free to conjure up fantasies of the past.**

### The Facts...
The lane is tucked away in the castle's northeast corner, beyond klášter sv Jiří (St George Convent, ➤ 106). It has been here since the 16th century when poor shopkeepers and artisans fled a town fire to settle here. The artisans included goldbeaters, after whom the street was named Zlatnická (Golden Lane).

In 1916, **Franz Kafka** came to work at night in his sister Ottla's cottage (No 22) and wrote six of his finest short stories. He described the lane in *The Castle* (➤ 32). **Jaroslav Seifert** lived here in 1929, writing some of the poems that were to win him a Nobel Prize. Today you will find various souvenir shops in the colourful little house, restored in 2010/2011.

### ...and the Fantasy
It was the German Romantics of the 19th century who decided the artisans working in Golden Lane were alchemists seeking to turn lead into gold for Rudolf II. The emperor posted his guards there not to watch out for foreign enemies but, so legend has it, to make sure the alchemists didn't shirk their duties. Hey presto, Zlatá ulička became known as Alchimistengasse (Alchemist Lane).

The Czechs also have their Golden Lane legends. One of the prison towers

# Zlatá ulička (Golden Lane)

where shopkeepers sold their wares to captives was – and, of course, still is – haunted by the noble knight **Dalibor**, imprisoned for heading a peasant revolt in the 15th century. To fight the boredom of solitude, it is said he learned to play the violin; beautiful laments were heard in Zlatá ulička even after he had been executed. A pity to spoil a good story, but *housle*, the Czech word for violin, was prison slang for the torturer's rack. Apparently his moans of pain under torture can still be heard on moonlit nights – by some, anyway.

## Prison Towers

At the west end of Zlatá ulička, take the stairs at **No 24** to a covered walk leading west to the castle's main prison, **Bílá věž** (White Tower). The tower at the other end is the haunted **Daliborka** where Dalibor is said to have played the violin.

**The Golden Lane in the twilight**

# Hradčany, Malá Strana and Beyond

One of several Golden Lane houses promoting the legend of Dalibor

### TAKING A BREAK
There's an **open-air cafe** in the courtyard between the Daliborka and Černá věž (Black Tower, not open to the public).

🕂 205 D4  ✉ Zlatá ulička
☎ Prague Castle information centre: 224 373 368
🕓 Apr–Oct daily 5am–midnight; Nov–Mar 6am–11pm.
Ⓜ Malostranská  🚊 22
🎫 Golden Lane: 250Kč; Combined ticket with Prague Castle: 350Kč

### INSIDER INFO

The **alchemists** of Zlatá ulička actually had laboratories in Vikářská, the lane between St Vitus Cathedral and Prašná věž (Powder Tower).

# ㉔ Zahrady (Castle Gardens)

**The gardens south and north of Pražský hrad (Prague Castle) are a delight both for their charm and for their great views of Prague and the castle. Lovely as they are, the gardens are rarely crowded so they are also ideal for a quick siesta.**

*From the wall gardens south of the castle, you have a magnificent view of the Old Town and Petřín Hill*

### King's Garden (Královská zahrada)
The most luxuriant of the castle's gardens lie north of the *hrad* across the 16th-century **Powder Bridge** (Pražný most), accessible from the north gate of the castle's second courtyard. The bridge spans the **Stag Moat** (Jelení příkop), a broad wooded ditch in which the Habsburgs planted lemon and fig trees and kept wild game for their hunts.

Across the street from the garden entrance is the 17th-century **Riding School** (Jízdárna), baroque but in simple, sober style, now an art gallery used for exhibitions.

Created by Ferdinand I in 1534, the gardens have an appropriately regal air – fountains playing among impeccable green lawns surrounded by almond trees, azaleas and a spectacular

> **POLITICALLY CORRECT**
>
> During restoration on the Míčovna pavilion in 1950, at the height of the Stalinist era, Pavel Janák added a nice touch to the row of allegorical figures flanking the sandstone pilasters. Between Peace and Justice, the fellow representing Industry is holding a hammer and sickle.

# Hradčany, Malá Strana and Beyond

spring display of tulips. Tulips made their appearance here in 1551 (some 10 years before the Dutch got hold of them), grown from Turkish seeds brought back by the Austrian ambassador to the Ottoman Court.

On the north terrace is the 16th-century **Míčovna**, a Renaissance pavilion where the Habsburgs whiled away the time with an early form of badminton. The facade is decorated with *sgraffiti* and a frieze of allegorical figures. In front is Matyás Braun's sculpture of *The Night* (1734).

To the right of the pavilion is **Royal House** (Zahradní dům), which is 18th century with some modern additions (unfortunately it is closed to the public).

At the east end of the gardens, the **Belvedér** is an exquisite example of pure Italian Renaissance style, probably the finest in Central Europe. Ferdinand I built this summer palace in 1537 as a little summer palace for Queen Anna. In the middle of the garden terrace, a Renaissance *giardinetto*, is Francesco Terzio's **Singing Fountain** (Zpívající fontána, 1568). Its music can be heard as the water drips from one basin to the other.

Mythological heroes on the Singing Fountain

## South Gardens

The South Gardens are accessible from the castle via a modern copper-canopied staircase in the southeast corner of the third courtyard. In charge of 20th-century renovations, Slovene architect Josip Plečnik designed the staircase so that its balconies on the way down to the gardens look out in an absolutely straight line over St Nicholas Church of Malá Strana (➤ 105) across the river and down to Vyšehrad Castle (➤ 157).

## Garden on the Ramparts (Zahrada na valech)

What was originally a single stretch of formal geometric baroque garden running the length of the castle's south facade has been re-landscaped as a charming, more varied little

### BEST VANTAGE POINTS

Most of the Royal Gardens offer fine views of the castle, but the **Belvedér's garden terrace** is the best place from which to see the fortifications, Daliborka and White Towers (➤ 100), and above all, the north side and chancel of St Vitus Cathedral (➤ 90). You also get a great view over the bridges on the Vltava River.

*The Allegory of Night* statue by Antonin Braun outside the Ballroom in the Royal Gardens

park. From the staircase, an esplanade leads across to a large semicircular observation terrace. In front of the Old Royal Palace (➤ 86) a monument marks the spot where the defenestrated governors landed in 1618 (➤ 24). You will also see an Alpine arboretum, an aviary, pergola and other pavilions. At the west end, a piece of the baroque garden has been preserved with a sculpture of Samson at the centre of an 18th-century fountain.

**Insider Tip**

### Paradise Garden (Rajská zahrada)

Beyond the Samson Fountain, the smaller garden has at the centre of its immaculate green lawn a giant granite basin made from one monolithic slab. At the far end, a monumental staircase leads to Castle Square, ➤ 108).

#### TAKING A BREAK

**Lví dvůr** (Lion's Court) restaurant, at the entrance to the Royal Gardens, is housed in Rudolf II's private zoo, where the emperor heated the cages in winter for his beloved lynxes, leopards, lions and wolves.

➕ 205 D4  ✉ Pražský hrad  ☎ 224 373 368
🕒 Apr–Oct daily 10–6, May, Sep 10–7, June, July 10–9, Aug 10–8
🚇 South Gardens, Malostranská; Royal Gardens, Hradčanská
🚌 South Gardens, 12, 22 Malostranské náměstí; Royal Gardens, 2, 8, 18
Pražný most  💳 Free, except for concerts and exhibitions

## INSIDER INFO

**Concerts and exhibitions** in the gardens are usually inexpensive. For latest programmes check with the Information Centre in the third courtyard at Prague Castle (tel: 224 373 368).

Hradčany, Malá Strana and Beyond

# 25 Malostranské náměstí
## (Malá Strana Square)

**The bustling centre of public life in the Malá Strana district, this cobbled square is a major landmark on the Royal Route that brought Bohemia's kings from the Old Town across Charles Bridge up to their castle. In effect, the square is divided in two by the magnificent Church of St Nicholas Malá Strana.**

A fire in 1541 destroyed the square's modest medieval houses, largely the homes of Protestants later expelled in the Thirty Years War. Reasserting Catholic influence at the end of the 17th century, the Jesuits and their supporters at court began turning Malostranské náměstí into a triumphant spiritual fortress of the Counter-Reformation. They created the square's dramatic decor of predominantly neo-classical facades around an exultant baroque church adjoining what was then a Jesuit college.

**Looking down on Malá Strana Square from St Nicholas church tower**

### Liechtenstein Palace (Lichtenštejnský palác)

Occupying the west side of the square, the Lichtenštejnský palác houses the Academy of Performing Art's music faculty, offering occasional concerts, exhibitions and a pleasant cafe. Its place in Prague's history is less agreeable. The palace's first owner was Karl von Liechtenstein, the Habsburgs' imperial governor who ordered the execution of 27 Czech Protestants in 1621 (➤ 57). In 1648, the palace was occupied by commanders of the invading Swedish army who fought the last battle of the Thirty Years War on Charles Bridge. Exactly 200 years later, it was the HQ of Austro-Hungarian Field Marshal Alfred Windischgrätz, brought in to crush the 1848 Prague revolt.

# Malostranské náměstí (Malá Strana Square)

The baroque church of St Nicholas – an 18th-century gem

### Church of St Nicholas Malá Strana (sv Mikuláš)

As the centrepiece of St Nicholas Malá Strana, the 18th-century church is the finest jewel of Prague's many baroque monuments. Its blend of power and elegance can be seen in the gently curving western facade and the dome and bell-tower. The design was a family affair. Bavarian-born Kryštof Dienzenhofer built the facade and nave. His son, Kilián Ignác, began the nave ceiling, choir and dome in 1737, and the bell-tower was added in 1755 by Anselmo Lurago (Ignác's son-in-law).

The **interior** of the church adorned with stucco marble and rich sculptural ornamentation is a stunning example of high baroque and a jubilant symphony of light and colour. The nave and choir are formed by a succession of ellipses and their arches, columns, larger-than-life sculptures and altars all carry the eye up to the ceiling frescoes. Above the nave is Johann Lukas Kracker's vast painting, *Apotheosis of St Nicholas*. Concerts are held regularly in the church.

### TAKING A BREAK

Just around the corner of the square, in Karmelitzka 12, is one of the oldest patisseries in Prague, **U Bílého Preclíku**, which first opened its doors in 1678. It offers a tantalising selection of sweet pastries and cakes, light meals and, of course, its namesake: white pretzels.

---

🗺 205 D3   ✉ Malostranské náměstí
☎ 251 512 516; www.psalterium.cz
🕒 St Nicholas Church: guided tours daily March–Oct. 9–5; Nov–Feb 9–5:
bell tower Nov–Feb Mon–Sun 10–6, March–Oct until 8, April–Sep until 10
🚇 Malostranská   🚊 12, 22   💰 St Nicholas Church: 70Kč, bell tower: 75Kč

## INSIDER INFO

- Many of the patrician palaces surrounding the square have been converted into restaurants and Gothic-vaulted basement bars.
- At the corner of Mostecká Street on the square's south side (No 1), the Renaissance **Parsley House** (Dům U petržílka) has a fine example of a typical Prague *pavlač* (balconied courtyard).

Hradčany, Malá Strana and Beyond

# At Your Leisure

## 26 Bazilika and klášter sv Jiří (St George Basilica and Convent)

Behind its handsome, russet-hued baroque facade, Prague Castle's second church reveals itself as in fact much older than the Gothic St Vitus Cathedral. The basilica's interior is a beautifully restored and well-preserved Romanesque structure dating to 1142. The long, narrow nave leads to the choir via an unusual but strangely not incongruous double baroque staircase. To the right of the choir is the **burial chapel of St Ludmilla**, Bohemia's first Christian martyr and grandmother of St Václav (Wenceslas). Beneath the choir, the **crypt** contains the tombs of the convent's first abbesses. On the altar to the right is a macabre 16th-century allegorical sculpture of Vanitas, showing snakes and lizards crawling through a saint's entrails. The basilica provides a wonderful atmosphere for early evening classical concerts.

The adjoining convent, **klášter sv Jiří**, founded in 973 and closed by Emperor Joseph II in 1782, is now part of the National Gallery with a permanent exhibition on 19th-century art in Bohemia.

✚ 205 D4
✉ Jiřské náměstí 33, Pražský hrad
☎ 224 372 434; www.hrad.cz
🕐 April–Oct daily 9–, Nov–March until 4
🚊 22 Pražský hrad 🎫 250Kč; combined ticket with Prague Castle: 350Kč

## 27 Lobkovický palác (Palais Lobkowitz)

Tucked in and among the castle attractions is a relatively new and highly recommended private museum operated by descendants of the Lobkowicz family to highlight the noble family's holdings through the ages. The museum's holdings include works by Brueghel the Elder and Velazquez, among others. The headphone audio guide personalizes the experience in a way the Prague Castle audio guide does not. Entry is not included in the general castle admission. The museum has a very good cafe and small restaurant.

✚ 204 C3 ✉ Jiřská 3
☎ 602 595 998 🕐 Tue–Sun 9–5
Ⓜ Malostranská
🚊 22 to Pražský hrad 🎫 20Kč

## 28 Malostranské věž (Malá Strana Bridge Towers)

The fortified gate-arch on the left bank of the Karlův most (Charles Bridge, ➤ 54) is flanked by two towers. The shorter one, built in

**A baroque staircase in St George Basilica and Convent**

# At Your Leisure

1166, was part of the earlier Judith Bridge, with *sgraffiti* decoration and Renaissance gables added in the 16th century. The taller tower (1464) matches the right bank's bridge tower with its similar chisel-blade roof, turrets and battlemented gallery. Besides an impressive view over Malá Strana and the river, the tower has a display relating the history of the bridge and the myth-laden life of John of Nepomuk.

✚ 205 E3  ✉ Karlův most
☎ 607 050 434
⏰ Nov–Feb daily 10–6,
March, Oct until 8, April–Sep until 10
🚋 12, 22  💰 Tower: 90Kč

## 29 Franz Kafka Museum

Brace yourself for a sensory journey through the author's life and imaginary world using the latest audio-visual wizardry, including soundtrack, projectors, mirrors, distorted film footage and special lighting effects. Fascinating displays on Prague's Jewish Quarter, Kafka's family circle, his friendship with fellow writer Max Brod, his incurable restlessness and his troubled relations with women set the scene for a succession of thoroughly eerie installations downstairs. They include black filing cabinets labelled with the names of Kafka's characters, a semi-animate Prague Castle, insect noises and barbed wire. The exhibition also includes all of Kafka's first editions.

✚ 205 E3
✉ Cihelná 2b
☎ 257 535 373;
www.kafkamuseum.cz
⏰ Daily 10–6
🚇 Malostranská  💰 200 Kč

## 30 Kampa Island

Any time a place has a couple of waterways around some houses, it is likely to be dubbed the Venice of somewhere. So this quaint little river island, reached from Charles Bridge by a double flight of stairs, is known as the "Venice of Prague". It is separated from Malá Strana by an arm of the Vltava called the **Čertovka** (Devil's Channel) which activated mill-wheels – still there but non-functional.

**Na Kampě**, the square running south of Charles Bridge, is bordered by some pretty 18th-century houses, notably No 7, **House of the Golden Lion** (Dům U zlatého lva).

✚ 197 E3  🚋 12, 22

## 31 Panny Marie Vítězné (Our Lady of Victory Church)

This unprepossessing 17th-century church is one of Malá Strana's great tourist attractions. Originally built by German Lutherans, it was handed over in 1624 to the Carmelite order, which made it a monument to the victory at White Mountain (Bílá Hora, ➤ 64).

107

# Hradčany, Malá Strana and Beyond

### HISTORY IN AN EMBASSY GARDEN
The splendid 18th-century baroque Lobkovický palác (which should not be confused with the building of the same name in Prague Castle) at Vlašská ulice 19, now the German Embassy, witnessed a turning point in history in the summer of 1989. Thousands of East Germans "on holiday" climbed into the embassy garden and camped there while seeking West German citizenship. They left their rickety Trabant cars in surrounding streets. The East German and Czech governments eventually relented and approved their emigration. It was not long afterwards that the Berlin Wall crumbled. Today, from behind the embassy in Petřin Park, you can see Giovanni Battista Alliprandi's beautiful undulating rear facade of 1713. And in the garden stands David Černy's modern sculpture, *Quo Vadis?*, a gold-painted Trabant raised on legs.

But what really draws both devout pilgrims and disrespectful fans of high kitsch is the **Infant Jesus of Prague** (Pražské Jezulátko). This wax-covered wooden figure, brought to Prague in 1628 as part of the dowry of a Spanish bride, is said to have miraculous powers, in honour of which scores of luxurious little costumes have been sent here from all over the world. [Insider Tip] The silk, satin, velvet and lace clothing is displayed, along with some astonishing jewellery, in a little museum on a spiral staircase in the church's south aisle.
✚ 205 D3   ✉ Karmelitská 9
☎ 257 533 646
🕐 Mon–Sat 8:30–7; Sun 8:30–8
🚋 12, 20, 22   💰 Museum: free

## 32 Nerudova
Once the main thoroughfare linking the castle to the town, Nerudova Street has some of the city's finest baroque palaces and mansions. It is named after Jan Neruda, a prominent 19th-century Czech writer famous for his portraits of life in Malá Strana's artists' quarter. This activity has been revived in recent years as galleries and studios have reappeared along the street. Coming from Malá Strana Square, look on the left for the elegant **Morzinský palác** (No 5, now the Romanian Embassy) with Ferdinand Maximilian Brokof's sculptures of two giant Moors holding up its ornate balcony. Across the street is the Italian Embassy, housed in the imposing **Thun-Hohenšteinský palác** (No 20, 1725). Jan Neruda lived in **House of the Two Suns** (Dům U Dvou slunců; No 47).
✚ 204 C3   🚋 12, 22

## 33 Hradčanské náměstí (Castle Square)
The great fire of 1541 cleared away Castle Square's artisans' homes and butchers' shops, to be replaced by the palaces of Bohemian and foreign nobility. On the south side of the square, notice the highly decorative **Schwarzenberský palác** with its stepped gables and elaborate *sgraffiti* imitating diamond-point masonry, a whimsical design for the Museum of Late Renaissance Baroque Art and Sculpture. It

**Three crossed violins adorn the facade of Three Little Fiddles on Nerudova Street**

# At Your Leisure

makes a sharp contrast to the rococo Archbishop's palace (Arcibiskupský palác) across the square at No 16.

The **Martinický palác** in the northwest corner is a quaint Renaissance reworking of three Gothic houses, with *sgraffiti* biblical and mythological scenes between the first-floor windows. On the north side, the 18th-century **Šternberský palác** (No 15) houses the National Gallery's collection of European masters, including Albrecht Dürer's *Feast of the Rosary* and works by Bernardo Daddi, Tintoretto, Bronzino, Simon Vouet, El Greco, Goya, Rembrandt, Rubens, Frans Hals, Jan van Goyen and Jan Steen.
🏠 204 C4 ☎ Šternberský palác museum: 233 090 570; www.ngprague.cz
🕐 Tue–Sun 10–6 💰 Moderate 🚌 22
💰 Šternberský palác museum: 150Kč

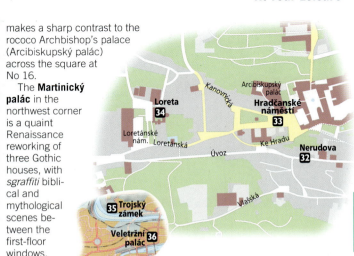

## 34 Loreta

The Loreta pilgrimage sanctuary, one of 50 throughout Bohemia, was founded here in a concerted campaign to re-Catholicize the country after the Protestant defeat at Bílá Hora (White Mountain, ►64).

Within a cloister, **Mary's Santa Casa** (sacred home) is reproduced, miraculously transported first to Italy (after the Crusades, by the Angeli family) and thence, as replicas, to wherever the faith needed to be bolstered. Inside the shrine is a wooden *Black Madonna and Child* and beside the shrine a Nativity Church displaying the gruesome martyrdoms of female saints.

Krýstof Dienzenhofer and his son Kilián Ignác added the cloister's monumental baroque facade facing the square in 1722. The bells in the tower play hymns on the hour throughout the day. *(Insider Tip)*
🏠 204 B4 ✉ Loretánské náměstí 7
☎ 220 516 740; www.loreta.cz
🕐 April–Oct daily 9–12:15, 1–5, Nov–March 9:30–12:15, 1–4
🚌 22 💰 130Kč

## 35 Trojský zámek (Villa Troja)

This French-style baroque château out in the northern suburbs was built by Jean-Baptiste Mathey for the Šternberk family in 1685. Surrounded by French-style formal gardens, the villa is in a charming country setting, most agreeably reached in summer by boat along the Vltava River. Mathey designed a handsome monumental double staircase modelled on that of Fontainebleau in France and enlivened by heroic sculptures of fighting giants by Georg and Paul Hermann. The interior has some extravagant ceiling frescoes celebrating Habsburg victories over

**Villa Troja (Trojský zámek) is an Italian-style chateau outside the city centre**

the Turks in a style compatible with the Hermann sculptures of giants.

🕂 202 A5 ✉ U trojského zámku 6
☎ 283 851 614; www.ghmp.cz
🕘 Apr–Oct Tue–Thu, Sat, Sun 10–6, Fri 1–6; Nov–Mar Sat, Sun 10–5
🚇 Nádraží Holešovice, then 🚌 112, or Vltava River boat from mooring near Palackého most 💰 Park: free, villa: 120Kč

### 36 Veletržní palác (Trade Fair Palace)

The huge 1928 Functionalist building has been transformed into a **Museum of Contemporary Art** – mainly from 1900 onwards. On six floors, accessible by lift, you can visit the excellent permanent exhibition; temporary exhibitions are also organised from time to time. Czech artists include abstract master František Kupka, sculptor František Bílek, Cubists Emil Filla, Bohumil Kubišta and Josef Čapek. Other European artists exhibited include Rodin, Renoir, Van Gogh, Henri Rousseau, Picasso, Matisse, Klimt, Schiele and Munch.

🕂 207 D5 ✉ Dukelských hrdinů 47, Holešovice
☎ 224 301 111; www.ngprague.cz
🕘 Tue–Sun 10–6 🚇 12 💰 180Kč

### 37 Petřín

Prague's biggest park is a wooded hill extending southeast from Strahov Monastery (➤ 95) to Malá Strana. From the monastery garden, follow the old **Hunger Wall** (Hladová zed), begun in the 15th century, to mark the southern boundary of the old city. As it winds southeast, the wall passes the **Rozhledna**, a miniature 1891 version of the Eiffel Tower, and **Bludiště**, a mini-Gothic castle with a Mirror Maze inside. Just beyond the funicular railway are the **rose garden** (Růžový sad) and the **observatory** (Štefánikova hvězdárna). The funicular railway (public transport tickets and passes are valid) takes you to Malá Strana and buses into the centre.

🕂 204 C2 ℹ www.petrinska-rozhledna.cz
🕘 Tower, observatory and Maze: Mar Sat, Sun 10–6; Apr daily 10–7; May–Sep 10–10; Oct 10–8; Nov–Feb 10–6 🚋 22
💰 Funicular railway: tickets cost the same as for the underground, tram and bus: 32 Kč per trip (➤ 38)

# Where to...
# Eat and Drink

**Prices**
Expect to pay per person for a meal, including drinks, tax and service:
**£** under 500Kč     **££** 500Kč–1,000Kč     **£££** over 1,000Kč

## RESTAURANTS

### Alchymist ££
The interior may be overwrought, with candles and knick-knacks, but the overall effect is secluded and romantic. Good Continental cuisine and an excellent wine list. Perfect choice for a special meal.

✚ 205 D2
✉ Nosticova 1
☎ 257 312 518; www.alchymist.cz
🕒 Daily noon–11  🚌 22

### Baráčnická rychta £/££
Climb the twisting street above the American embassy to find this quintessential Czech *hospoda*: dark, warm, welcoming and non-smoking, with lots of wood, perfunctory but professional service, and all the pork knuckle and beer you can down. The fruit dumplings are excellent. A very comfortable place for a good meal. There's often a weekend band.

✚ 204 C3
✉ Tržiště 23
☎ 257 532 461; www.baracnickarychta.cz
🕒 Mon–Sat 11–11, Sun 11–9
Ⓜ Malostranská  🚌 12, 20, 22

### Café Savoy £/££
The restaurant is a member of the popular Ambiente chain, which ensures excellent food and service. The menu is heavy on international dishes, but this is also a good place to sample *Svíčkova*, a classic Czech dish of beef tenderloin served in a cream sauce with dumplings and cranberries.

✚ 205 D1  ✉ Vítězná 5
☎ 257 311 562; www.ambi.cz
🕒 Mon–Sat 8–10:30; Sun 9–10:30
🚌 6, 9, 12, 22

### Černý orel ££
Italian wines and Czech Pilsner accompany their respective cuisines in the two comfortably luxurious low-ceilinged rooms. The popularity of this neighbourhood among Italian tourists ensures that plenty of their nation's favourite dishes (generous and inexpensive portions) appear on the menu here, along with traditional Czech cuisine.

✚ 205 D3  ✉ Malostranské náměstí 14 (entrance from Zámecká)
☎ 257 533 207; www.cernyorel.com
🕒 Daily 11–11
Ⓜ Malostranská  🚌 12, 20, 22

### Cowboys ££/£££
Another jewel in the local chain of eateries that runs Kampa Park – it's the best restaurant within easy walk of the castle complex, just down the road in the direction of Malostranské náměstí. It is not only the location that is a winner however, it serves magnificent steaks. It's not cheap, but at lunch you can get away with burgers and sandwiches. Dinner revolves around well-prepared steaks and seafood in a casual but upscale setting. In nice weather ask for a rooftop terrace table.

✚ 204 C3  ✉ Nerudova 40
☎ 296 826 107; www.kampagroup.com
🕒 Daily noon–1am

# Hradčany, Malá Strana and Beyond

### Essensia £££
A bit like being in Asia and a bit like being right out in the Bohemian countryside: the finest, most varied dishes are available in the hotel restaurant of the Mandarin Oriental: Czech or Asian cuisine – it's up to you!
✚ 205 D2 ✉ Nebovídská 1, Malá Strana
☎ 233 088 888; www.mandarinoriental.com/prague ⏰ Daily 11am–midnight 🚌 12, 20, 22

### Gitanes ££
Gitanes specializes in Balkan cuisine. Seafood and roasted meat dishes dominate the menu: *čevapčiči* for beef-lovers, or the simmered pork dish, *mučkalica*. There's plenty for the non-meat eater, too: stuffed peppers, roasted beans simmered with spices. There are wines from the Balkans, France and the Czech Republic.
✚ 205 D3 ✉ Tržiště 7
☎ 257 530 163; www.gitanes.cz
⏰ Daily noon–midnight 🚇 Malostranská

### Hergetova Cihelná £££
This restaurant on Kampa Island has a terrace with views across the river and what some would call the city's best wood-fired gourmet pizzas. The large menu also offers plenty of excellent salads, meat and fish entrées. Reservations are recommended, and essential in summer for a seat on the terrace.
✚ 205 E3 ✉ Cihelná 2b, Malá Strana
☎ 296 826 103; www.kampagroup.com
⏰ Daily 11:30am–1am
🚇 Malostranská 🚌 18

### Kampa Park £££
One of the leading restaurants in the city. It's expensive, so make it a night to remember with high-toned Continental cuisine, excellent wines and service, and a table on the -terrace in good weather. Book in advance.
✚ 205 E2 ✉ Na Kampě 8b
☎ 296 826 112; www.kampagroup.com
⏰ Daily 11:30am–1am
🚇 Malostranská 🚌 12, 20, 22

### Nebozízek ££
This historic restaurant serves fine examples of the national cuisine: game, duck, pork, fruit-based sauces, and pancakes for dessert. But the main reason to dine here is ==the view over Prague and onto the castle.== Reservations are essential. *Inside Tip*
✚ 204 C2 ✉ Petřínské sady 411
☎ 257 315 329; www.nebozizek.cz
⏰ Daily noon–11 🚋 Tram 12, 22 to Újezd, then funicular to halfway up Petřín

### NOI £
This Thai restaurant has been wowing customers ever since it opened in 2008. Some praise the cool Zen decor, some the relaxing garden terrace, while others value the discreet but attentive service. But everyone agrees that NOI produces authentic Thai food at knock-down prices. What's more, most of the mains are available as vegetarian dishes.
✚ 205 D2 ✉ Újezd 19
☎ 257 311 411; www.noirestaurant.cz
⏰ Daily 11–midnight
🚌 6, 9, 12, 20

### Pálffy Palác £££
The Pálffy's charmingly shabby palace ==houses the most romantic dining room in the city,== decorated with subdued colours and old prints. It is a favourite brunch spot, as much for the atmosphere as the food. At dinner the menu is contemporary, with delicacies such as shiitake mushroom-stuffed chicken breast in tarragon sauce.
✚ 205 E4 ✉ Valdštejnská 14
☎ 257 530 522; www.palffy.cz
⏰ Daily 11–11

### Perpetuum ££
A restaurant with a gimmick, albeit a pleasant one – especially if you like duck, because that's about all you'll find on the menu. It's a Czech staple, but here you'll find it prepared in different ways, in-cluding country duck with sweet

# Where to...

and sour cabbage, and duck confit with potato pancakes. Excellent wines, good service and a refined environment round off a perfect evening. Take your map to find this place on a side street not far from Dejvická metro station.

✚ 205 off C5
✉ Na hutích 9
☎ 233 323 429; www.restauraceperpetuum.cz (in Czech only) ⏰ Mon–Sat noon–11

### Rybářský klub ££

If it swims in a Czech river or pond, they serve it here. The pike in black sauce and the river eel are local favourites. Or try the national fish, carp, although this bony beast is something of an acquired taste. In the summer a few small tables make for splendid riverside dining.

✚ 205 E2
✉ U Sovových mlýnů 1, Kampa
☎ 257 534 200; www.rybklub.cz
⏰ Daily noon–11

### Sushi Bar ££/£££

Minimalistic decor with pale laminated tables and chairs: this bar exudes California-esque style. Seafood is delivered twice weekly, so you might want to call ahead to make sure of getting fresh eel, scallops, sea bass or crab, then watch the Czech chefs whip up sushi rolls, sashimi or tempura.

✚ 205 D1 ✉ Zborovská 49
☎ 603 244 882; www.sushi.cz
⏰ Daily noon–10 🚋 5, 14

### Terasa U Zlaté studně £££

Opinion is divided on whether the food at this stylish restaurant matches the view. Most would say it doesn't, but that's nothing against the food, for the view will knock your socks off. The cuisine is international, and the menu lists some specialities that are still hard to come by in Prague, like baked goose liver. The restaurant is somewhat hidden in a cul-de-sac above Valdštejnské náměstí.

✚ 205 D4 ✉ U Zlaté studně 166/4 (off the north end of Sněmovní)
☎ 257 533 322; www.terasauzlatestudne.cz
⏰ Daily 7am–11pm 🚋 12, 20, 22

### U malé velryby ££

Good-value tapas and international dishes, like steaks and grilled salmon, but also with a nod towards local tastes, with the addition of seared lamb and roast duck. The seven-course fish menu with oysters and spiny lobsters is highly recommended. Only a half-dozen tables, so book in advance.

✚ 205 D2 ✉ Maltézské náměstí 15
☎ 257 214 703; www.umalevelryby.cz
⏰ Daily 10–10 🚋 17, 18, 22

### U Ševce Matouše ££

You can easily guess that this long-established steakhouse was once a cobbler's shop from the ancient bronzed shoes that decorate the entrance and perch on stands in the dining room. The decor is simple, and the food is, of course, steaks with sauces, although poultry and fish are also served.

✚ 204 B3 ✉ Loretánské náměstí 4
☎ 220 514 536; www.usevcematouse.cz
⏰ Daily 11–11 🚋 22

### Valdštejnská hospoda ££/£££

The medieval "House of the Three Storks" received its present facade in the 18th century. The house reopened in 2008 as an upscale hotel, and the restaurant is comfortable and refined. The cooking leans towards game, fowl and traditional Czech dishes.

✚ 205 D3 ✉ Tomášská 20/16
☎ 257 212 989 ⏰ Daily 10–11
Ⓜ Malostranská 🚋 18, 20, 22

## INNS, PUBS AND BARS

### BarBar

This friendly cellar bar-restaurant popular with expats and locals. Sweet and savoury crêpes and comfort food like *halušky* and *goulaš* are served in the back

# Hradčany, Malá Strana and Beyond

**Insider Tip:** room. The changing lunch menu is good and very inexpensive. A soup and main dish cost about 120Kč.
✚ 205 D2 ✉ Všehrdova 17 ☎ 257 312 246; www.bar-bar.cz ⏰ Mon–Sat 11–midnight, Fri, Sat noon–6 Ⓜ Malostranská

### Fraktal
Nice bar for everyone staying in Letná or Holešovice. English-speaking staff, decent bar food and a relaxed vibe that varies from a bustling student pub to "Cheers". An easy choice to stay in all night. WiFi is available.
✚ 202 C2 ✉ Šmeralová 1
☎ 777 794 094; www.fraktalbar.cz
⏰ Daily 11–midnight 🚋 17 to Výstaviště

### J.J. Murphy's
A mere stone's throw from the Irish Embassy, this popular hostelry makes a great lunch stop after a busy morning's sightseeing. The atmosphere is convivial, the menu caters for most tastes and Staropramen, Granat and, of course, Guinness are all available on draught.
✚ 205 D3 ✉ Tržiště 4
☎ 257 535 575; www.jjmurphys.cz
⏰ Sun–Wed 10–midnight, Thu–Sat 10am–1am
Ⓜ Malostranská 🚋 12, 22

### Klášterní pivovar
St Norbert's brewery was founded in the 13th century in grounds of the Strahov Monastery, although the present microbrewery dates only from 2000. **Insider Tip:** Sample the famous dark beer while tucking in to a plate of typical Czech pub grub. Tip: At times like Easter or Christmas, there are special seasonal beers.
✚ 204 A3 ✉ Strahovské nádvoří 301
☎ 233 353 155; www.klasterni-pivovar.cz
⏰ Daily 10–10 🚋 22

### Kolkovna/Olympia
Part of the Kolkovna chain of Pilsner-Urquell pubs and restaurants. The food gets mixed reviews, but the beer is some of the best near Malá Strana. The large space improves the odds you'll find a table. Strong on typical Czech dishes.
✚ 205 D1 ✉ Vítězná 7
☎ 251 511 080; www.kolkovna.cz
⏰ Daily 11am–midnight 🚋 6, 9, 12, 20

### U Malého Glena
There's no cover charge for the bar at this popular jazz and rock music club. The music plays in the cellar. Funky mismatched furnishings and a big wooden bar create a laid-back atmosphere.
✚ 205 D3 ✉ Karmelitská 23
☎ 257 531 717; www.malyglen.cz
⏰ Fri, Sat 10am–3am, Sun–Thu 10am–2am
Ⓜ Malostranská 🚋 12, 20, 22

### U sedmi Švábů
The best time to visit many Czech pubs is summer but here the open hearth is particularly welcome when it's cold. It's a bit on the kitsch side, but the hearty Bohemian food, costumed staff and environment are entertaining.
✚ 204 C3 ✉ Jánský vršek 14 14 (corner Nerudova) ☎ 257 531 455; www.7svabu.cz
⏰ Daily 11–11 🚋 22

### Zlatý klas
Picture-perfect Czech pub, not far from the Nový Smíchov shopping mall at Anděl. It's a good place to sample Czech standards like *gulaš* and *vepřo, knedlo, zelo* (roast pork, bread dumplings and sauerkraut). Good beer.
✚ 208 A3 ✉ Plzeňská 9
☎ 251 562 539; www.zlatyklas.cz
⏰ Mon–Thu 11–midnight, Fri 11am–1am, Sat 11:30am–1am, Sun 11–11 Ⓜ Anděl

## CAFÉS AND TEAROOMS

### Bohemia Bagel £
This informal sandwich and bagel shop is just on the Malá Strana side. **Insider Tip:** It is one of the few places in Prague open early for breakfast.
✚ 2005 D3 ✉ Lázenská 19
☎ 257 218 192; www.bohemiabagel.cz
⏰ Daily 7:30–7 Ⓜ Staromestská

## Where to...

### Café de Paris
A cross between a French cafe and a classic bistro. Serving a full range of espressos and teas, the menu features traditional French dishes, but also salads and fresh seafood – all at excellent prices.
🕀 205 D3  ✉ Maltézské náměstí 4
☎ 603 160 718; www.cafedeparis.cz
🕓 Mon–Fri 8am–midnight, Sat, Sun 11:30–midnight  Ⓜ Malostranská

### Malý Buddha
A soothing tearoom serving simple vegetarian "temple foods". The heady aroma from the steaming teapots brewing Tibetan clove, Royal Nepalese and Hong Kong-style fruit teas promotes a meditative mood.
🕀 204 B3  ✉ Úvoz 46  ☎ 220 513 894; www.malybuddha.cz (in Czech only)
🕓 Tue–Sun noon–10:30

# Where to...
# Shop

**The best options are around the point where the Charles Bridge merges into Mostecká Street. On the hill running up towards the castle, Nerudova is the main street (▶ 108). Behind Pražský hrad quirky shops and arty galleries are good for gifts around Pohořelec Square and in the rather twee neighbourhood near Nový Svět.**

### LOWER MALÁ STRANA

Visitors to the Franz Kafka Museum (▶ 107) near the Charles Bridge may get ideas for gifts from its shop which sells posters, mugs, calendars, postcards and so forth.

**Capriccio** (Újezd 15, tel: 257 320 165) has a vast stock of sheet music, including jazz as well as classical scores. More shops huddle on the ground floors of the looming baroque palaces on Maltézské náměstí, a couple of blocks towards the river.

Just off the square at **Antique Ahasver** (Prokopská 3, tel: 257 531 404. Closed Mon) you'll find old textiles and the excellent contemporary photographs of Pavel Ahasver.

In Vlašská, at No 13, tiny **Pavla & Olga** (tel: 728 939 872) is brimming with fantastic one-of-a-kind dresses, costume jewellery, skirts and shirts for women.

A few steps on is **Signet** (Vlašská 15, tel: 257 530 083), where you'll find rare and special old Czech, German and Russian books and maps. North of the bridge, U Lužického seminare Street has a wide variety of possibilities.

### UPPER MALÁ STRANA

**Antiques** at Loretanské náměstí 9 (tel: 233 353 780) deals in everything from coins to vintage model cars.

At Úvoz 1, look for **Factory Shop** which specializes in hand-made and -painted porcelain houses (tel: 257 530 634).

Picture-perfect Nerudova Street oozes alluring little shops such as **Katrák Antiques** (No 51) dealing in old coins, stamps, watches, porcelain and jewellery, as well as some almost priceless individual pieces (tel: 257 532 200; www.antiquekatrak.cz).

Look out, too, for the rare hand-carved wooden dolls in the **Marionety** an (Nerudova 51, tel: 774 418 236).

Walk a few more steps up this steep street to charming **U Zeleného čaje** (No 19, tel: 257 530 027), where you can buy Czech ceramics and order gourmet coffees, 150 kinds of tea and delicious sweets.

Browse through old books, postcards, stamps and prints at **Antikvariát U Zlaté Číše** (No 16, tel: 731 472 753).

# Hradčany, Malá Strana and Beyond

## PRAŽSKÝ HRAD AND HRADČANY

Fortunately, the castle's keepers have not allowed the precinct to become over-commercialized.

**The Museum Store** (off Zlata ulička, also accessible by a stairway from Jiřská, tel: 224 371 111) is the most comprehensive shop of its kind in town, full of replicas, books, and toys.

**Galerie Gambra** (Černínská 5, tel: 220 514 527; http://gambra.jex.cz) is the headquarters of the Czech Surrealist movement and the sales point for head-spinning art, ceramics and books by animator Jan Švankmajer and other members of the group.

For excellent, high-quality Czech artworks, visit the changing sales exhibitions mounted by **Galerie Miro** (Strahovské nádvoří 1/132, tel: 233 354 066; www.galeriemiro.cz), in the grounds of the Strahov Monastery.

Shops selling glassware, antiques and jewellery can be found on the stepped streets to the south of Prague Castle (Zámecké schody and Radnické schody).

# Where to... Go Out

## MUSIC

### Cross Club
The underground rock and dance club of the moment. Occupies a grungy spot in up-and-coming Holešovice.
🚇 off map ✉ Plynarní 1092/23
☎ 722 498 317; www.crossclub.cz

### Lichtenštejnský palác
During the summer lively operatic productions are staged in the courtyard of this palace opposite Malá Strana's Church of St Nicholas (➤ 105). The palace is the seat of the Prague music academy, and faculty and students perform regularly. There are also regular concerts of contemporary classical music.
🚇 205 D3 ✉ Malostranské náměstí 13
☎ 257 534 206 or 603 296 327 (reservations)

### SaSaZu
Very popular disco catering for up to 2500 people and with an elegant Asian restaurant.
🚇 off map ✉ Bubenské Nábřeží 306, Hološovice ☎ 284 097 444; www.sasazu.com
🕐 Daily 7pm–5am

## SPORT

### Generali Arena (Sparta Stadium)
This is the home of Prague's top soccer team, Sparta Praha, and the national team. The season runs from August to December and February to May. Tickets are easily obtainable at the gate. Sparta Praha regularly tops the Czech league table and takes part in European competitions.
🚇 202 A1 ✉ Milady Horákové 98 ☎ 220 570 323; www.prague.net/stadion-sparta

### Tipsport Arena (Sportovní hala)
Home to one of Prague's top ice hockey clubs, HC Sparta Praha. Books rock concerts occasionally.
🚇 203 E3 ✉ Za Electrárnou 419, Výstaviště
☎ 266 727 443

## FAMILY ENTERTAINMENT

### 🎡 Výstaviště Fairgrounds
This is a 100-year-old amusement park with an exhibition hall and a small funfair. Two modern theatres stage Czech-language musicals, and the low-budget replica of the Globe Theatre in London stages summer Shakespeare in both Czech and English.
🚇 202 D2 ✉ Výstaviště (eastern end of Stromovka Park), Holešovice
🕐 Daily 10–7, summer until 11

# Josefov

| | |
|---|---|
| Getting Your Bearings | 118 |
| In a Day | 120 |
| TOP 10 | 122 |
| Don't Miss | 125 |
| At Your Leisure | 130 |
| Where to... | 135 |

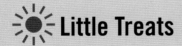
## Little Treats

### Cubism at Home
Often overlooked and yet remarkable: the **Cubist houses** (Kubistické Domy) near the **Spanish Synagogue** (➤ 133).

### See and be Seen
Celebrity spotting is all part of the fun at **Pravda** (➤ 136)...and you should leave yourself enough time to enjoy the experience.

### 🛈 Picture Puzzle
Let your fantasy run wild at the **Old Jewish Cemetery**: What do the symbols mean on the graves (➤ 124).

Josefov

# Getting Your Bearings

In the 19th century, much of the area now called Josefov had become a slum, so Prague's city council ordered the buildings to be demolished and rebuilt. Nonetheless, the Jewish heritage still remains very apparent. Wandering through this district is an encounter with the rich and often emotional history of what was once a vibrant Jewish community (➤ 21). Not even the tourist shops with their overly poignant knickknacks can detract from the beauty of the Old Jewish Cemetery or the Old-New Synagogue.

Roughly speaking, the neighbourhood fills the corner of the right bank's river bend. From Old Town Square, it extends northeast to Anežský klášter (Convent of St Agnes) and west to the Rudolfinum. Most of the synagogues and the cemetery cluster on either side of Maiselova Street. The Spanish Synagogue is over to the east, closer to the quarter's other main thoroughfare, Pařížská třída (Paris Boulevard). There are plenty of cafes and restaurants, even a couple that are kosher.

## TOP 10

⭐ Starý židovský hřbitov
(Old Jewish Cemetery) ➤ 122

## Don't Miss

㊳ Pinkasova synagoga
(Pinkas Synagogue) ➤ 125

㊴ Staronová synagoga
(Old-New Synagogue) ➤ 127

The exterior of the Spanish Synagogue exudes a Moorish air

# Getting Your Bearings

**TICKETS FOR THE JEWISH MUSEUM**

The Jewish Museum includes the Old Jewish Cemetery, the Ceremonial Hall and four of Josefov's five synagogues. The fifth synagogue, the Old-New Synagogue, is separate. Combined tickets (480Kč) are available at the synagogues or tourist agencies around Maiselova Street. To avoid crowding, tickets specify a timetable granting about 20 minutes for each "sight". For reservations, phone: 222 317 191 or send a mail to: rezervacni.centrum@jewishmuseum.cz.

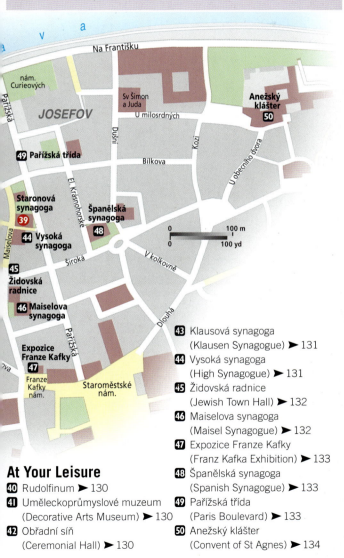

## At Your Leisure

- ④⓪ Rudolfinum ➤ 130
- ④① Uměleckoprůmyslové muzeum (Decorative Arts Museum) ➤ 130
- ④② Obřadní síň (Ceremonial Hall) ➤ 130
- ④③ Klausová synagoga (Klausen Synagogue) ➤ 131
- ④④ Vysoká synagoga (High Synagogue) ➤ 131
- ④⑤ Židovská radnice (Jewish Town Hall) ➤ 132
- ④⑥ Maiselova synagoga (Maisel Synagogue) ➤ 132
- ④⑦ Expozice Franze Kafky (Franz Kafka Exhibition) ➤ 133
- ④⑧ Španělská synagoga (Spanish Synagogue) ➤ 133
- ④⑨ Pařížská třída (Paris Boulevard) ➤ 133
- ⑤⓪ Anežský klášter (Convent of St Agnes) ➤ 134

*Perfect Days in...*

## Josefov

# The Perfect Day

Josefov, Prague's old Jewish district, is compact and you can tour the main sights in one day without any problem. Follow our itinerary and you will not miss any of the highlights. For more information see the main entries (➤ 122–134).

### 🕙 10:00am
Start at the ㊵ **Rudolfinum** (➤ 140) to enjoy the 1900s decor of its cafe. You might also take in one of the usually excellent temporary art exhibitions.

### 🕚 11:00am
Take a look on náměstí Jana Palacha at the Dvořák statue, then make for the ㊶ **Decorative Arts Museum** (➤ 130). While most people are still doing the Jewish Museum tour, have an early lunch at either **Les Moules** (➤ 135) or **Shelanu Deli** (➤ 136).

### 🕐 1:00pm
Around midday, the flood of visitors to the Jewish museum gradually subsides, so the chances of a more peaceful tour are best at this time. It is well worth starting with the poignant exhibition in the ㊳ **Pinkas Synagogue** (➤ 125).

### 🕐 1:30pm
Don't be hurried on your walk through the ⭐ **Old Jewish Cemetery** (detail pictured right, ➤ 122).

# The Perfect Day

## 🕒 2:00pm
On either side of the cemetery exit, the exhibits at the ㊷ **Ceremonial Hall** (➤ 130) and the ㊸ **Klausen Synagogue** (➤ 131) should take about half an hour between them.

## 🕒 2:30pm
Give yourself more time for the ㊴ **Old-New Synagogue** (➤ 127), the most important stop after the cemetery. Stroll around the ㊺ **Jewish Town Hall** (➤ 132), check the time – backwards and forwards – on the Hebrew and Roman-numeral clocks, pictured left, and walk south to ㊻ **Maisel Synagogue** (➤ 132).

## 🕒 3:30pm
Double back north on Maiselova and head east along Siroka to end the museum tour at the spectacular ㊽ **Spanish Synagogue** (➤ 133).

## 🕒 4:00pm
Coming back west on Široka, it's time for some chic profanity at ㊾ **Paris Boulevard** (➤ 133). You may have done enough architectural sightseeing by now, so this is the place to stop at one of the cafes before some window-shopping and people-watching.

## 🕒 6:00pm
Before the evening starts, head back to the heart of Josefov for a beer at **U Pivrnce**, an honest-to-goodness old-fashioned pub at Maiselova 3 (➤ 16).

Josefov

# ⭐ 9 Starý židovský hřbitov (Old Jewish Cemetery)

**There is a chaotic beauty here that gives particular meaning to the Hebrew name for a cemetery, *beit hayim* (House of Life). With Prague's Jewish population all but gone the cemetery sustains the memory of the community. The monumental tombs of the proud and the simple stones of the humble crowd together in a glorious, disorderly affirmation of life.**

Founded in the first half of the 15th century and closed to new burials in 1787, the cemetery today numbers around 12,000 tombs on the surface and tens of thousands more in uncounted layers beneath. Subsidence, erosion and the weathering of time have created an undulating landscape of crooked and tottering tombstones. The cemetery's oldest tomb is dated 1439 – a few older stones brought here from other cemeteries are inserted in a wall by the Klausová synagoga (▶ 131), while some wooden burial tablets are displayed in the museum of the Ceremonial Hall (▶ 130).

### Tomb Styles
You can practically date the tombstones according to their style. After the first simple flat limestone or granite markers of the 15th century, more ornate rounded or pointed red and white marble tombs appear in the 16th century, with Hebrew inscriptions. Poems or passages from the Bible extol the virtues of the deceased, and homage is paid to worldly success or scholarship. In the 17th century, wealthier Jews followed the Christian fashion for monumental baroque sepulchres simulating a miniature chapel.

*The Old Jewish Cemetery looks like a sea of stones*

### Household Names in the Ghetto
Best known of the people buried here, and the most visited tomb, is that of the community's most revered scholar, **Rabbi Yehuda Loew ben Bezalel**, who died in 1609. His monumental double tomb (shared with his wife Perl) was remodelled in the 18th century with a lion for his name, beneath a bunch of grapes to symbolize his ripe old age of 96. Visitors place pebbles on his grave as a mark of respect. Just across the way, his contemporary, financier **Mordechai Maisel**

> **STONES AND MORE**
> As a sign of respect, it is the Jewish custom to place on a tomb not flowers but a small stone. Formerly, visitors would also put coins on the tombs of the rabbis. The destitute would visit the cemetery at night to collect the money as alms.

# Josefov

### PICTORIAL SYMBOLS
Animals or other emblems are often carved on tombstones as visual puns on the Hebrew or German name of the deceased or in order to symbolize a profession. Thus there may be a lion for Yehuda, Loeb or Loewe; two hands in blessing for the priestly family of Cohen; a pitcher for their temple assistants, the Levites and thus Levy; a deer for Hirsch; a cockerel for Hahn; a mouse for Maisel; a violin for a musician; scissors for a tailor, and so on.

(died 1601), was the mayor of what was then known as the Jewish Town and one of its greatest benefactors. One of Prague's most renowned Jewish sons, **Franz Kafka**, is buried in the New Jewish Cemetery over in Žižkov (➤ 163).

In the male-dominated world of Orthodox Jewry, **Hendel Bashevi** (died 1628) stands out as the only woman here to have a truly monumental tomb of her own. Indeed, in its sheer size and the splendour of its late Renaissance decoration, it outshines that of the sages and rabbis around her. The wife of wealthy community leader Jacob Bashevi, whose letters of nobility won her the right to place two heraldic lions on her monument, she was renowned for her work with the poor of Josefov.

### TAKING A BREAK
Head over to the Vltava river and outdoor **cafes on the Vltava embankment** (Alšovo nábžeží), or try the **Café Franz Kafka** for an atmospheric coffee or light meal (➤ 137).

---

🚩 206 A3
✉ Entrance by Pinkasova synagoga, Siroká 3
☎ Jewish Museum: 222 317 191
🕐 Apr–Oct Sun–Fri 9–6; Nov–Mar Sun–Fri 9–4:30
🚇 Staroměstská 🚋 17, 18
🎟 Jewish Museum ticket: 480Kč

### INSIDER INFO

- Entrance to the cemetery, as part of the Jewish Museum tour, is from the Pinkasova synagoga (➤ 125) on Siroka Street with the exit by the Klausová synagoga on U Starého hřbitova (➤ 131). A cemetery **map** is provided with the museum's tour brochure showing the location of its most famous tombs.
- Men **cover their heads**, just as in a synagogue, as a Jewish cemetery is considered holy ground. Paper *kippah* are available.

# 38 Pinkasova synagoga (Pinkas Synagogue)

**The Renaissance synagogue, built in the 16th century as a private synagogue, is now a sober memorial to the Czechoslovak Jews killed in World War II.**

The synagogue was founded in 1479 by Rabbi Pinkas and enlarged by his great-nephew Aaron Meshullam Horowitz. It was then taken over in 1535 by Žalman Horowitz and integrated into the family residence abutting directly on the south side of the Old Jewish Cemetery (▶ 122). The original late Gothic building was remodelled a century later in its present Renaissance style with the addition of a women's gallery in the 17th century vestibule and council room, creating a charming inner courtyard for the entrance. It has been rebuilt many times over the centuries.

The *bima* pulpit with wrought-iron grille in Pinkas Synagogue

## The Interior

Inside, the synagogue is an interesting blend of the two styles, with richly coloured Renaissance motifs edging the Flamboyant Gothic rib-vaulting. There is no attempt here, as in the Staronová synagoga (▶ 127), to avoid ribs forming a cross. The central *bima* (pulpit for leading the service) has kept its rococo, wrought-iron grille on gilded spiral supports.

**Memorial 77,297** is the title of the wall-monument to Czechoslovak Jewish victims in the Nazi concentration camps. It took Václav Boštík and Jiří John five years (1954–59) to cover the synagogue's walls with all 77,297 names, dates of birth and dates of death written in simple black and red letters. In 1968, the

# Josefov

synagogue was closed and the names removed, as the Communist authorities insisted, because of the deteriorating state of the building. The Communist regime's Czech critics say the decision was strictly political, in the heated "anti-Zionist" atmosphere following Israel's victory in the Six-Day War in 1967.

The synagogue was renovated in the 1990s and the Memorial names were restored. Against the east wall, around the Tabernacle that once held the scrolls of the Law and the Prophets, are written the names of the principal concentration camps where the Czechoslovak Jews died.

### "Children's Drawings From Terezín (1942–1944)"

A permanent exhibition here is devoted to drawings by Jewish children in the German concentration camp of Theresienstadt, an hour's drive from Prague (➤ 178). The Jewish Museum keeps in the synagogue a collection of 4,500 drawings saved and hidden by the children's art teacher, Bauhaus painter Friedl Dicker-Brandeisová. The children continued to draw, mostly pictures of a fantasy world outside the camp, until many of them, like their teacher, were deported to Auschwitz.

The 77,297 memorial is thought-provoking

### TAKING A BREAK

Get away from it all at the delightful first-floor 19th-century cafe in the **Rudolfinum concert hall** (Alšovo nábreží 12, ➤ 130), in which you can ponder on the impressions.

---

🕂 206 A3  ✉ Široká 3
☎ Jewish Museum: 222 317 191
🛈 Apr–Oct 9–6; Nov–Mar 9–4:30; closed Sat, Jewish holidays
🚇 Staroměstská  🚌 17, 18
🎫 Jewish Museum ticket: 480Kč

## INSIDER INFO

Excavations in the synagogue basement in the 1970s uncovered a **ritual bath** *(mikveh)* dating back to the 15th century, at least 100 years before the present synagogue was built.

# ③⑨ Staronová synagoga (Old-New Synagogue)

The oldest surviving synagogue in Europe – completed in 1275 – still being used regularly for worship. Quite apart from being a treasure for Prague's dwindling Jewish community, it is a significant monument for anyone interested in what makes Prague such a special city.

Architecture being a profession denied to Jews at the time, the Staronová was probably erected by master builders and masons from the site of the nearby Convent of St Agnes (Anežský klášter, ➤ 134). Deceptively small on the outside, the synagogue is simple in form, distinguished only by the crenellated, steeply sloping brick gable of its facade. The entrance is on the south side through a Gothic portal. The finely carved stone pediment's stylized vine has 12 roots and 12 bunches of grapes – symbolic of the 12 tribes of Israel.

*The Bima (pulpit) of the Old-New Synagogue*

# Josefov

## The Interior

The long vestibule and a parallel area along the other side of the hall of worship have window-slits through which women, separated from the men in Orthodox Judaism, could follow the service. The hall itself is unexpectedly loftier because the floor's level is today so much lower than that of the improved street outside. Marrying function and faith, the Gothic vaults each have five load-bearing ribs rather than four so as not to form a cross, forbidden in a Jewish house of worship. Sturdy octagonal pillars with the *bima* (a rectangular platform-like pulpit), between them divide the hall into twin naves, unique among Bohemia's medieval religious buildings. Above the elegant wrought-iron frame of the *bima* is the Jewish community's red banner (1716) with a Star of David and the traditional hat then worn in public.

**Simple yet striking at the same time – the gabled roof of the Old-New Synagogue**

## The Tabernacle

Built into the east wall in the 16th century, the Tabernacle (*aron ha-kodesh*) houses the scrolls of the Law (Torah, the first five books of the Bible) and the books of the Prophets (Haftarah). During the Sabbath service (Saturday), the two scrolls are carried ceremonially to the *bima,* where seven

---

### SO WHAT'S NEW?

The story of the synagogue's name sounds like a Jewish joke. When it was first built, the community already had an Old Synagogue – Altschul in Yiddish – so they called this one Neuschul, New Synagogue. In the 16th century, the wealthy and powerful Wechsler family built another synagogue and told the rabbis: "We're calling it the New Synagogue. Yours is old now. You'll have to find a different name." "But," said the rabbis, "we have an Old Synagogue already. What do we do?" Every Jewish community has a Solomon and, whoever he was, he came up with the name Old-New Synagogue. He had God on his side: in the slum-clearance of 1900 (▶ 133), the Old Synagogue and Wechslers' New Synagogue disappeared. The Old-New Synagogue survived.

Another explanation for the etymology of the name is that it derives from the Hebrew word *altnai*, which means: "On condition that". According to legend, angels brought stones for the construction of the temple in Prague from the ruins of the destroyed temple in Jerusalem, but only "on condition" that these stones were returned when they were needed for rebuilding the temple in Jerusalem upon the arrival of the Messiah.

# Staronová synagoga (Old-New Synagogue)

members of the congregation are called up in turn to share in the reading of a chapter from the Prophets. A quorum (*minyan*) of at least 10 men must be present for a properly constituted service to be held.

### Survival
In a town where so many older buildings have had to be reconstructed after devastating fires, the Staronová has escaped unscathed – blessed, say the faithful, by the most revered of its sages, Rabbi Loew. Perversely, it also benefited from the decision of Adolf Hitler to preserve it and the other synagogues of Josefov (in the Klausen and Maisel synagogues ➤ 131, 132) as an "Exotic Museum for an Extinct Race". The Nazis had treasures from synagogues all over Bohemia transported to Prague, which are exhibited today in testimony to a people still very much alive.

### TAKING A BREAK
For a culinary break, head over to Belgian **Café Les Moules** (➤ 135) for fresh seafood.

Detailed stonework on the Old-New Synagogue

🕂 206 A3  ✉ Červená 2  ☎ Reservations 224 800 812
🕐 Apr–Oct 9–6; Nov–Mar 9–5; closed Sat, Jewish holidays
Ⓜ Staroměstská  🚊 17, 18
💰 200Kč (Staronová is separate from the Jewish Museum ticket)

## INSIDER INFO

- People are expected to **dress appropriately** for a house of worship. Men are requested to cover their heads – paper *kippah* are available at the ticket office or synagogue entrance.
- In the little park north of the synagogue is Symbolist (and Protestant) sculptor František Bílek's 1905 **statue of Moses**, at his feet the fragments of his shattered tablets of the Law. Read into this what you will – like beauty, the meaning of a symbol is in the eye of the beholder.

Josefov

# At Your Leisure

### ⓸⓪ Rudolfinum
The imposing 19th-century neo-Renaissance concert hall is home to the Czech Philharmonic Orchestra, and is one of the venues for the annual Prague Spring and Prague Autumn music festivals. Besides the orchestra's splendid Dvořák Hall (the composer's statue is in the square outside), its galleries host prestigious temporary art exhibitions and there is a delightful spacious cafe on the first floor. The building served as the first Czechoslovak parliament (1918–38) and the German Army HQ in World War II. The hall faces onto náměstí Jana Palacha, the square honouring Jan Palach, the Czech student-martyr who committed suicide in 1969 to try to rouse the people from their apathy following the Warsaw Pact invasion in 1968 (➤ 150).
✚ 206 A3 ✉ Alšovo nábřeží 12
☎ Concerts: 227 059 227, guided tours: 221 714 152; www.ceskafilharmonie.cz
🕒 Rudolfinum: July–Aug Mon–Fri 10–3, Sep–June 10–6; cafe: Tue–Sun 10–7:30
Ⓜ Staroměstská 🚋 18 💰 50Kč

### ⓸⓵ Uměleckoprůmyslové muzeum (Decorative Arts Museum)
Even the Czechs admit this museum's name may be hard to say and simplify it from Uměleckoprůmyslové Muzeum to UPM. The 19th-century building (many parts of which have undergone a thorough restoration) houses first-rate Bohemian and European glass, porcelain, ceramics, furniture and metalware collections from the 16th to the 20th century. There is a special emphasis on Art Nouveau and Czech Cubism, but not all of the exhibits are always on display. The ground-floor Espresso UPM is also worth a visit.
✚ 206 A3 ✉ 17 listopadu 2
☎ 251 093 111; www.upm.cz
🕒 Wed–Sun 10–6; Tue 10–7
Ⓜ Staroměstská 🚋 17, 18 💰 80Kč

### ⓸⓶ Obřadní síň (Ceremonial Hall)
On the left as you leave the Old Jewish Cemetery, the stone neo-Romanesque building (1908), with its little round corner turret, was once the ceremonial hall of the Jewish Burial Society. Until the 1920s, bodies were prepared here for burial in the New Jewish Cemetery over in Žižkov (➤ 163). Don't let the hall's appearance put you off visiting its intriguing exhibition of Jewish burial customs and its explanations of the tombstone imagery and inscriptions.
✚ 206 A3 ✉ U starého hřbitova 3
☎ Jewish Museum: 222 317 191
🕒 Apr–Oct 9–6; Nov–Mar 9–4:30; closed Sat, Jewish holidays
Ⓜ Staroměstská 🚋 17, 18
💰 Jewish Museum ticket: 480Kč

**Stained glass on stairs of the Decorative Arts Museum**

# At Your Leisure

The Klausen Synagogue conducted funeral services for people buried in the Old Jewish Cemetery

### 43 Klausová synagoga (Klausen Synagogue)

To the right of the cemetery exit, the Klausen Synagogue, created by Mordechai Maisel in 1573, originally consisted of three smaller buildings (*Klausen* in German) – a synagogue, *mikveh* ritual bath, and *yeshiva* Talmudic school. Destroyed by fire in 1689, they were replaced five years later by the present synagogue, second in importance only to the Staronová synagoga (➤ 127). It was used for the funeral ceremonies of the adjacent cemetery, of which there is a fine view from upstairs windows. The handsomely restored baroque interior today houses an exhibition of **Hebrew manuscripts** and traditional artefacts of everyday Jewish life.

🕀 206 A3
✉ U starého hřbitova 4
☎ Jewish Museum: 222 317 191
🕐 Apr–Oct 9–6; Nov–Mar 9–4:30; closed Sat, Jewish holidays
Ⓜ Staroměstská 🚋 17, 18
🎫 Jewish Museum ticket: 480Kč

### 44 Vysoká synagoga (High Synagogue)

Next door to the Židovská radnice (Jewish Town Hall), the High Synagogue's plain grey building conceals in its interior an ornate hall of worship located upstairs – hence the name. The decoration, restored after the fire of 1689, makes an elegant adaptation in Renaissance style of the building's original Gothic ribbed-vaulting. The synagogue is generally reserved

# Josefov

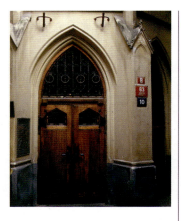

**The Jewish community's greatest benefactor, Mordechai Maisel, left his name on this synagogue**

for non-Orthodox Jewish services and is only open to worshippers.
🏠 206 A3 ✉ Červená 4
🕒 Fri, Sat (Sabbath services), Jewish holidays
🚇 Staroměstská 🚋 17, 18

## ㊺ Židovská radnice (Jewish Town Hall)

The baroque town hall and clock tower were reconstructed in 1765 on the site of an earlier building founded in the 1560s by its mayor, Mordechai Maisel. It brought the ghetto's administration into line with those of the Old Town, New Town and Malá Strana. Besides the four Roman-numeral clocks, there is a **Hebrew clock** on which the hands run "counter-clockwise". Over the main entrance on Maiselova is the Jewish Town's coat of arms, a Star of David with a traditional Jewish hat. Use of the emblem, also on the clock tower, was granted by Ferdinand III after the Jews had fought against Swedish troops on Charles Bridge in 1648. The assembly rooms are used for Jewish festivals and other community activities and by the kosher restaurant Shalom (tel: 224 800 806, open Mon–Sat noon–1:30).
🏠 206 A3 ✉ Maiselova 18
🚇 Staroměstská 🚋 17, 18

## ㊻ Maiselova synagoga (Maisel Synagogue)

Halfway up Maiselova Street, Maisel Synagogue is often the first one visited on the Jewish Museum tour for anyone coming from Staroměstské náměstí (Old Town Square). When the Jewish Town's illustrious and very wealthy 16th-century mayor, Mordechai Maisel, built this synagogue in 1592, towards the end of his life, it was the most lavishly decorated building the Prague ghetto had ever seen. The simpler neo-Gothic structure you see today is the result of frequent remodelling after a devastating fire in 1689. The hall of worship and upstairs women's gallery are now used as an exhibition space for some beautiful silver and gold ritual objects collected from various disbanded Czechoslovak

# At Your Leisure

Jewish communities. They include wine goblets, spice caskets *(besamim)* and intricately patterned plaques and crowns that adorned scrolls of the Torah. These are treasures originally assembled, not by the Jewish community itself, but by the German Nazis in the 1940s for their own aborted "Exotic Museum for an Extinct Race" (➤ 129).

🟥 206 A3  ✉ Maiselova 10
☎ Jewish Museum: office 221 711 511; reservations 222 317 191
🕐 Apr–Oct 9–6; Nov–Mar 9–4:30; closed Sat, Jewish holidays
Ⓜ Staroměstská 🚋 17, 18
💷 Jewish Museum ticket: 480Kč

### 47 Expozice Franze Kafky (Franz Kafka Exhibition)

Near the western facade of the Church of St Nicholas, a small museum is installed in the building standing on the site of Franz Kafka's birthplace. The bronze bust on the corner was mounted during a brief 1960s thaw in the general Socialist hostility to this profoundly subversive writer (➤ 32). Today, his rehabilitation is such that the little square in front of the museum has been given his name. The exhibits include photographs of him and his family, his many homes around the city, and copies of his manuscripts and drawings. (Make sure you don't confuse this with the Gallery Franz Kafka, which is devoted to temporary art exhibitions.)

🟥 206 A3  ✉ Náměstí Franze Kafky 5
☎ 222 321 675  🕐 Tue–Fri 10–6, Sat 10–5
Ⓜ Staroměstská 🚋 17, 18  💷 40Kč

### 48 Španělská synagoga (Spanish Synagogue)

On the east side of the neighbourhood, the most recent of Josefov's synagogues, the Spanish Synagogue, is also the most lavish.

**The Spanish Synagogue symbolizes the prestige and prosperity of Prague's Jewish community in the 19th century**

It was built in 1868 in Moorish style, with an interior inspired by Spain's Alhambra Palace. It stands on the site of the Altschul (Old Synagogue), house of worship of a Byzantine Jewish community arriving in the 11th century. The interior is a riot of gilded geometric and floral motifs in reds, blues and greens. Its exhibits document the history of Czech Jews from the 19th century to the present. Up in the women's gallery are some remarkable photos of the ghetto before and after its demolition in the 1900s. Outside stands a controversial statue of Franz Kafka, which, whether you love it or hate it, makes for a great photo-op.

🟥 206 B3  ✉ Vězeňská 1
☎ Jewish Museum: 222 749 211
🕐 Apr–Oct 9–6; Nov–Mar 9–4:30; closed Sat, Jewish holidays
Ⓜ Staroměstská 🚋 17, 18
💷 Jewish Museum ticket: 480Kč

### 49 Pařížská třída (Paris Boulevard)

Elegant and leafy Paris Boulevard is an urban showpiece epitomizing the neighbourhood's brash break with the past. In the 1900s, ruthless slum clearance in dank and overcrowded Josefov made way for

# Josefov

**Ornate facades characterize the exuberant architecture of Pařížská třída**

the new boulevard. Today, exuberant neo-baroque and Art Nouveau architecture, fashionable shops, cafes and chic restaurants amply justify its name.

It runs from Old Town Square to Čechův most (bridge) at the Vltava river. Starting at Old Town Square, the grand four-storey neo-baroque house on the northeast corner was the home of the Kafka family in 1913. (Next door is the Image Theatre, which puts on flashy shows of pantomime, dance and "blacklight theatre", ➤ 48.) Across the street are two fine houses, Nos 7 and 9, on opposite corners of Jáchymova Street. Peek into Matej Blecha's ornate neo-Gothic building at No 15 (corner of Široká) to see **Insider Tip** its splendid Art Nouveau oval stairwell. Two other Art Nouveau gems are at Nos 28 and 19, the latter by Bedřich Bendelmayer, designer of the Grand Hotel Evropa on Wenceslas Square (➤ 148).

Reflecting a lingering need to latch on to the past, the street began as Mikulášska třida (Nicholas Boulevard), named after the nearby church (➤ 58) on Old Town Square. In 1926, when the French capital was very much in vogue, the street became what it most looked like: Pařížská třída (Paris Boulevard). Then, under German occupation during World War II, SS commanders renamed it Nuremberg Avenue after their favourite town back home. Today, the name is once more reminiscent of France.

✚ 206 B4  Staroměstská  17, 18

### 50 Anežský klášter (Convent of St Agnes)

On the northeast edge of Josefov, the 13th-century Convent of St Agnes holds a place of honour in the life of the Old Jewish Town inasmuch as its master builders and masons also worked on the Staronová synagoga (➤ 127). It was founded in 1231 for the Order of Poor Clares by Agnes, daughter of King Přemysl Otakar I. The convent was closed in 1782 but, following restoration, reopened as a **Museum of Medieval Art in Bohemia and Central Europe**. The high-quality works on display, part of the Czech National Gallery, consist mainly of altar panels, carved wooden statues and stone sculptures.

✚ 206 B4  U Milosrdných 17
☎ 224 810 628; www.ngprague.cz
🕐 Tue–Sun 10–6  Náměstí Republiky
🚋 5, 8, 14  150Kč

# Where to...
# Eat and Drink

**Prices**
Expect to pay per person for a meal, including drinks, tax and service:
**£** under 500Kč    **££** 500Kč–1,000Kč    **£££** over 1,000Kč

## RESTAURANTS

### Barock £££
From the people who brought Pravda (➤ 136) to Prague comes this *très chic* joint across the street. The staff are friendly and cool, the patrons just plain cool. Why not order salad, sushi or Thai-style fish to accompany your cold drink?
➕ 206 A3 ✉ Pařížská 24
☎ 222 329 221; www.barockrestaurant.cz
🕐 Daily 10am–1am 🚇 Staroměstská

### Café Les Moules ££
You can get mussels in coconut milk with chilli and fresh coriander and a side of *pommes frites* at this brasserie. The stunning double-height windows that look out onto the Old-New Synagogue and Pařížská Boulevard make the view here so pleasant that it's easy to overlook the restaurant's inner charms: traditional dark wood panelling, comfortable tables and ornate light fixtures.
➕ 206 A3 ✉ Pařížská 19/203
☎ 222 315 0 22; www.lesmoules.cz
🕐 Daily 11.30–midnight 🚇 Staroměstská

### Casa Andina ££
Prague's one and only Peruvian restaurant occupies a prime site just across the street from the Spanish Synagogue. The spicy cuisine reflects an exotic mix of Spanish, Incan and Chinese influences (Chinese labourers built the Peruvian railways in the 19th century). Beef, duck, chicken and fish dishes feature on a tempting menu which changes with the seasons. Reserve a table at the weekend to enjoy live Andean music in the restaurant and adjoining night club.
➕ 206 B3 ✉ Dušní 15
☎ 224 815 996; www.casaandina.cz
🕐 Sun Tue 11–11, Wed–Sat 2–2
🚇 Staroměststká

### Chez Marcel £/££
If your languages run to French rather than Czech, no problem! The same goes for the staff and much of the regular crowd at Chez Marcel. They eat and drink with insouciance, but at Czech prices. Jazz tunes and old French advertising posters add to ==the bistro atmosphere as patrons dine== **Insider Tip** on steaks, *poulet frites* (chicken and chips), or a simple *croque monsieur* (ham and cheese toasted sandwich).
➕ 206 B3 ✉ Haštalské náměstí 12
☎ 222 315 676; www.chezmarcel.cz
🕐 Daily 11:30–11 🚇 Staroměstská

### King Solomon ££
This kosher restaurant holds true to its name with a warm interior intended to resemble the Temple of Jerusalem. If that's not your preferred environment in which to dig into *gefilte fisch* or *blintzes*, ask to be seated in the glazed atrium. They'll also send a Sabbath lunch box to your hotel on request. US First Lady, Michelle Obama was a guest here in 2009.
➕ 206 A3 ✉ Široká 8
☎ 224 818 752; www.kosher.cz
🕐 Mon–Sun 1pm–2am Fri dinner and Sat lunch by reservation only 🚇 Staroměstská

# Josefov

### Le Café Colonial ££
International standards such as steaks, grilled salmon and chicken are served here in this inviting set of rooms. This place buzzes with both drinkers and diners all day long, which is a record most other local eateries could envy. Also fine just for a coffee or a glass of wine.

🗺 206 A3 ✉ Široká 6
☎ 224 818 322; www.lecafecolonial.cz
🕐 Daily 10–midnight 🚇 Staroměstská

### Pravda ££/£££
The restaurant/club called "Truth" feels like a stray from some glitzy Mediterranean port. The lunchtime scene is relaxed, reflecting the many walk-ins strolling near Staronová synagoga (Old-New Synagogue). Dinner becomes a more glamorous affair – although still relaxed by European standards. The food is eclectic world food – adventurous for Prague – including Vietnamese spring rolls, lobster soup and tacos.

🗺 206 A3 ✉ Pařížská 17
☎ 222 326 203; www.pravdarestaurant.cz
🕐 Daily noon–1am 🚇 Staroměstská

### Shelanu Deli £
Informal lunch counter and small restaurant serving kosher sandwiches and salads is a good spot for breakfast or lunch, or a quick snack. It has a great location, just down from the main sites of the former Jewish ghetto.

🗺 206 A3 ✉ Břehová 8
☎ 221 665 141; www.shelanu.cz
🕐 Sun–Thu 9–9, Fri 9–5 🚇 Staroměstská

### La Veranda £££
One of the city's leading restaurants, which is also listed in the Michelin Guide. Lunches and dinners here are exquisitely and carefully prepared, with a focus on intense flavours. So whether you choose the baked duck breast with thyme, cannellini beans, caramelized shallots or the tuna "grillé-cru" with roasted mushrooms and spinach, the chances are you'll be well pleased.

🗺 206 B3 ✉ Elišky Krásnohorské 2
☎ 224 814 733; www.laveranda.cz
🕐 Mon–Sat noon–midnight 🚇 Staroměstská

## INNS, PUBS AND BARS

### Bugsy's
Many consider Bugsy's to be Prague's best cocktail bar, not for the atmosphere necessarily, but for the quality of the drinks. These bartenders take their cocktails seriously. A magnet for Prague's well-to-do and non-package tourists.

🗺 206 A3 ✉ Pařížská 10
☎ 840 284 797; www.bugsysbar.cz
🕐 Daily 7pm–2am 🚇 Staroměstská

### Molly Malone's
The crackling fireplace and menu of Irish favourites are two reasons to call on this friendly pub; Guinness on draught and the convivial mix of expats and locals are two more. Try to get the cosy table tucked into the upstairs.

🗺 206 B3 ✉ U Obecního dvora 4
☎ 224 818 851; www.mollymalones.cz
🕐 Sun–Thu 11am–1am, Fri, Sat 11am–2am
🚇 Náměstí Republiky

### Potrefená husa
Admire the restored Cubist interior here while enjoying the house beers and Belgian bottled varieties. Food specials include a succulent beefsteak braised in dark beer.

🗺 206 B3 ✉ Bílkova 5
☎ 266 313 108; www.pivovary-staropramen.cz
🕐 Tue–Thu 11am–midnight, Fri, Sat 11–1, Sun 11–11 🚇 Staroměstská

### U Pivrnce
The ancient vaulted ceilings here are decorated with contemporary and naughty scenes by the cartoonist Urban. There's an extensive menu of beef, chicken and pork dishes. Try "Mydlář the Executioner's Sword", a beef and pork skewer commemorating the famous Prague executioner.

# Where to...

🏠 206 A3 ✉ Maiselova 3
☎ 222 329 404; www.upivrnce.cz (Czech only)
🕐 Daily 11am–midnight 🚇 Staroměstská

### Zlatá Praha
In summer, the ninth-floor terrace bar attached to the Inter-Continental Hotel's restaurant commands an unbeatable panorama of the Old Town. And you can order drinks and light meals.
🏠 206 A4 ✉ Pařížská 30
☎ 296 631 111; www.zlatapraharestaurant.cz
🕐 Daily 6pm–11:30pm; Sun brunch 11–3
🚇 Staroměstská

## CAFÉS

### Au Gourmand
Choose from a mouth-watering array of cakes, pastries and sandwiches while admiring the restored Art Nouveau interior of this delicatessen and bakery.
🏠 206 B3 ✉ Dlouhá 10
☎ 222 329 060; www.augourmand.cz
🕐 Mon–Fri 8–7, Sat 8:30–7; Sun 9–7
🚇 Staroměstská

### Café Franz Kafka
Admittedly touristy, but fun to get yourself in the mood for exploring the Jewish quarter and learning about Prague's most famous Jewish resident. The menu includes excellent hot drinks, plus some salads and sandwiches. Evocative photos on the walls capture a bit of this quarter as it once looked.
🏠 206 A3 ✉ Široká 12 ☎ 222 318 945
🕐 Daily 10–9 🚇 Staroměstská

### Café UPM
The café connected to the Museum of Decorative Arts is a hidden gem. Convenient, cheap, and almost unknown to the legions of people around the corner at the Jewish Museum. To find the café, walk into the UPM and go through the door to the right.
🏠 206 A3 ✉ 17 listopadu 2
☎ 251 093 111; www.upm.cz
🕐 Mon–Fri 10–7 🚇 Staroměstská

### Kavárna Rudolfinum
You can always find plenty of soft seating in this elegantly dressed room in the Rudolfinum (➤ 130). To reach the cafe, find the entrance along the riverside of the building and tell the cash desk attendant you only want to go to the café.
🏠 206 A3 ✉ Alšovo nábřeží 12
☎ 224 893 317
🕐 Exhibitions only Tue–Sun 10–6
🚇 Staroměstská

# Where to... Shop

**On Pařížská and Maiselova are most of the city's ultra high-end fashion shops, a sprinkling of antiques and art dealers. In the immediate area of the Jewish Museum you will pay over the odds.**

## PARIS BOULEVARD

Pařížská třída runs from Old Town Square to the Čechův most (bridge) over the Vltava. The names start at **Cartier** at Pařížská 2 (tel: 221 790 000), and roll on like a "Who's Who" of international luxury: **Louis Vuitton, Gucci, Christian Dior, Hugo Boss**, and **Hermes**, to name but a few. Sales are frequent, though, particularly during the spring and autumn clear-outs. Otherwise, it all depends on what the exchange rate is like at the time. Scattered among the big-brand names are a couple of shops of local interest.

Look in at **Obchod mincemi** at Pařížská 8 (tel: 222 313 285; www.mince.cz) if you're interested in historic coins. Adjacent at the same address is an **Antikvariát** (tel: 222 321 402) with excellent old books and maps.

Away from Pařížská the stores thin out, but are still worth a visit.

## Josefov

Try Bilková between Pařížská and Kozí streets, which has an interesting gallery dedicated to art featuring women, the **Galerie La Femme** (Bilková 2, tel: 224 812 656; www.glf.cz).

Czech fashion for the ladies is available at **Navarila** (Elišky Krašnohorské 4; tel: 271 742 091; www.navarila.cz).

The cramped shop in the **Decorative Arts Museum** (➤ 130) has good posters, books and calendars highlighting its collections.

### JEWISH HERITAGE

The small gift shop at the **Maisel Synagogue** (Maiselova 10, ➤ 132) stocks a comparatively dignified selection of replicas, such as Torah pointers.

**Antikvariát V Široké** (Široká 7, tel: 222 318 876) sells books on Judaism, a few guides to the Jewish Quarter, prints and modern artworks.

*Insider Tip:* For inexpensive gifts, try the **Franz Kafka Exhibition** (Náměstí Franze Kafky 5, tel: 222 321 675, ➤ 133).

# Where to... Go Out

**Prague has always been known for its artistic heritage. Many concerts are performed in churches and palaces and are extremely popular. Sometimes it is the only way to see the church, which may be closed to the public otherwise.**

### MUSIC

#### Rudolfinum
The Dvořák Hall is a jewel of an auditorium where the best local and visiting talent performs. This is home to the Czech Philharmonic Orchestra, the country's best travelled, most respected cultural institution, which upholds the great musical traditions of Central Europe. The excellent Prague Philharmonia Chamber Orchestra and the Czech National Symphony Orchestra make regular appearances. Chamber concerts take place in the Suk Hall.
🕀 206 A3 ✉ Alšovo nábřeží 12
☎ 227 059 227; www.ceskafilharmonie.cz

#### St Agnes Convent (Klášter sv Anežký České)
The historic St Agnes Convent complex includes a concert hall built in the 1980s from the ruins of an early Gothic church. It is one of the better venues in town for serious classical music, and one of the few where Praguers outnumber tourists.
🕀 206 B4 ✉ U Milosrdných 17, Staré Město
☎ 224 810 628, 222 002 336 (tickets); www.fok.cz

#### Church of SS Simon and Jude (Kostel sv Šimona a Judy)
High-quality chamber concerts take place in this large baroque Church of SS Simon and Jude. Check online for forthcoming performances. Advance tickets are sold at the FOK agency, U Obecního domu 2, in Staré Město (Old Town).
🕀 198 B4 ✉ Dušní at U Milosrdných, Staré Město ☎ 222 002 336 (FOK), 222 002 336 (tickets); www.fok.cz

### BOAT RIDES

Excursion boats dock at the quayside below Na Františku Street, across from the Inter-Continental Hotel. You can simply pick from the available craft or reserve through the largest tour operator, **EVD** (from the booth on the quay or telephone 224 810 030; www.evd.cz), which runs brief sightseeing rides, lunch trips and evening cruises. Prices vary depending on the ride.

# New Town and Beyond

| | |
|---|---|
| Getting Your Bearings | 140 |
| In a Day | 142 |
| Top 10 | 144 |
| Don't Miss | 152 |
| At Your Leisure | 160 |
| Where to… | 165 |

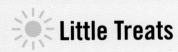 **Little Treats**

### Rendezvous with the "Green Fairy"
Lap up the literary spirit in **Café Slavia** (➤ 162) and admire the painting of the *Absinthe Drinker* in the clutches of the "Green Fairy".

### Sunshine Break
Enjoy a relaxing break in the park area around **Charles Square** (➤ 162) mingling with the people of Prague.

### Pulsating Centre
There are few other places that represent the beating heart of Prague better than **Wenceslas Square** (➤ 148). A stroll reveals a whole array of architectural gems.

**Josefov**

# Getting Your Bearings

**Despite its name and modern buildings, Nové Město (New Town) has a place well anchored in history. If its monuments proudly proclaim the Czechs' rise to nationhood, Vyšehrad Castle is bathed in the legendary mists of Prague's medieval beginnings. And from Vltava Embankment you can enjoy the blithely unhistoric pleasures of open-air cafes and dancing.**

With the Art Nouveau Municipal House (Obecní dům) as its bright beacon on the southeast corner of Old Town, New Town extends from the avenues of Na příkopě and Národní south along the Vltava River to the heights of Vyšehrad. To the east lie the residential and nightlife districts of Vinohrady and Žižkov.

**The Municipal House, Art Nouveau jewel and symbol of the Czech nation**

This is the liveliest part of modern Prague. Wenceslas Square is the bright and busy centre where young and old like to stroll. Národní třída has two cultural monuments, the august National Theatre and, opposite, Café Slavia, once the haunt of the dissidents and now a tourist-friendly cafe with a great view of Prague Castle across the river.

# Getting Your Bearings

## TOP 10
- ★ Vlatva ➤ 144
- ★ Obecní dům (Municipal House) ➤ 146
- ★ Václavské náměstí (Wenceslas Square) ➤ 148

## Don't Miss
- 51 Muchově muzeu ➤ 152
- 52 Národní divadlo (National Theatre) ➤ 153
- 53 Vyšehrad ➤ 157

## At Your Leisure
- 54 Prašná brána (Powder Tower) ➤ 160
- 55 Na příkopé ➤ 160
- 56 Státní opera (State Opera House) ➤ 160
- 57 Národní muzeum ➤ 161
- 58 Muzeum voskových figurín (Wax Museum) ➤ 161
- 59 Café Slavia ➤ 162
- 60 Karlovo náměstí (Charles Square) ➤ 162
- 61 Nový židovský hřbitov (New Jewish Cemetery) ➤ 163
- 62 Žižkovská televizni věž (Žižkov TV Tower) ➤ 164
- 63 Vítkov ➤ 164
- 64 Muzeum Hlavního města Prahy (Prague Municipal Museum) ➤ 164

*Perfect Days in...*

Josefov

# The Perfect Day

The distances in the New Town are slightly greater than for example in the more compact Old Town. Thanks to the trams, however, you can still visit all the main sights in one day. Follow our itinerary and you will not miss any of the highlights. For more information see the main entries (➤ 144–164).

## 🕙 10:00am
Make a bright start at ⭐**Municipal House** (➤ 146) and maybe visit the cafe. At the southern end of the building, climb the **54 Powder Tower** (➤ 160) for a good rooftop view of the monuments you'll be visiting.

## 🕚 11:00am
Stroll west along **55 Na příkopě** (➤ 160) and maybe do some shopping before heading south on Panská to the **51 Mucha Museum** (➤ 152).

## 🕛 12:00noon
Cut over on Jindřišská west to ⭐**Wenceslas Square** (➤ 148). Walk up to the Wenceslas Monument and then back down, ending up at the Grand Hotel Evropa for a pre-lunch cocktail in its elegant cafe (➤ 149).

## 🕐 1:00pm
At the Vodičkova junction with Václavské náměstí, hop on the No 9 tram, which turns north and west to run along Národní třída to the ⭐**Vltava Embankment** (below, ➤ 144). From Masarykovo nábřeží, walk down the causeway over to **Slavonic Island** (➤ 144) for lunch at one of the restau-

# The Perfect Day

rants, perhaps out on the terrace. After lunch, choose between a siesta in the garden and renting a rowing boat for a closer look at the river.

### 🕒 3:00pm
Back up on Masarykovo nábřeží, walk south to **Mánes Gallery** (➤ 144) to see one of its excellent temporary exhibitions of modern art. Just south of that is the futuristic Rašín building by Frank Gehry and Vladimír Milunič, also called "**Ginger and Fred**" (➤ 145) or "The Dancing House". Then hop on a No 17 or 21 tram down to Vyšehrad.

### 🕒 4:00pm
This is the ideal time to explore the grounds of 53 **Vyšehrad Castle** (➤ 157) and pay your respects to Dvořák (left) and Smetana in the cemetery. Leave yourself time to see Josef Chochol's unique **Villa Kovařovič** (➤ 159).

### 🕒 5:30pm
From the embankment – Rašínovo nábřeží – take the No 17 or 21 tram back north to Národní and tea or an apéritif in 59 **Café Slavia** (➤ 161).

### 🕒 7:00pm
Round off the evening with some opera or ballet at 52 **National Theatre** (Národní divadlo, ➤ 153).

143

Josefov

# ⭐5 Vltava Embankment

**When you stroll along the Vltava Embankment, you pass some of the most impressive buildings in New Town. After stopping off on Slavonic island with its dance hall, café and beer garden, you can compare the historical architectural styles with the modern "Ginger and Fred" office building, which as the name suggests looks like a dancing couple gliding along the river bank.**

South of the National Theatre (➤ 153), the buildings on the **Masaryk Embankment** (Masarykovo nábřeží) offer showcases of early 20th-century architecture, an eclectic mixture of Art Nouveau, historicist and modern functionalist styles. On the corner of Na Struze, at No 32, the Goethe-Institut (German Cultural Centre) occupies the attractive building that was the East German Embassy. The Art Nouveau ornament is by Ladislav Šaloun. No 16 is the concert hall (1906) of the historic **Hlahol Choral Society**, a major contributor to the Czech national revival. In the gable, the facade bears a characteristic inscription: *Zpěvem k srdci – srdcm k vlasti* ("Let the song reach the heart, let the heart reach the homeland").

**The Dancing House – Architecture that has real rhythm**

### Mánes Art Gallery
Forming a bridge between the embankment and Slavonic Island, the gallery is housed in Otakar Novotný's handsome, white, concrete and glass functionalist building of the 1920s, in sharp contrast to the adjoining black onion-domed tower of the old Šítek watermill. The gallery, founded by the Josef Mánes Fine Arts Association, exhibits major contemporary art rather than the 19th-century folksy genre painting associated with Mánes.

### Slavonic Island (Slovanský ostrov)
On the island you will find a popular concert and dance hall, which honours Archduchess Sophie, mother of Emperor Franz-Joseph. The island was originally called Sophie Island (Žofín ostrov) after the Emperor's mother. Formed by a sandbank

# Vltava Embankment

### THE PALACKÝ MONUMENT
On a square beside the bridge is a gigantic monument to František Palacký, 19th-century historian, politician and leader of the Czech national movement. "Father of the Nation" *(Otec národy)*, Palacký produced the five-volume *History of the Czech Nation* at a time when the Austro-Hungarian Empire had almost obliterated the Czechs as a separate entity. Palacký fought Engels' dismissal of the Czechs as "an absolutely non-existent nation" who "have never had a history of their own".

Stonework detail on Most Legií bridge (near Mánes Art Gallery)

and landfill, the island has been a favourite pleasure park for nearly 200 years. Facilities include **rowing boats** in the summer (May–Oct), open-air cafes, restaurants, concerts – jazz and classical – and dancing in the gardens.

### "Ginger and Fred"
On the embankment just south of Jiráskův most (Jiraský Bridge) is one of the city's more imaginative edifices, two modern towers clinging to each other in a dancers' embrace. The Dutch company offices were built in 1996 by US architect Frank Gehry and his Yugoslav associate Vlado Milunič. The building is known variously as "Dancing House" (Tančicí dům) and "Ginger and Fred", after Ginger Rogers and Fred Astaire.

Nestling up against the thoroughly modern couple is a now inevitably quaint-looking 1900s apartment building. It was built by Václav Havel, grandfather of the Czech president. The latter lived in the top-floor apartment with his first wife, Olga.

### TAKING A BREAK
There is a cafe and restaurant in the **Mánes Gallery** but you might like to duck away from the embankment to the city's most historic pub, **U Fleků** (➤ 166).

---

🕂 206 C4
✉ Mánes Gallery: Masarykovo nábřeží 250; Palác Žofín: Slovanský ostrov 226
☎ Mánes Art Gallery: 224 930 754; Palác Žofín: 224 934 880; www.zofin.cz
🕔 Mánes Gallery: Tue–Sun 11–7; Palác Žofín gardens: daily 11–7; theatre box office: noon–4:30  🚋 17, 21  💰 Mánes Gallery: 30Kč; Palác Žofín gardens: 30Kč

## INSIDER INFO

Do you want to dance the night away? At weekends the Mánes Art Gallery has become a favourite rendezvous for **Latin American dancing**.

Josefov

#  Obecní dům (Municipal House)

**For many people, this masterpiece of Art Nouveau architecture is the city's grandest 20th-century building. Its ornate cafe and restaurants and splendid concert hall, all lovingly renovated, certainly make it one of the most popular.**

Long before the word "multi-functional" had entered the modern urban planner's vocabulary, the city of Prague was commissioning its architects to design a home for art exhibitions, classical music concerts and a traditional coffee house with good cuisine to add a touch of class to the municipal offices. In an unabashed expression of the Czech national revival that rejected the Habsburg past, it replaced an old royal palace turned military academy. It was completed in 1911 and independent Czechoslovakia was proclaimed there seven years later, on 28 October 1918.

## On the Square
Antonín Balšanek and Osvald Polívka erected a lofty domed rotunda from which two bold wings spread to embrace the west side of busy náměstí Republiky (Republican Square). In the archway over the rotunda's entrance is Karel Špillar's mosaic, a somewhat pompous allegorical *Homage to Prague*.

**Art Nouveau design at its most exuberant**

## The Interior
The building's artwork inside has a much lighter touch. Lobbies, cloakrooms, elevators and stairways are all decorated with Art Nouveau floral motifs or the geometric patterns of the Czech *secesní* (Secession/Art Nouveau). Leading artists competed to contribute – Jan Preisler, Max Švabinský, Mikoláš Aleš and sculptor Ladislav Šaloun. **Alphonse Mucha** (► 152), most famous of them all since moving to Paris, wanted to do all the interior painting himself, and did a grand job on the **Mayoral Hall**, but had to

# Obecní dům (Municipal House)

**Time appears to have stopped in the magnificent café in the Municipal House**

accept his colleagues' participation in the cafe and restaurants. Exhibitions, often of the artists who decorated the Obecní dům, are held on upper floors.

### Smetana Hall (Smetanova síň)
On the first floor, this is the city's largest concert hall with a monumental elliptical glazed dome. It is principally the home of the **Prague Symphony Orchestra**, though the Czech Philharmonic plays here during the annual Prague Spring Music Festival (➤ 48).

A traditional – and highly emotional – event is the festival's opening night when Smetana's *My Country (Má vlast)* is played in the presence of the president. On either side of the stage, Šaloun's sculptures represent *Má vlast* on the left and Dvořák's Slavonic Dances on the right.

#### TAKING A BREAK
The grand **cafe has a delightful ambience and** is good for morning or late afternoon coffee; for lunch there's French cuisine in the elegant surroundings of **Francouzská Restaurace** (➤ 165); and in the evening Czech specialities and beer in the tavern-like basement **Plzeňská Restaurace** (➤ 166).

---

✚ 206 C2   ✉ Náměstí Republiky 5
☎ 222 002 101; www.obecnidum.cz   🕐 Ticket/information office 10–8
🚇 Náměstí Republiky   🚊 5, 8, 14   💰 Free; tours 290Kč

## INSIDER INFO

On the ground floor is a charming Art Nouveau **American Bar,** which can also be reached by a side staircase from a rear entrance on U Prašné brány street.

*Insider Tip*

Josefov

# ⭐10 Václavské náměstí (Wenceslas Square)

**The unquestioned centre of modern Prague bustles night and day. Czechs and tourists alike flock here, drawn by the cinemas, restaurants, casinos and shopping arcades. In the past, they came here, often in their thousands, to witness some of the most dramatic events in modern Czech history.**

Less a square, more of a long and broad sloping esplanade, Václavské náměstí (Wenceslas Square) was originally created by Charles IV in 1348 as the New Town's Horse Market. It extends from National Museum (➤ 161) down to Můstek Metro station on Na příkopě avenue (➤ 160).

### Wenceslas Monument

At the top of the square, the equestrian **statue** of patron saint sv Václav (Wenceslas) is surrounded by four other national saints – his grandmother Ludmila, Vojtěk, Prokop and Anežska (Agnes). Sculptor Josef Myslbek took 25 years to complete the monument, in 1912, of the man who led the Christian conversion of the country. On more than one occasion, his monument has been the backdrop of passionate political demonstrations.

### The Buildings

Blending innovative use of steel and glass with more ornate Art Nouveau facades, Václavské náměstí epitomizes the Czechs' early enthusiastic embrace of modernity in the

Václavské náměstí (Wenceslas Square) slopes away from the Wenceslas Monument

# Václavské náměstí (Wenceslas Square)

Visit the Grand Hotel Evropa and the Café Evropa within

20th century. The 1920s and 1930s were boom years for big stores and cinemas. For a state funeral, die-hard traditionalists had the neon signs draped in black. Spared bombardment in World War II, the square is a living museum of 20th-century architecture.

Downhill from Wenceslas Monument on the right, the **Jalta Hotel** (No 45) is a classical piece of 1950s Stalinist design, bleak and charmless. Much more attractive, on the left at the corner of Stepanská, is the imposing rotunda of the old **Moravian Bank** building (1916). Next door (No 36) is the historic **Melantrich** publishing house where, on its balcony in 1989, Václav Havel joined the beloved but hapless Alexander Dubček who tried 20 years before to introduce "Socialism with a human face".

Directly opposite, the **Grand Hotel Evropa** (1906) by Bendřich Bendelmayer and Alois Dryák is a landmark among Art Nouveau buildings on the square. Besides the facade's splendid double bay windows, notice, perhaps on your way into the ornately decorated

> **TOURIST'S LAMENT**
> The fourth verse of the Christmas carol *Good King Wenceslas* might well have been written for a footsore sightseer:
> *Sire, the night is darker now,*
> *And the wind blows stronger.*
> *Fails my heart, I know not how.*
> *I can go no longer.*
> *Mark my footsteps, my good page,*
> *Tread thou in them boldly;*
> *Thou shalt find the winter's rage*
> *Freeze thy blood less co-oldly.*

# Josefov

restaurants or cafe, the lofty oval gallery around the hotel's stairwell. Down the street on the other side of Jindřišská, Osvald Polívka's neo-baroque corner building (No 19), is best known as the **Assicurazione Generali** where Franz Kafka got his first job as an insurance clerk.

The square's other Art Nouveau jewel is across the street at No 12, the **Peterka House**, a subtle design by Jan Kotěra, a pupil of Vienna's Secession master, Otto Wagner. Side by side at the bottom end are the famous shops of **Bat'a Shoes** (No 6) and **Lindt Chocolate** (No 4), both pioneering buildings for their 1920s functionalist design in steel and glass on a reinforced concrete frame. (A great patron of Czech art before World War II, Tomás Bat'a fled when his shoe factories and shops were

### TRAGEDY AND JOY ON THE SQUARE

**1848** Crowds met here to celebrate an open-air Mass before their abortive revolt, the first "Prague Spring", was brutally repressed by Austrian artillery. Overnight, the Horse Market became Václavské náměstí (Wenceslas Square).
**1918** Thousands gathered at the foot of the Wenceslas Monument to celebrate the proclamation of the new Czechoslovak Republic.
**1939** A demonstration against the German occupation ended in the fatal shooting of medical student Jan Opletal.
**1948** Armed factory workers paraded here in support of the Communist Party's February coup d'état.
**1968** The new "Prague Spring" of social reforms was ended in August by Soviet tanks. They fired at the Národní muzeum, mistaking it – according to conflicting reports – either for the Czechoslovak Parliament or the Czechoslovak Radio Station. Five months later, philosophy student Jan Palach burned himself alive near the Wenceslas Monument in protest at the people's lethargy and apathy. His gesture is marked by a small memorial.
**1989** Hundreds of thousands staged the Velvet Revolution's candle-lit demonstration to force the end of the Communist regime and call for Václav Havel to become President.

# Václavské náměstí (Wenceslas Square)

**Two figures of classical mythology bear the weight of a bay window**

expropriated by the Communists in 1948. His family retrieved the business after 1989.)

Opposite, **Palác Koruna** offers the square a fitting, if somewhat overpoweringly monumental No 1. The majestic tower's spangled crown (*koruna*) lights up at night. When it was first built, Ladislav Machoň designed a Cubist cinema in the basement, a fast-food restaurant on the ground floor – Europe's first – and an apartment for himself at the top of the tower.

### TAKING A BREAK

This is a good place to try out one of Prague's teahouses, the easygoing **Dobřá čajovna** (literally "good teahouse"), on Václavské náměstí 14, next to the Peterka House.

✚ 206 C1  ✉ Václavské náměstí  🚇 Muzeum, Můstek  🚊 3, 9, 14, 24

## INSIDER INFO

The people of Prague like to meet "under the tail" or "by the horse"; what is meant is the Wenceslas Monument. But the Czechs would not be the Czechs if they didn't also turn the highly respected Wenceslas and his horse upside down. Which is exactly what David Černý did with his knight under the glass dome of the **Lucerna Passage**; the knight is sitting on the stomach of a dead horse hanging up by its legs. The Prague sculptor present yet another tongue-in-cheek look at the monument...

Josefov

# 51 Muchově muzeu
# (Mucha Museum)

**Around one hundred works by the master of Art Nouveau, painter and decorative artist Alphonse Mucha (1860–1939), are on display in this popular museum. Yet the artist who made his name in Paris during the belle époque with his highly decorative poster art remains more appreciated by visitors than by his fellow countrymen.**

Housed in the Kaunický palác south of Na příkopě avenue, the museum presents Mucha's paintings, lithographs, drawings, pastels, sculpture and personal memorabilia. Best known are his theatre posters for plays featuring the great actress Sarah Bernhardt – *Gismonda, Médée, Lorenzaccio* and *La Samaritaine* – guaranteeing his commercial success in the 1890s. Mucha served Parisian society and the design departments for Nestlé's baby food and Moët et Chandon champagne. In 1900, his work for the Paris World Exhibition made the headlines.

In 1910, after a spell in Chicago and New York, Mucha was desperate to prove himself a truly Czech painter. Back in Prague, he painted lofty allegorical themes for the Municipal House (➤ 149) as well as stained-glass windows for St Vitus Cathedral (➤ 90).

Mucha's *Princess Hyacinth* lithographs used in a promotional poster

### Slav Epic
In an English-language video, the museum tells the story of Mucha's most ambitious work – the *Slovaská epopej (Slav Epic)* of 20 giant canvases, which took him 18 years to complete. In 1928 he bequeathed this series of paintings to the state.

### TAKING A BREAK
In memory of Mucha's good times, have a good French coffee at **Paris-Praha** on Jindřišská.

---

🚇 206 C2  ✉ Panská 7
☎ 224 216 415; www.mucha.cz
🕐 Daily 10–6  💰 Moderate  Ⓜ Můstek  💵 240Kč

## INSIDER INFO

Be sure to see Mucha's collection of **personal snapshots** of models and famous friends – including fellow painter Paul Gauguin playing the harmonium in his underwear.

Národní divadlo (National Theatre)

# 52 Národní divadlo (National Theatre)

**Like a cathedral or royal palace, this theatre is a veritable national shrine, paid for by the Czech people themselves. The massive, long-domed building is Nové Město's most prominent landmark overlooking the Vltava River. Profit from an evening at the opera here, both for the festive atmosphere and a close-up view of the grand interior.**

The neo-Renaissance beauty of the National Theatre reflected in the modern glass building of the New Stage (➤ 156)

The imposing neo-Renaissance building was designed by Josef Zítek, architect of the Rudolfinum (➤ 130). Above the stately portico at the entrance are Bohuslav Schnirch's statues of Apollo and the nine Muses.

### The Interior

Paintings and sculptures in the sumptuous interior are by leading artists later known collectively as "The Generation of the National Theatre". For the lobby, Mikoláš Aleš and František Ženišek painted 14 scenes inspired by Smetana's symphonic poem *My Country (Má vlast)*. Many of the sculptures are by Josef Myslbek, creator of the Wenceslas Monument (➤ 148). The majestic, four-tiered auditorium is lavishly decorated in gold and red. Vojtěch Hynais created the spectacular allegorical painting for the safety curtain. Written in gold over the arch is the theatre's aspiration: *Národ sobě* (The Nation to Itself).

Josefov

# Golden Temple on the Vltava

**The National Theatre was funded to a large extent by donations from Czech citizens, and intended as a symbol of Czech national identity. Inaugurated in 1881, it suffered a devastating fire just two months later. Renovation work started straightaway, however, and it was possible to celebrate the second opening in 1883 – once again with Smetana's opera *Libuše* dedicated to the mythical city founder of Prague.**

❶ **Triga:** The chariot of the goddess of victory on the Prague National Theatre is pulled by three horses (triga) – not actually a method used in antiquity – a peculiarity of the sculptor Bohuslav Schnirch (1845–1901).

❷ **Facade:** The portico on the front of the building has a pillared loggia which highlights the front of the building. On the embankment side, there is a passage for carriages.

❸ **Foyer:** Mikoláš Aleš (1852 to 1913) designed the 14 lunette pictures on the subject of *My Fatherland for the foyer*. They depict mythical figures drawn in the spirit of neo-Romanticism and important sites in Czech history. The fresco by František Ženíšek (1849–1916) exalts the golden era of art, including its fall and rebirth. It also includes the bronze bust of Czech composers.

❹ **Auditorium:** The semicircular auditorium with its frescoes by František Ženíšek, also exalting the fine arts, has four tiers and offers space for a total of 17,000 visitors.

# Národní divadlo (National Theatre)

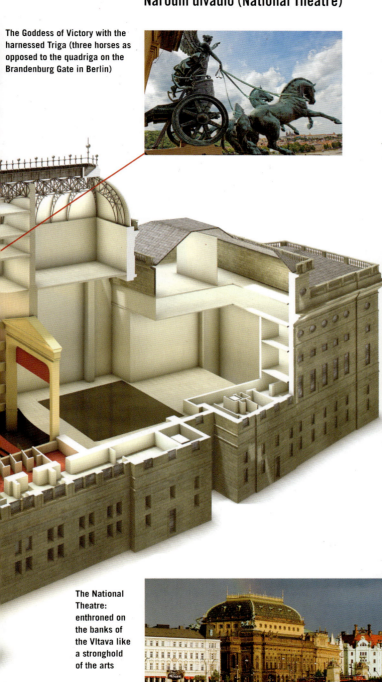

The Goddess of Victory with the harnessed Triga (three horses as opposed to the quadriga on the Brandenburg Gate in Berlin)

The National Theatre: enthroned on the banks of the Vltava like a stronghold of the arts

# Josefov

## The People's Theatre

At the height of the Czech nationalist movement in the 19th century, the Národní was built as a Czech counterpoint to the German-speaking community's Stavovské divadlo (Estates Theatre, ➤ 65). The people wanted a theatre specifically for Czech opera and drama. Under Austrian pressure, parliament refused funds, but a public subscription raised donations. Over 50,000 people brought the foundation stones to the building site in 1868. The stones came from historic sites in Bohemia and Moravia – but also from Chicago, sent by Czech émigrés with the inscription: "What blood unites, the sea will not sunder". The theatre opened in June 1881 with Smetana's patriotic opera *Libuše* and, just two months later, after only 12 performances, was gutted by fire. It was rebuilt with a public subscription, this time with a donation by Emperor Franz Joseph, who was conscious of the need to keep his subjects happy.

**Audiences here have enjoyed some of the most sublime acoustics in European music**

### TAKING A BREAK

You can have a cocktail in the elegant and historic **Café Slavia** (➤ 162); just across the street.

---

🚇 208 C5  ✉ Národní třída 2
☎ 224 901 448; www.narodni-divadlo.cz
🕐 Box office: daily 10–6; also open 45 minutes before performances
Ⓜ Národní třída  🚊 6, 9, 17, 18, 22
🎭 Opera: 50Kč (standing room) to 950Kč (stalls, first row)

## INSIDER INFO

- During the interval in the theatre bar, try the **Czech champagne – Bohemia sekt** – it's really pretty good.
- People who may find the Národní divadlo's architecture pompous are immediately reconciled when they see the starkly modern, almost brutally cold glass box of the **New Stage** (Nová scéna) next door. Devoted principally to the National Theatre's repertoire of modern Czech drama, it was designed by Karel Prager in 1983 while he was renovating the Národní.

# ⓷ Vyšehrad

The castle rock at the southern edge of Nové Město is a place bathed in myth as much as in reality. It is the romantic site of an 11th-century clifftop fortress above the Vltava River – Vyšehrad means "Castle on the Heights". Redbrick ramparts enclose vestiges of its ancient buildings and a national cemetery honouring the country's creative genius. The gardens are ideal for picnics – with wonderful sunset views.

### The Fortress

Castle signposts from Vyšehrad Metro station lead along V Pevnosti Street to the southeast entrance, through the **Leopold Gate** (Leopoldova brána). Fork right to the **sv Martin Rotunda**, one of the few structures remaining from the original castle. This 11th-century chapel, restored in 1878 and used now only for funeral services for Vyšehrad Cemetery, is the city's oldest surviving Romanesque building. Over to the left, on Soběslavova Street, archaeologists have excavated foundations of the even older **Basilica of St Lawrence** (sv Vavřince), built before the castle. The **Church of SS Peter and Paul** (kostel sv Petra a Pavla) is a neo-Gothic reconstruction (1887, towers 1903).

*The Rotunda of St Martin is the oldest Roman building in Prague*

In a garden, Vyšehrad's fanciful origins are reinforced by Josef Myslbek's 19th-century statues of mythical couples. Closest to the river are *Libuše and Přemysl*, the ancestress of the first Bohemian royal dynasty and her husband. At the other end of the garden are *Šárka and Ctirad*, a woman warrior and her lover.

### The Cemetery (Vyšehradský hřbitov)

North and east of St Peter and St Paul Church, the medieval cemetery became in 1869, as part of Vyšehrad's nationalist mission, a Pantheon for Czech musicians, opera singers, actors, writers, painters and sculptors. Here, the country celebrates its artists, not its politicians and generals. Surrounded by Antonín Wiehl's neo-Renaissance arcaded portico, their graves are shown on a map at the entrance next to the church.

# Josefov

Graves along the arcaded portico of the Vyšehrad Cemetery

Designed by Ladislav Šaloun, the monumental tomb of **Antonín Dvořák** is set in the arcade behind a wrought-iron railing. The more modest tomb of **Bedřich Smetana** stands near the formidable **Slavín Monument**. Also designed by Wiehl, the column and sarcophagus mark a communal tomb for 50 artists, including painter Alphonse Mucha and sculptors Šaloun and Myslbek.

### The Dungeons
Beside Vyšehrad's north entrance/exit, the **Brick Gate** (Cihelná brána), a guided tour takes you under the ramparts into the castle dungeons and Gorlice Hall, housing original baroque statues from Charles Bridge.

### The Myth…
The Vyšehrad cliff was discovered by Princess Libuše, legendary heroine celebrated in Smetana's opera. Standing with her husband Přemysl, she looked across the river at where Prague Castle now stands and prophesied: "I see a great city whose fame will touch the stars." They hurried over and found an old man already building the threshold – *prah* (hence the city's name). A mosaic designed by Mikuláš Aléš depicts the myth in the lobby of the Old Town Hall (➤ 59).

### …and the Reality
A church and fortified trading post were built on the heights of Vyšehrad in the 10th century, 70 years after the establishment of Prague Castle. To counter his rivals, Vratislav II, a prince of Bohemia's founding Přemyslid dynasty, built a castle here in 1085. Forty years later, his successors returned to Prague Castle and Vyšehrad was abandoned until restored by Charles IV from the House of Luxembourg. The fortress was destroyed by the Hussites and later the Habsburgs left only the redbrick ramparts.

### Vyšehrad Cubist Buildings
Prague offers Europe's only examples of Cubist art applied to architecture. Along with the Black Madonna House on Staré Město's Celetná Street (➤ 70), the finest are Josef Chochol's two villas and an apartment building (1912–14) north of Vyšehrad.

# Vyšehrad

An example of Cubist buildings and garden that can be seen around Vyšehrad

From the north side of the castle, cut through to Neklanova (No 30) to see the great **Hodek Apartment House** on the corner of Hostivitova. In characteristic Cubist style, the prismatic shapes of balconies and windows make an intricate play of light and shade beneath a dramatically projecting cornice.

In the **Villa Kovařovič** (Libušina 3) set back in a garden facing Rašínovo nábřeží (embankment), Chochol uses more restrained Cubist shapes to create the appearance of an elegant country manor. South along the embankment, his **Three-Family House** (Rodinný trojdům; Rašínovo nábřeží 6–10) is an elongated building with handsomely framed windows and Cubist gables for the upper floors. They are private homes and not open to the public, but their main interest is their exterior.

### TAKING A BREAK

If you haven't brought your own picnic, **Rio Vyšehradě** near St Peter and St Paul Church is a pleasant little wine bar serving good snacks.

**Vyšehrad Castle**
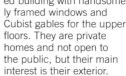 209 D1
✉ V Pevnosti 159/5
☎ 241 410 348;
www.praha-vysehrad.cz
🕐 Grounds dawn to sunset; exhibits Apr–Oct daily 9:30–6; Nov–Mar daily 9:30–5
Ⓜ Vyšehrad
🚌 7, 8, 24 to Albertov
🎟 Dungeons: 25Kč

**Cubist Buildings**
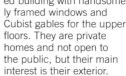 209 D1
🚌 3, 6, 14, 18, 21, 22

## INSIDER INFO

- The best **view** over New Town, Old Town and across the river to Prague Castle is up on the ramparts on the north side of the fortress.
- Below the ramparts are the remains of a wall referred to as **Libuše's Bath** – all that is left of the medieval palace that once stood on this spot. According to legend, it was here that Libuše cavorted with her lovers. When they displeased her, she pushed them through a rock crevice into the Vltava.

Josefov

# At Your Leisure

### 54 Prašná brána (Powder Tower)

Looming dark and incongruous on the edge of the garish modern náměstí Republiky (Republican Square), this sturdy, 15th-century Gothic tower was the starting point for the grand procession of kings along the *králova cesta* (Royal Route) over to Prague Castle. When the Habsburgs abandoned this tradition, the tower served as a gunpowder store. It blew up in the Prussian siege of 1757 and was restored in the late 19th century. It is well worth going up the tower for the rooftop view across Old and New Town's domes and spires.

🕂 206 C2   ✉ Na příkopě
🕘 Daily Jan–Feb, Nov–Dec 10–6, March, Oct until 8, April–Sep until 10
🚇 Náměstí Republiky   🚌 5, 8, 24, 26   💰 90Kč

### 55 Na Příkopě

Bordering the Staré Město and Nové Město (Old and New Town) districts, this popular pedestrianized shopping street was, during its fashionable heyday nearly 150 years ago, the German-speaking community's favourite avenue. Known then as Am Graben (meaning, like Na příkopě, "On the Moat"), it competed with the equally emphatically Czech atmosphere of Národní třída.

At the centre, on the south side facing Havířská Street, the splendid **baroque palace** at No 10 was once the "Deutsches Kasino". Designed by Kilián Ignac Dienzenhofer in 1743, today it serves once more as a casino and as the **Museum of Communism**.

Apart from two noteworthy adjacent bank buildings (Nos 18 and 20) by Osvald Polívka, mixing Art Nouveau and neo-Renaissance, the street succumbed to the functionalist building boom of the 1930s.

🕂 206 B2
☎ 224 212 966; www.muzeum komunismu.cz
🕘 Daily 9–9   🚇 Můstek   💰 190Kč

### 56 Státní opera (State Opera House)

Opened in 1888 as the Neues Deutsches Theater (New German Theatre). The impressive neo-Classical building is based on a design by the Viennese architects Ferdinand Fellner und Hermann Helmer. Many musicians regard the acoustics of its neo-Rococo auditorium as even better than those of the National Theatre (Národní di-

**The Powder Tower has recovered well from its gunpowder explosion**

# At Your Leisure

**The Wax Museum's trio: Havel, Klaus and Dubček**

vadlo, ➤ 153) and Estates Theatre (Stavovské divadlo, ➤ 63).
🚇 209 F5  ✉ Wilsonova 4  ☎ 224 227 266; www.opera.cz  Ⓜ Muzeum

## 57 Národní muzeum (National Museum)

The colossal pile at the top of Wenceslas Square is a deliberate but clumsy expression of the 19th-century movement for Czech national renewal. The neo-Renaissance building, designed by Josef Schulz, was opened in 1890 as a monumental companion-piece to the National Theatre.

The museum does have a vast collection of plants, minerals, animals and human prehistoric stones and bones, but for most people the real interest is at the top of the ceremonial staircase leading from the grand marble entrance hall.

There, under the great glass dome, are the statues of those who led the way to Czechoslovakia's national independence – a display that many young Czechs regard as the monumental fossil of a bygone age.
🚇 209 F4  ✉ Václavské náměstí 68
☎ 224 497 111; www.nm.cz
ℹ Currently closed for renovation.
Ⓜ Muzeum  🚋 11

## 58 Muzeum voskových figurín (Wax Museum)

Close to Wenceslas Square, this popular museum requires a certain knowledge of Czech history in order to appreciate the scenes of famous characters. The most easily recognizable figures are from the 20th century – Soviet leaders, their Czechoslovak underlings and their (generally) more democratic successors.
🚇 206 A2  ✉ Celetná 6
☎ 224 229 852; www.waxmuseumprague.cz
🕐 Daily 10–9
Ⓜ Můstek  💰 160Kč

# Josefov

**Franz Kafka's burial place in the New Jewish Cemetery**

## 59 Café Slavia

This landmark cafe opposite the National Theatre has been a meeting place for artists, writers and political dissidents from the 1920s to the Velvet Revolution of 1989 (➤ 17).

They included Karel Teige's avant-garde Devětsil group, poet Jaroslav Seifert, Cubist architect Josef Chochol and journalists Milena Jesenská and Egon Erwin Kisch. During easier times, the intellectuals complain that gentrification destroys the old atmosphere, but the cosmopolitan mix of coffee, apple strudel and foreign newspapers (as well as the more recent WLAN) remains.

✚ 205 F1
✉ Smetanovo nábřeží 2
☎ 224 218 493; www.cafeslavia.cz
🕒 Mon–Fri 8am–midnight, Sat, Sun 9am–midnight
Ⓜ Národní třída
🚋 6, 9, 17, 18, 22

## 60 Karlovo náměstí (Charles Square)

Its extended, tree-lined gardens now give Prague's biggest square more the appearance of a public park than the city square it was in the 18th century. It was originally a cattle market, set up by Charles IV when he created Nové Město in 1348 – along with the horse market at Wenceslas Square (➤ 148) and a hay market farther east (Senovážné náměstí).

In the northeast corner, the well-restored Gothic gabled building, largely 15th century, is **Nové Město's town hall** (Novo-městska radnice), the scene of Prague's first Defenestration (➤ 24). On the east side, next to the old Jesuit college, now a hospital, is the 17th-century **Church of St Ignatius** (kostel sv Ignác). The portal/entrance is adorned with a statue of St Ignatius. Inside, the baroque interior is particularly lavish. On the southwest corner of the square, a baroque building associated with several alchemists, including the Englishman Edward

# At Your Leisure

Kelley (➤ 11), is fancifully known as the **Faust House** (Faustův dům).
🕂 209 D4  🚇 Karlovo náměstí
🚍 4, 6, 10, 16, 22

### 61 Nový židovský hřbitov (New Jewish Cemetery)

East of Olšanské municipal cemeteries, tombstones in the New Jewish Cemetery tell the story of the community's last years. Laid out in the 1890s, it is a place of pilgrimage not just for the (signposted) **grave of Franz Kafka**, but also for the tombs and memorials of Prague's Jewish citizens, prominent and otherwise, with tombstones bearing the inscription *1944 v Osviětimí* ("1944 in Auschwitz").

On the simple tomb of Kafka and his parents is a plaque in memory of his three sisters, who died in concentration camps. On a wall opposite is a tribute to Kafka's friend **Max Brod**, "born in Prague, writer and thinker who carried Czech culture abroad" – among the first to champion Jaroslav Hašek, author of *Good Soldier Švejk*, and composer Leoš Janáček.
🕂 210 off C4  ✉ Izraelská
🕐 Apr–Sep Sun–Thu 9–5, Fri 9–2; Oct–Mar Sun–Thu 9–4, Fri 9–2
🚇 Želivského  🚍 10, 11, 16  💰 50Kč

---

**MORE MONUMENTAL ARCHITECTURE IN THE NEW TOWN**

A monument among Prague's classical hotels, the **Hotel Paříž** (U Obecního domů 1; tel: 222 195 195) stands behind the Municipal House (➤ 146). Its architecture (1907) is a palatial combination of neo-Gothic and Art Nouveau. In the elegant cafe, bar and restaurant, everything is designed with exquisite attention to detail. Prague's **Main Station** (Praha hlavní nádraží, photo below) on Wilsonova is a slice of history. With some Art Nouveau frills, Josef Fanta's grand design of 1909 was appropriate to what began as Franz-Joseph Station, Prague's swansong for the Habsburg Empire. Nine years later, in gratitude for the American president's help in gaining independence, the Czechs renamed it Woodrow Wilson Station. Much of the station's character was destroyed in an insensitive reconstruction in the 1980s. It is currently undergoing renewed renovation work.

163

# Josefov

**Žižkov TV Tower, a legacy of the Communist regime's**

## 62 🛈 Žižkovský vysílač (Žižkov TV Tower)
Completed in the early 1990s after its Communist builders had left power, the tower is 260m (853ft) above sea level; the view from the observation deck at 100m (328ft) is spectacular. On a clear day you can see up to 100km (62mi). Don't miss the surreal giant bronze babies, by local artist David Černy, that "climb" up the sides. There is a restaurant up on the fifth floor, at 66m (216.5ft) high, which does not charge an entrance fee.
🕂 210 off C5  ✉ Mahlerovy sady 1, Žižkov
☎ 210 320 081; www.towerpark.cz
⊚ Observation platform and restaurant: Daily 8am–midnight
🚇 Jiřího z Poděbrad  💵 150Kč

## 63 Vítkov Hill
On the north side of the working-class neighbourhood of Žižkov, overlooking the city centre, a monument building was erected in 1932 on the hilltop site of a famous Hussite victory over papal forces in 1420. Created by Bohumil Kafka (no relation), the gigantic **bronze equestrian statue** of the Hussites' one-eyed general, Jan Žižka, was added in 1950. Originally honouring the Slavic fight against the Habsburgs, the monument building served as a mausoleum for Czech Communist leaders, including Klement Gottwald whose body was embalmed, like Lenin's in Moscow, but less expertly, so that its deteriorated remains had to be cremated.

In the Ceremonial Hall there's a fascinating exhibition on 20th-century Czech and Slovak history. Using rarely seen archive film and newsreel footage it focuses on key turning points: the founding of the republic; the Nazi occupation; the Communist takeover; the Soviet invasion following the "Prague Spring" and the Velvet Revolution.
🕂 207 F2  ✉ U památníku 2 Žižkov
☎ 222 540308
⊚ Exhibition: April–Oct Wed–Sun 10–6, Nov–March Thu–Sun 10–6
🚌 133 to Husitská  💵 Exhibition: 110Kč

## 64 Muzeum hlavního města Prahy (Prague Municipal Museum)
Off the beaten track, but well worth seeking out, the Prague Municipal Museum traces the city's story from prehistoric times to the present. Its superb collection of Gothic, Renaissance and baroque sculptures and painting are beautifully displayed. Of particular interest are the scale-model of 19th-century Prague and fine architectural models of major monuments that have now disappeared.
🕂 207 E3  ✉ Na Poříčí 52, Karlin
☎ 224 816 773  ⊚ Tue–Sun 9–6
🚌 8, 25  🚇 Florenc  💵 120Kč

# Where to...
# Eat and Drink

**Prices**
Expect to pay per person for a meal, including drinks, tax and service:
**£** under 500Kč          **££** 500Kč–1,000Kč          **£££** over 1,000Kč

## RESTAURANTS

### Aromi £££
The perfect neighbourhood Italian restaurant, with warm service. Try sea bass in white wine sauce, with olives and potatoes or the ravioli with truffle and cheese-truffle fondue.
🞢 210 C4 ✉ Mánesova 78 ☎ 222 713 222; www.aromi.cz 🕔 Mon–Sat noon–11, Sun noon–10 🚇 Jiřího z Poděbrad

### Francouzská Restaurace £££
All glistening brass and exquisite woodwork, the restaurant on the ground floor of the Municipal House (► 146) is a spacious, stylish spot for French cuisine.
🞢 199 D3 ✉ Náměstí Republiky 5
☎ 222 002 770; www.obecnidum.cz
🕔 Daily 11:30–4, 6–11 🚇 Náměstí Republiky

### Grosseto £
Four reasons to come here – good, low-cost pizzas, the Vinohrady location, a secluded garden in the back and a good al fresco selection. Decent Italian starters and good desserts.
🞢 210 B3 ✉ Francouzská 2
☎ 224 252 778; www.grosseto.cz
🕔 Daily 11:30–11 🚇 Náměstí Miru

### Jiná Krajina £
This unpretentious little restaurant, which opened in 2009, will appeal not only to non-smoking vegetarians (its target clientele) but anyone seeking a tasty, reasonably priced meal. The soft glow of pumpkin lamps creates a mellow ambience in which to delve into a refreshingly adventurous menu which includes cream of carrot soup with ginger and roasted pumpkin seeds, vegetable red curry and aubergine (eggplant) moussaka. Fish dishes are also available.
🞢 209 D4 ✉ Řeznická 4
☎ 222 231 148; www.jinakrajina.cz
🕔 Daily 11–11 🚇 Můstek 🚋 5

### Korea House £
Though on the outside it is not very inviting, the inside tells a different story: Every table has its own barbecue, an iron plate installed in the middle of the table on which you can prepare the served ingredients exactly as you wish. Easy to reach on the underground.

🞢 209 E3 ✉ Sokolská 52 ☎ 224 266 246
🕔 Daily 5:30pm–11:30pm 🚇 I.P. Pavlova

### Le Grill £££
In summer, Le Grill offers an enchanting oasis in the garden of the elegant Kempinski, but you can also eat very well inside too: modern, but down-to-earth, international, but also with a touch of Czech style. 150 sorts of wine and homemade chocolates.
🞢 206 C2 ✉ Hybernska 12, Staré Město
☎ 226 226 111; www.kempinski.com/Prague
🕔 Daily 11–11 🚇 Náměsti Republiky

### Mozaika ££
A recently renovated restaurant offering good quality. Although on the outer streets of Vinohrady, the Metro whisks you here in a few minutes. The cooking ranges from fusion food to local dishes with an international twist. The sleek interior has a hushed vibe. Reserve in advance.

# Josefov

📍 202 B1 ✉ Nítranská 13
☎ 224 253 011; www.restaurantmozaika.cz
🕐 Mon–Fri 11:30–midnight, Sat 2–midnight, Sun 4–midnight 🚇 Jiřího z Poděbrad

### Oliva ££

Although Oliva feels a little remote it's a good option if you've visited Vyšehrad castle. It offers great value and is popular with locals. Mediterranean cooking is the theme. Candlelit tables at night and highly professional staff. Reserve in advance.
📍 208 C2 ✉ Plavecká 4
☎ 222 520 288; www.olivarestaurant.cz
🕐 Mon–Fri 11:30–3, 6–11, Sat 6pm–11pm
🚇 Karlovo Náměstí

### Universal £

This restaurant's inexpensive French and Mediterranean dishes, as well as huge helpings of scalloped potatoes and large salads, keep the regulars coming back for more. No credit cards.
📍 208 C5 ✉ V Jirchářích 6
☎ 224 934 416; www.universalrestaurant.cz
🕐 Daily noon–11 🚇 Národní třída

## INNS, PUBS AND BARS

### Pivovarský dům

A Czech emigré from America brews his own Bohemian-style light and dark beers in sight of drinkers at this cheerful pub-restaurant. Try home-made banana beer, a few imports, and Czech liqueurs such as *medovina* (mead).
📍 209 D4 ✉ Lipová 15
☎ 296 216 666; www.gastroinfo.cz/pivodum
🕐 Daily 11am–11:30pm 🚇 Karlovo náměstí

### Plzeňská Restaurace

This tavern in the basement of the Municipal House is an extravagant piece of Art Nouveau design. Ceramic murals by leading Czech artists glow in the dim lighting. The food is standard pub fare such as goulash and the similar *svičková na smetaně* (tenderloin in a cream sauce with bread dumplings).
📍 206 C2 ✉ Náměsti Republiky 5
☎ 222 002 780; www.plzenskarestaurace.cz
🕐 Daily 11:30–11 🚇 Náměstí Republiky

### U Fleků

Two spacious beer halls and an even roomier garden ensure plenty of space at this admittedly touristy beer palace. They've been brewing rich, dark beer here since 1499. Dig into steaming plates of "Fleck's treat" – duck, pork and sausages.
📍 209 D5 ✉ Křemencova 11
☎ 224 934 019; www.ufleku.cz 🕐 Sun–Wed 10am–11pm, Thu–Sat 10am–midnight

## CAFÉS AND TEAROOMS

### Café Imperial

This used to be a rather scruffy place where for a few crowns you could buy a bowl of doughnuts and have a doughnut fight. In the meantime however, the beautifully restored Art Nouveau café can compete with the cafe in Municipal House.
📍 207 D3 ✉ Na Poříčí 15
☎ 246 011 440; www.cafeimperial.cz
🕐 Daily 7am–11pm 🚇 Florenc

### Café Louvre

This grand cafe of Prague's heyday offers a range of Czech dishes, salads and home-made ice cream as well as billiards. The Louvre is open for breakfast every day. ==There is also a non-smoking area – something which is a bit of a rarity in Prague.==
📍 209 D5 ✉ Národní třída 22 ☎ 224 930 949; www.cafelouvre.cz 🕐 Mon–Fri 8am–11:30pm, Sat, Sun 9am–11:30pm 🚇 Národní třídá

### Dobřá Čajovna

A Czech gift to serious relaxing was born in the early 1990s here at the "Good Tea Room". Teas from the world over are brewed here. Mobile phones and smoking are both forbidden.
📍 206 B1 ✉ Václavské náměstí 14
☎ 224 231 480; www.tea.cz
🕐 Mon–Fri 10am–11:30pm, Sat, Sun 2pm–11:30pm 🚇 Můstek

# Where to... Shop

Bigger stores, lots of familiar brand names and the hustle and bustle of city life – shopping in Nové Město certainly feels different from shopping in some older historic districts. Wenceslas Square (Václavské náměstí) forms the area's main artery, with a mix of department stores and shops offering *levné* (cheap) goods. At the bottom of Wenceslas Square is the crowded pedestrian zone on Na příkopě, which leads via 28 Října into another major shopping street, Národní třída.

### WENCESLAS SQUARE

Among the baubles of this long "square", look for the fine selection of traditionally painted Easter eggs at **Original Souvenir** (Peterkův dům, Václavské náměstí 12).

In the mazelike Lucerna Arcade, between Vodičkova and Štěpánská streets, shops worth seeking out include **Galerie Módy** (tel: 242 211 514; on the top floor opposite the cinema), which stocks fashions and accessories by half a dozen Czech designers.

**Cellarius** (also in the Pasáž Lucerna; tel: 224 210 979) is a good choice for wines and spirits.

### AROUND WENCESLAS SQUARE

Offices, government ministries and shops pack the grid of streets either side of Václavské náměstí (Wenceslas Square). The densest concentration of shops lies on Vodičkova Street.

On the right hand side of the bottom of the square is **Bontonland Megastore** (Václavské náměstí 1, tel: 224 226 242), a massive CD store that covers all genres of music in depth, and has a brilliant selection of Czech and Eastern European music.

The **Mucha Museum gift shop** (Panská 7; tel: 224 216 415, ▶ 152) has items inspired by Alphonse Mucha's work.

A few blocks off the square's upper end, **Dům Porcelánu Praha** (Jugoslávská 8, Vinohrády, near I P Pavlova Metro station, tel: 221 505 320; www.dumporcelanu.cz) has two floors of Czech porcelain from most of the major factories.

### NA PŘÍKOPĚ

For replica Art Nouveau jewellery and glass visit **Art Décoratif** (U Obecního domu, tel: 222 002 350).

Closer to Wenceslas Square is a shop worth making a detour for. **Moser** (Na příkopě 12, inside the Černa růže shopping arcade, tel: 224 211 293) has been displaying its lead-free glassware here since 1925.

Also on this street is a branch of the **Zara** clothing store chain (tel: 224 239 870), a **Korres** herbal pharmacy (www.korres.cz) which also stocks i.a. cosmetics, perfumes, a mobile phone shop with "non-stop internet" (tel: 214 414 900) and no less than three shopping arcades.

### AROUND NÁRODNÍ TŘÍDA

One of the city's largest musical-instrument emporia is **Hudební nástroje Kliment** (Jungmannovo náměstí 17, tel: 224 213 966).

The nearby Palác Adria has a lovely **Antikvariát "Můstek"** on the ground floor (tel: 224 217 189).

**Platýz Courtyard** (Národní třída 37) offers shops with classy women's fashions and shoes.

Finally, there's even a **Tesco** supermarket (Národní třída at Spálená, tel: 222 003 111).

# Josefov

# Where to... Go Out

## THEATRE

### Archa
Prague's all-purpose stage for avant-garde drama, music, dance, film – you name it. Tickets are scarce, but worth the trouble to find.
✚ 207 D3 ✉ Na Poříčí 26
☎ 221 716 333; www.archatheatre.cz

### Laterna Magika
The Magic Lantern is the most famous of the blacklight (mime, clowning and lighting effects in front of a black screen) and multi-media theatres.
✚ 208 C5 ✉ Národní třída 4
☎ 224 901 442; www.laterna.cz

## MUSIC

### Duplex
The most sophisticated club in the city looks out over the roofs of Wenceslas Square. Mick Jagger celebrated his 60th birthday here.
✚ 206 B1 ✉ Václavské Náměstí 21
☎ 732 221 111; www.duplex.cz
Ⓜ Můstek

### Lucerna Music Bar
A cavernous club hosting touring bands and Saturday night DJs.
✚ 206 B1 ✉ Vodičkova 36
☎ 224 217 108; www.musicbar.cz
Ⓜ Můstek

### Národní divadlo (National Theatre)
The National Theatre is distinguished by its high-level cultural venue. Good seats can sometimes be had from the box office for around 250Kč. Book by post, email or internet five months in advance for any show here or at the Estates Theatre (➤ 63).
✚ 209 D5 ✉ Národní třída 2
☎ 224 668 901, 224 291 448 (tickets); www.narodni-divadlo.cz

### Radost FX
Trendies flock to this popular club to dance, mingle and socialize. Late night eats can be enjoyed in the on-site all-night veggie cafe which is open until 5 o'clock in the morning.
✚ 209 F4 ✉ Belehradská 120
☎ 224 547 776; www.radostfx.cz

### Reduta
Jazz is played in the city's oldest music club. In 1994, former US President Bill Clinton spontaneously took part in a session on a saxophone.
✚ 209 D5 ✉ Národní třída 20
☎ 224 933 487; www.redutajazzclub.cz
Ⓜ Národní trída

### Smetana Hall (Smetanova síň)
Home to the Prague Symphony Orchestra, this hall is a work of art in its own right – the music too!
✚ 206 C2 ✉ Náměstí Republiky 5
☎ 222 002 101, 222 002 336 (tickets); www.fok.cz

### State Opera House (Státní opera Praha)
Verdi operas and ballet feature on the programme of this neo-Classical establishment (➤ 160) as do experimental works by the music theatre.
✚ 209 F5 ✉ Wilsonova 4
☎ 224 227 266, 296 117 111; www.opera.cz

## FILM

Most of the cinemas in the district can be found on Wenceslas Square or Na příkopě. Try Palace Cinemas in **Slovanský dům** (Na příkopě 22) for Hollywood releases or see current cinema listings in *Prague Post*.

# Excursions

| | |
|---|---|
| Kutná Hora | 170 |
| Mělník | 175 |
| Terezín | 178 |

## Excursions

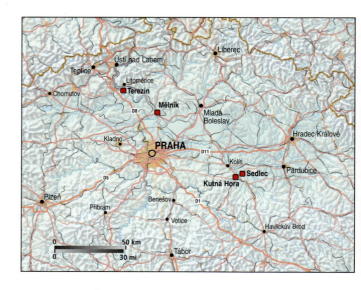

# Kutná Hora

**Kutná Hora's silver mines made this the second most important town in medieval Bohemia and an economic, political and cultural rival to Prague. The silver has gone but not the unique beauty of the great Church of St Barbara where the miners had their own chapel.**

Find out more about the life of a silver miner at the Castle (Hrádek) before donning a helmet and white coat to explore the disused shafts and galleries. At the Italian Court it's time to learn about minting by watching a smithy at work. And don't leave Kutná Hora without enjoying a gruesome thrill in the Cistercian cemetery chapel at Sedlec where the baroque decor is fashioned from human bones.

### Mines and Minting
For more than four centuries, Kutná Hora's fortunes were inextricably linked to the mining of silver for coin making. It was the Cistercian monks at Sedlec who set the town on the road to fame and fortune when, in 1260, they put German miners to work on their estates. Forty years later Václav II of Bohemia issued regulations for the burgeoning industry, a sign of its importance to the national economy. By the 15th century Kutná Hora's silver *groschen* were in circulation throughout Central Europe, the town benefiting from numerous royal privileges, prompting an ambitious building programme. Then, in 1546 disaster struck when the most valuable mine flooded beyond repair. Decline set

# Kutná Hora

in, a fire in 1770 proving to be the final straw. Kutná Hora's magnificent architectural heritage was recognized by UNESCO in 1995 when the town was declared a World Heritage Site.

### Church of St Barbara (Chrám sv Barbora)
Dedicated to the patron saint of miners, this remarkable building is one of the great treasures of the Czech nation. Its dramatic, tent-like silhouette is without parallel in Gothic architecture.

The mining confraternity invited architects working on Prague's St Vitus Cathedral (▶ 90) including Peter Parleř's son, Jan, to supervise construction here in 1380, but the church only assumed its present shape following the intervention of Benedikt Ried (builder of Prague Castle's Vladislav Hall) when work resumed after the Hussite Wars. It was Ried's lofty rib-vaulting that created the need for the roof's fascinating canopy of cones. Much of the church's medieval decoration has survived and you will marvel at the Gothic statuary, altarpieces and frescoes. Don't miss the depictions of minters and silver miners in their respective chapels (Minicířská kaple and Hašplířská kaple).

**The mining magnates paid for the Church of St Barbara from their own pockets**

### Chapel of Corpus Christi (Kaple Božího těla)
Within the grounds of St Barbara is the restored 14th century "cemetery chapel" that originally served as an ossuary (bone chapel) – in deliberate competition with its more

# Excursions

famous counterpart at Sedlec (▶ below). There are excellent views of the town's wooded valley from the terrace.

## Sedlec
The star attraction of Sedlec's former monastery, Panna Maria (St Mary) is the seriously spooky Ossuary (Kostnice) – a place for storing the bones of the dead. In the course of 600 years, the subterranean "bone chapel" accumulated 40,000 skeletons. In 1870 František Rint, a woodcarver by trade, was hired to fashion the bones into bells, a chandelier, chalices and other bizarre decor – even the coat-of-arms of the Schwarzenberg family, former owners of the chapel.

## Jesuit College (Jezuitská kolej)
The baroque facade of the former Jesuit seminary was completed in 1667 by the shock troops of the Counter Reformation. Focus on František Baugut's 18th-century statues of saints, which decorate the adjoining parapet. They were inspired, as you will probably guess, by the sculptures on Prague's Charles Bridge (Karlův most, ▶ 54). Baugut also carved the Plague Column (Morový sloup) which stands in front of the College and dates from 1715. It was a thanksgiving offering following an epidemic that killed 6,000 townspeople.

## Castle (Hrádek)
Once a silver-smelting factory, Kutná Hora's old fortress is now a 🏛 **Mining Museum** and open for guided tours. It stands directly over the medieval 🏛 **mineshafts and tunnels** which are a "must see" providing you're reasonably fit (▶ 174). You'll only visit a small section of the mines, which once covered an area of more than 40km² (15.5mi²). After descending to a depth of 70m (230ft) and experiencing the dank, the cold, the dark and the confinement of the labyrinthine corridors you'll appreciate what life was like for the medieval miner, who operated without a safety helmet and armed only with a pair of hammers and a tiny oil lamp. Working in complete isolation, it would have taken him two or three hours to get to the surface. If fires, explosions and other accidents didn't kill him, respiratory diseases would – average life expectancy was 35.

## Italian Court (Vlašský dvůr)
It was in this graceful building, sensitively restored in the 19th century, that Kutná Hora's *groschen* and *Thalers* were minted, originally under the direction of Florentine

**Statue of a miner in the Italian Court of Kutná Hora**

# Kutná Hora

**Spooky decoration in the Ossuary Sedlec**

masters – hence "Italian" Court. Understandably security was the watchword. Not only was the place heavily fortified with moats and ramparts, the minters even had their own en-suite toilet so they would never have to leave their work unguarded! The guided tour begins at the royal treasury, with its warning over the door "Noli me tangere" (Don't touch me). You're then shown a splendid sequence of royal portraits (the Court was a royal residence after all), a replica workshop, the superb Knight's Hall (Rytíšký sal) and the Royal Chapel, redesigned in Art Nouveau style, but with its original medieval altarpieces intact. At the rear of Vlašský dvůr, the gardens slope down to the Vrchlice River offering a spectacular view across the hillside towards St Barbara.

## Town Squares

The city's two main squares are lined with patrician mansions dating from the 15th to 17th centuries. One you're certain to come across at some point, on the east side of Palackého náměstí is the Sankturinovský dům, a baroque reconstruction of one of the town's oldest houses and now the tourist information office and Alchemy Museum. On the opposite side of the square, look out for a niche containing a beautiful sculpture of the Virgin surrounded by angels, and for the U Stříbného groše bookshop with trademark *groschen* on the outer wall. On Rejskovo náměstí you'll find the Kamenná kašna, a handsomely carved polygonal stone well designed in 1495 by Matyáš Rejsek.

*Insider Tip*

# Excursions

### TAKING A BREAK
**Piazza Navona** (Palackého náměstí 90, tel: 327 512 588) for pizzas made by Italians. Alternatively **U Hrnčiře** on Barborská (tel: 327 512 113), a hotel restaurant with a country pub atmosphere and summer beer garden.

### Tourist Information Offices

**Kutná Hora**
✉ Palackého náměstí 377 ☎ 327 512 378; www.kutnahora.cz
🕐 Apr–Sep daily 9–6; Oct–Mar Mon–Fri 9–5, Sat, Sun 10–4

**Sedlec**
✉ Zámecká 279 ☎ 326 551 049
🕐 April–Sep daily 9–5 Oct–March Mon–Fri 9–4

**Vlašsky dvůr (Italian Court)**
☎ 327 512 873
🕐 Apr–Sep daily 9–6; Mar, Oct 10–5; Nov–Feb 10–4 💰 100Kč

**Hrádek Mining Museum**
☎ 327 512 159 🕐 July–Aug Tue–Sun 10–6; May–June, Sep Tue–Sun 9–6; Apr, Oct Tue–Sun 9–5. Closed Nov–Mar 💰 150Kč

**Ossuary Sedlec**
☎ 326 551 049
🕐 Apr–Sep daily 9–5, Oct–Mar 9–4 💰 60Kč

## INSIDER INFO

- There's so much to see that you'll be hard pressed to cover everything even in a day. Factor in three hours to get there and back, 90 minutes for the mine and one hour at the Italian Court.
- While trains do run to Kutná Hora, the station is in Sedlec, close to the "bone chapel" but a good 45-minute walk to the centre of town.
- Visitors under age 7 or those suffering from claustrophobia, obesity, heart disease or visual impairment may not join the castle mine tour.
- You'll save time at the Italian Court by joining a tour in Czech if no English-speaking guide is on hand. You'll be given a printed summary in English and most of the Czech guides have at least a smattering of the language.

**Getting there:** Kutná Hora is 80km (50mi) from Prague.
**By car:** From behind Národní muzeum (➤ 161) take Vinohradská street east, continuing as Černokostelecká. This becomes Highway 2, signposted Kutná Hora via Kostelec nad Černými lesy, and takes you right into town.
**By bus:** Coaches leave from Florenc bus station, journey time approximately 1 hour 40 minutes. It's then a 15-minute walk into town. Guided tours from Prague to Kutná Hora are offered by **Martin Tour** (224 212 473; www.martintour.cz) and **Gray Line Tours** (224 826 262; www.grayline.com)
**Sedlec:** You'll have to drive or take a taxi the 3km (2mi) to this suburb. The route takes you to Sedlec's former monastery church of Panna Maria (St Mary). Turn left up Zámecká to the Ossuary – you'll find parking nearby.

# Mělník

This historic town offers a rare opportunity to taste home-grown Czech wines in the romantic surroundings of a nicely restored Renaissance castle. Add to this the magnificent view over the vineyards towards the confluence of the Vltava and Labe (Elbe) rivers and you have all the makings of a delightful half-day trip.

### Mělník Castle (Zámek Mělník)
The original Gothic castle was given an extensive makeover during the 16th and 17th centuries when it was transformed into a graceful Renaissance chateau. It was acquired by the Lobkowicz family in 1753, nationalised in 1948 and restored to them in 1992 after the fall of Communism. Pick up the English-language text from the ticket desk and take a self-guided tour of the tastefully decorated rooms, including the Great Hall and the exquisite baroque chapel, originally commissioned by Charles IV's wife, who lived in the castle at one time. On your way out, take a closer look at the arcaded courtyard and the handsome *sgraffiti* on the facades.

### The Cellars
A separate English-language text will help you find your way around the cellars, some of which are up to seven hundred years old. These labyrinthine vaults and passageways cover an area of 1,500m² (16,145ft²) and are linked to a series of tunnels running under Mělník's main squares. The Lobkowicz family uses Princess Ludmila, grandmother of Good King Wenceslas, on their label, even though she lived 500 years before Charles IV brought the first vines here from Burgundy. Today, the Bettina Lobkowicz vinařství

*Mělník Castle stands proudly above its terraced vineyards and the Labe (Elbe) River*

# Excursions

vineyard (www.lobkowicz-vinarstvi.cz) produces two cuvées worth special mention, the white *Lady Lobkowicz* a Müller-Thurgau and Muscat blend, a fruity wine, light yellow in colour and the red of the same name, which is a blend of Blue Portuguese and Zweigelt – to create a deep ruby colour and a bouquet of strawberries. The vineyards also turn out a rosé and a champagne-style bubbly: Château Mělník (www.lobkowicz-melnik.cz). Wine tastings are organized here but you have to join a group tour in Czech only (30–45 mins). If this doesn't appeal, you can sample the wines in the castle restaurant.

**The idyllic location of Mělník on the confluence of the Vltava and Labe (Elbe) makes it a popular choice for boat excursions**

### Church of St Peter and St Paul (Chrám sv Petra a Pavla)
The parish church is Mělník's other major landmark. Look for the side door leading to the Kostnice (Ossuary) where you'll encounter a macabre collection of up to 15,000 human bones, the skeletal remains of medieval plague victims fancifully arranged by a local professor in the early 20th century. When you're done here, climb the 177 steps to the top of the onion-domed belfry (separate entrance and admission charge) for panoramic views as far as Prague on a clear day.

### Prague Tower (Pražská brána)
The last remnant of the town's medieval walls and bastions was rebuilt in 1500. It now houses a contemporary art gallery.

# Mělník

## INSIDER INFO

- The Castle Restaurant is occasionally overrun with tour groups. A quieter alternative may be the excellent U Rytířů hotel just around the corner (Svato Václavská 9, tel: 315 621 440; www.urytiru.cz). The restaurant menu includes wild boar, venison and other game, also river fish – all great value.
- If the Ossuary is locked during opening hours, ask the ticket seller in the church tower to fetch the key. *Insider Tip*
- If you decide to make a day of it, there are boat trips on the Elbe to Mělník (approx. six hours, June–Sep mornings and evenings, 490Kč). You can obtain further details from the tourist office.
- If you only have an hour or so to spare, consider the **Regional Museum** (Okresní muzeum Mělník, Náměstí mírů 54, tel: 315 630 936, Tue–Sun 9–noon, 12:30–5; 50Kč) which has diverting displays on wine-growing, local village life and, more unusually, perambulators (baby carriages).

**Getting there** Mělník is 33km (21mi) from Prague.
**By Car:** From behind Národní museum, drive north on the Wilsonova Freeway through the Holešovice district onto the E55 Expressway and take the Mělník exit onto Highway 9. This leads straight into town on Pražská.
**By Bus:** There's a regular service from Holešovice bus station (adjoining train station). Buy tickets on board (journey time 40 minutes). When you arrive, follow the green signs to the castle (Zámek).

### Festivals
Mělník puts on its glad rags twice a year. The last weekend in September marks the grape harvest with all the fun of the fair, from fire-eaters and sword swallowers to folk music and country dancing. Contact the tourist office for more details. In June the castle hosts the week-long Jiří Lobkowicz International Music Festival with drama and classical music concerts. *Insider Tip*

### TAKING A BREAK
The **Zámecká restaurace** (Castle Restaurant) on the ground floor is the best place to sample the local wines if you're not joining a tasting tour. To make an advance booking, tel: 317 070 154. Restaurant closed Mondays.

---

**Mělník Tourist Information Office**
✉ Náměstí Míru 11
☎ 315 627 503; www.melnik.cz 🕐 Daily 9–5

**Mělník Castle (Zámek Mělník)**
☎ 315 622 108; www.lobkowicz-melnik.cz
🕐 Wine cellar 10–6 (last tour 5)
💰 Castle tour: 100Kč; wine tour with tasting: 1,000Kč

**Ossuary, Church of SS Peter and Paul (Chrám sv Petra a Pavla)**
☎ 315 622 337
🕐 Ossuary: Tue–Sun 10–12:30, 1:15–5 💰 30Kč

## Excursions

# Terezín (Theresienstadt)

**Of all Nazi concentration camps, Terezín was unique. As the propaganda film in the Ghetto Museum makes clear it was a "showcase", intended to convince the outside world (including inspectors from the International Red Cross) that rumours alleging the extermination of the Jews were untrue.**

The reality was different, Terezín was not the "Free Jewish City" of Nazi propaganda but a transit camp where the inmates were held in indescribably squalid conditions before being sent to their deaths at Auschwitz. But through the creative outpourings of its inmates, not least the children's drawings on show in Terezín's museums, it also bears witness to the indestructibility of the human spirit.

### Background

Hapsburg Emperor Joseph II founded Theresienstadt in 1782 as a garrison town, naming it after his mother, Maria Theresa. In October 1941, Reinhard Heydrich, Reich Protector of the German-occupied Czech lands, turned it into a Jewish ghetto. It was to receive, among others, German-Jewish war veterans decorated in World War 1 and the families of prominent Jews – artists, musicians, writers – whose internment elsewhere might arouse international protest. Life was to be as "normal" as possible, with theatre, opera, jazz, puppet shows and painting lessons for the children – there was even a soccer team.

**Of the 140,000 Jews who passed through the camp, 34,000 died**

# Terezín (Theresienstadt)

### Ghetto Museum (Muzeum Ghetta)
At the time of the ghetto, the main museum building was a home for 10- to 15-year-old boys who for two years turned out a clandestine newspaper, *Vedem* (We are Leading) in the attic. You can see some of the artwork produced here in a room on the ground floor. The main exhibition tells Theresienstadt's wartime story in graphic detail but without resorting to pathos. Even so, it is difficult not to be moved by the discarded combs and shaving brushes, the uniforms with the yellow Star of David badges sewn onto the pockets or the rag dolls made by female prisoners for their children.

### Magdeburg Barracks (Magdeburská kasarná)
From 1941 to 1944 this was the headquarters of the Jewish administration, the "self-governing" body that ran the camp under the supervision of the SS. The exhibition is devoted to the creative outpourings of Terezín's cultural elite and includes theatre sets, musical scores, watercolours, poems and magazines, all presented by the Nazis as evidence of "normality" at the camp. The museum also contains a reconstructed women's dormitory with three-tier wooden bunks and some of the prisoners' personal belongings.

### Czechoslovak Army Square (Náměstí Československé armády)
Leaving the Ghetto Museum, the corner building by the park was an SS headquarters. Heading south, beyond the church, was the home where young children painted the pictures now displayed in Pinkasova synagoga (▶ 116–117). On the southeast corner of the square, a shop re-sold clothes confiscated from the inmates' own suitcases.

### Small Fortress and Cemetery (Malá pevnost a hřbitov)
Terezín's secondary fortress is on the opposite side of the river. The road passes to the left of the Jewish Cemetery (Židovský hřbitov), its 2,300 graves dominated by a huge cross and a smaller Star of David. Beyond the cemetery is the old garrison's Malá pevnost (small fortress) which the

---

**IF YOU HAVE MORE TIME**
**The Bohušovice Gate and Columbarium** Three casements in the walls of the main fortress (Bohušovice Gate) were used for storing bodies and conducting funeral services for those who died in the camp. At first, the victims were buried in individual graves in the cemetery, later in mass graves. As early as 1942, however, the mortality rate was so high that a crematorium was opened and the ashes stored in urns in a room known as the Columbariusm. Then, in the last months of the war the fleeing SS guards, fearing their crimes would be discovered by the advancing Soviet forces, ordered the dispersal of the ashes in the river Ohře.

# Excursions

SS used as a concentration camp for political prisoners, mainly Communists, 32,000 in all. The former SS barracks is now used for an exhibition on the history of the prison. Also within the precincts are the hospital block, isolation cells, Commandant's house and execution ground.

### TAKING A BREAK
Options are limited. There is a restaurant in the restored **Hotel Memorial** at náměstí Československé armády 180, on the far side of the barrack square, opposite the Ghetto Museum (tel: 416 783 082; www.hotel-memorial.cz).

View over the Jewish Cemetery at the Small Fortress

---

**Information Office Památnik Terezín (Theresienstadt Memorial)**
✉ Principova alej 304, Terezín
☎ 416 782 225; www.pamatnik-terezin.cz
🕐 Memorial site: April–Oct daily 8–6, Nov–March until 4:30; Crematorium: April–Oct Sun–Fri 10–5, Nov–March until 4; Ghetto Museum: daily 9–6
💰 Combined ticket 210Kč

## INSIDER INFO

- When you arrive at the Ghetto Museum you'll be given a map with your ticket. This is so detailed, it is actually confusing and is best discarded!
- On arrival find out the time of the next English-language showing of the documentary film (▶ below). The theatre is in the basement where there's also a cafe selling soft drinks and a very limited selection of snacks.
- There are toilets in the basement of the Ghetto Museum and in the car park near the Small Fortress (small charge).
- The Ghetto Museum's 20-minute documentary film includes fascinating footage from *Theresienstadt. Ein Dokumentarfilm aus dem jüdischen Siedlungsgebiet (Terezin: A Documentary Film from the Jewish Settlement Area)*, a propaganda film made in 1944 under coercion by Kurt Gerron, a Jewish inmate and actor. Like most of the participants, he was deported to Auschwitz after completion of the film work where he was subsequently murdered.

**Getting there:** While the memorial site is a mere 50km (31mi) from the capital, treat this as a full-day excursion, as you'll need at least four hours to see everything.
**By car:** From Prague, behind Národní museum, drive north on the Wilsonova freeway through Holešovice onto the E55 expressway and take the exit for Roudnice onto Highway 8. Past Roudnice, follow signs to Terezín.
**By bus:** Buses leave Holešovice bus station (journey time 45 mins, buy ticket on board). Buses return to Prague from the blue bus stop (zastávka 1) on the main square. For guided tours with transportation, try **Martin Tour** (tel: 224 212 473; www.martintour.cz) or **Gray Line** (tel: 224 826 262 www.citytours.cz).

# Walks

| | |
|---|---|
| 1 On and Off the Royal Route | 182 |
| 2 Castle Hill | 186 |
| 3 Malá Strana | 190 |

# Walks & Tours

## 1 ON AND OFF THE ROYAL ROUTE
*Walk*

> **DISTANCE** 1.6km (1mi)   **TIME** 2 hours
> **START POINT** Metro náměstí Republiky ✚ 206 C3
> **END POINT** Novotného lávka, corner of Smetanovo nábřeží (Smetana Embankment) ✚ 205 F2

Start out where the kings paraded through Staré Město (Old Town), but then, unlike the monarchs of old (and most tourists), slip away from the main streets down the back lanes and along their covered passages. Without missing at least a glimpse of the monuments, you'll explore the heart of Staré Město along its medieval byways. Interesting enough by day, this walk is even more fun at night.

### ❶–❷

From Náměstí Republiky metro station, cross the square to the grand **Municipal House** (Obecní dům, ▶ 146) and walk around it to the left to the medieval **Powder Tower** (Prašná brána, ▶ 160). This is the last of 13 gates that used to guard the entrance to the Old Town. The ornately carved 19th-century facade pretties up what was once a store for black gunpowder.

### ❷–❸

From the west side of the gate tower, start out on the Royal Route (královska cesta) along **Celetná** street (▶ 70). This modern shopping street is also one of the town's most ancient – in English it would be Baker Street, Celetná referring to makers of medieval *calty* bread. (However, beware that the arcaded passages between and through the old Gothic-turned-baroque buildings here made great getaways for pickpockets working the crowds at the king's parade.)

On the right, at No 27, if it's open, duck through the arcade to peek into old Templova Street and duck back again to cross Celetná, passing the cubist **House of the Black Madonna** (dům U černé Matky Boží) on the west corner, south into Ovocný trh (the former Fruit Market).

# On And Off The Royal Route

**3-4**

At the far end of Ovocný trh is the rear entrance of the **Estates Theatre** (Stavovské divadlo, ➤ 65), famous as the venue for the premiere of Mozart's Don Giovanni and where today opera singers are still seen wandering around in 18th-century tunics over a pair of jeans. Round the front of the theatre, cut over to the right past the **church of St Havel** to stroll through Havelská street market (➤ 47) and back. Most of the market has now been given over to souvenir stands, but you can still find some fruit or small items to snack on during the walk. Return past the Church of sv Havel (not an ancestor of the President, but St Gall, a 6th-century Irish monk) to the redbrick **Karolinum** (➤ 70). The university's illustrious rebels include Jan Hus and Franz Kafka. Turn left on narrow

**The Old Town Square is the perfect place to stop for a break**

# Walks & Tours

Kamzíkova through either of the two covered passages back into Celetná.

## 4-5

Cross Celetná and bear to the right, past the south side of **Church of Our Lady Before the Týn** (chrám Matky Boží před Týnem, ➤62), onto Štupartská, passing on the left the charming little Hotel Ungelt. Turn left on Malá Štupartská, leading to an archway into **Ungelt Court** (➤63) on the left and, on the right, the baroque portal of the gothic church of **St James** (kostel sv Jakub, ➤69).

## 5-6

Back on Malá Štupartská, turn left at the bend into Týnská Street with two fine remodelled Gothic houses: on the right, Renaissance at No 6, **House of the Golden Ring** (dům U zlatého prstenu, ➤69) and baroque across the street at No 7. At the Týn Church (➤62), the street narrows into Týnská ulická, lined by souvenir vendors, which leads between the House of the Stone Bell and the old Týn School to the Old Town Square (Staroměstské náměstí, ➤58).

## 6-7

Walk left through the Týn School's Gothic arcade. On the south side of Old Town Square, the ornate stepgabled Storch publishing house has a *sgraffito* painting by Mikuláš Aléš of St Wenceslas on a white horse beside the neo-Gothic oriel window. Next door, the **House At the White Unicorn** (dům U bílého jednorožce) was renowned as Berta Fanta's literary salon. Besides rounding up the town's usual literary suspects, Franz Werfel, Max Brod and Franz Kafka, Berta also hosted those masters of science and parascience Albert Einstein and Rudolf Steiner.

Now for a sharp manoeuvre to escape the crowds on Old Town Square. Hurry on past the south side of the **Old Town Hall** (Staroměstská radnice), pausing only to admire the *sgraffito* facade on **The Minute House** (dům U minuty) in the far southwest corner of the square. Then cross Malé náměstí and, shunning the souvenir-hunters milling on Karlova, take a diagonal left on Jalovcová. Cross Husova and turn left into Řetězová.

## 7-8

This is the cobblestoned heart of Old Town's medieval maze. The house at Řetězová 3, **Palace of the Lords of Kunstat und Poděbrady** (dům Pánů z Kunštátu a Poděbrad,

**The painting in Café Slavia shows an absinthe drinker**

**Beautiful sgraffiti decoration adorns the front of *The Minute House***

► 67), is one of the oldest in the city. The museum commemorating its most illustrious resident, King George of Poděbrady, may be of only marginal interest, but it's worth going inside for a peek at the Romanesque vaults down in the basement. This was once the ground floor of what may have been a small town-palace which may date back at least to 1200. Continue west on Řetězová and its prolongation, Anenská. Just before the river, turn left into Anenské náměstí, home of the **Divadlo na zábradlí** (Balustrade Theatre), where the future President Václav Havel worked first as a stage-hand, then resident playwright in the 1960s. Converted from an old warehouse, this hub of Prague's absurdist satirical theatre is now making a comeback.

### 8–9

Back on Anenská and turn left to the embankment road, Smetanovo nábřeží. Cross over to Novotného lávka, a bridge that leads to the old waterworks that is now the **Muzeum Bedřicha Smetany** (Smetana Museum, ► 66).

> **TAKING A BREAK**
> If you feel like breaking the walk in two with an elegant meal, step into Ungelt Court where **Rybí trh** serves fine if expensive seafood (► 74).
>
> The **Smetana Museum** (Muzeum Bedřicha Smetany, ► 66) has a cafe with a beautiful view over the Vltava to the Charles Bridge. At **Café Slavia** (► 162), it's the same view as from the Smetana Museum, with the best of Czech cuisine on the embankment.

# Walks & Tours

## 2 CASTLE HILL
*Walk*

**DISTANCE** 3km (2mi) Time 3 hours
**START POINT** Belvedér (Královský Letohrádek) ✚ 205 E4
**END POINT** Malá Strana Bridge Towers on Charles Bridge ✚ 205 E3

Imagine you are the King or Queen of Bohemia. This visit to your royal domain gets away from Prague Castle to stroll through gardens, around the aristocrats' palaces on Castle Square and over to Hradčany's remaining medieval houses on Nový Svět. From there amble down – the great thing about this hill walk is that it is almost all downhill – past a couple of splendid embassies to Malá Strana's main square. Stop for lunch or continue down to the Charles Bridge. A majestic ramble.

### ❶–❷

The Belvedér entrance to the **Royal Gardens** (Královská zahrada, ➤ 101) is on the south side of the busy Mariánské hradby highway. Cross carefully if getting off at the west-bound tram stop. Walk around the lovely west facade of the 16th-century **Belvedér**. Queen Anna, for whom Ferdinand I built this summer palace (Královský Letohrádek), died before it was completed. If it's playing, listen to the "music" of the

# Castle Hill

Singing Fountain on the Italian-style giardinetto (garden-terrace). Take in the view of the castle, especially the north side of St Vitus Cathedral (➤ 90), which you don't get to see up close.

## 2–3

From the Belvedér's giardinetto, walk west past the long Orangery to the **Jeu de Paume** (Míčovna), where the Habsburgs played real (royal) tennis originally using the palm of the hand (paume) rather than a racquet. Stroll among the almond trees and, in season, the azaleas

**Floral splendour in the Royal Gardens**

and tulips, before leaving the gardens beside the **Lví dvůr** restaurant (Lion's Court, ➤ 103). Turn left onto **Powder Bridge** (Prašný most) over the wooded Jelení příkop (Stag Moat).

## 3–4

Powder Bridge leads to the north gate of the Second Courtyard in the castle precincts (free access). Cross the courtyard to the second exit, **Matthias Gate** (Matyášova brána) leading out of the castle through the first courtyard, where every hour you can watch the **Changing of the Guard** (➤ 84).

> **TAKING A BREAK**
> The chic **U Zlaté hrušky** (At the Golden Pear) is on Nový Svět 3 (➤ 107).

# Walks & Tours

### 4–5
Escape through the castle gates into **Castle Square** (Hradčanské náměstí). Walk left to the ramparts for the view south over Malá Strana and across the Vltava River to Staré Město (Old Town). Continue west along the south side of the square. The adjoining step-gabled **Schwarzenberský palác** (No 2), notable for its ornate *sgraffiti*, for years housed the Military History Museum, but following a long renovation is now the new museum of baroque art. Next door, the hotel in the converted Barnabite convent at No 3 is usually reserved for guests of the President. In the middle of the square, the baroque Plague Column was the work of Ferdinand Brokof, commemorating the victims of 1679.

### 5–6
On the west side of the square is the **Tuscany Palace** (Toskánský palác), which belonged to the Dukes of Tuscany from 1718. Leaving Castle Square on the northwest side, walk towards the 16th-century **Martinic Palace** (Martinický palác). Originally consisting of three Gothic houses, it was redesigned in the Renaissance style.

**Trams trundle across Malostranské náměstí**

### 6–7
Kanovnická curves round to the fine baroque church of **St John**

**Signpost in the Nový Svět (New World Street)**

# Castle Hill

of Nepomuk (kostel sv Jan Nepomucký), one of Kilián Ignác Dienzenhofer's first Prague buildings. Continue north past the church and turn left into **New World Street** (Nový Svět). Nothing American about it, but its charming, brightly painted cottages are a last vestige of Hradčany's medieval quarter – castle-workers' homes that have now been refurbished as smart wine bars and restaurants.

### 7-8

Turn left on Černínská for one of the few uphill stretches on this walk to Loretánské náměstí (Loreta Square). On the right is the monstrous **Černínský palác**, the Foreign Ministry building from which Jan Masaryk fell to his death from an upper window in 1948 (➤ 24) – the circumstances behind his death remain unclear to this day. Directly opposite is the more peaceful **Loreta** pilgrimage sanctuary with Casa Santa, one of the most beautiful architectural monuments to Bohemian Baroque (➤ 109).

### 8-9

At the southern end of Loretánské náměstí, turn left to walk east along Loretánská street just past the south side of Thun-Hohenšteinsky palác on Castle Square and turn right down the Radnické schody stairway. At the bottom of the stairs, leave cobbled Ke Hradu on your left and take the right fork down Nerudova. Past the old Dittrich pharmacy (1821) at No 32, turn right again down the Jánský vršek stairs.

Take another right on Šporkova which bends right to come out in front of the baroque **Lobkovický palác** (➤ 106), housing the German Embassy. To see the palace's splendid rear facade and historic garden (➤ 106), take a left into the Petřín woods and left again on a path leading to the embassy garden's railings.

**View of Little Quarter from Prague Castle**

### 10-11

Retrace your steps to turn right on Vlašská past the German Embassy. This merges into Tržiště, passing in front of the grand **Schörnbornský palác**, off-limits now that it houses the United States Embassy. Kafka had a second-floor apartment there in 1917. Continue on Tržiště to Karmelitská and turn left into the noisy bustle of **Malostranské náměstí** (➤ 104). Here you may choose to have lunch at one of the square's many cafes.

### 10-11

You can complete the walk by going down Mostecká at the southeast corner of the square leading straight to the **Malostranské věž** (Malá Strana Bridge Towers, ➤ 106) at the entrance to **Charles Bridge** (Karlův most, ➤ 54), a delightful walk on a pleasant evening.

# Walks & Tours

## 3  MALÁ STRANA
*Walk*

**DISTANCE** 3km (2mi)  **TIME** 2–3 hours (including funicular railway)
**START POINT** Strahov (Pohořelec tram-stop) ✚ 204 A3
**END POINT** Malostranská Metro ✚ 205 E4

This Left Bank walk mixes town and country. South of the Strahovský klášter (Strahov Monastery), head through the refreshing greenery of Petřín Hill, and then make your way down by the funicular railway to Malá Strana's riverside mansions and the different world of peaceful Kampa Island. End the walk with the bonus of Malá Strana's lovely terraced gardens, Kolovratská, Ledeburská and Pálffyovská.

### 1–2

From the tram-stop, cross through the gated entrance to **Strahov Monastery** (Strahovský klášter, ►95), with its magnificent libraries. If you do not want to see the libraries at this particular time, however, keep to the right and leave the monastery again by a doorway in the east wall leading to the orchards and gardens.

The Strahov Monastery's gardens stand at the northern end of **Petřín Hill** (►110). The views over the city are a joy. Make your way along the park's eastern perimeter wall, the so-called Hunger Wall (Hladová zed) that leads south to the unmissable mini-Eiffel Tower, **Rozhledna** (literally "look-out tower") built 60m (197ft) high as a tribute in 1891, just two years after the original in Paris.

### 2–3

East of the "Eiffel" is the irresistible little Bludiště mock-Gothic castle with a **mirror maze** inside. South of the mini-castle, hugging the Hunger Wall, is the church of **St Lawrence** (kostel sv Vavřinec), originally 12th-century Romanesque but given its present baroque form in 1770. The church gives the hill its German name, Laurenziberg. Behind the Hunger Wall is the **rose garden** (Růžový sad, ►110).

### 3–4

Walk past the funicular railway station to the **astronomical observatory** (Štefánikova hvězdárna). This is worth a look inside only at night.

# Malá Strana

### TAKING A BREAK
Have a snack or lunch (good venison and other wild game in season) on the terrace at **Nebozízek** (➤ 112, tel: 257 315 329), high above Malá Strana on a stop of the funicular railway.

Otherwise make your way back to the funicular railway and head downhill. The funicular terminus is at Újezd Street, but you can make a stop at the halfway stage to take in the view or to dine in the restaurant (Taking a Break ➤ above).

**Decorative baroque towers adorn the church of St Lawrence**

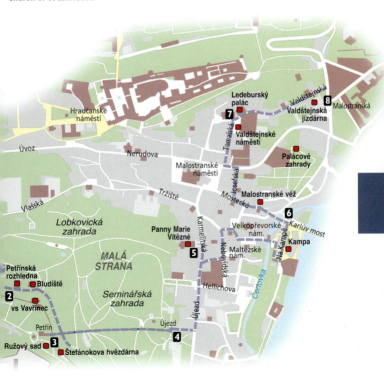

# Walks & Tours

## 4-5

Take the stairs from the funicular terminus and turn left on Újezd. After about 400m, where Újezd merges into Karmelitská, is the astonishing Church of **Panny Marie Vítězné** (➤ 107) on the left. Pilgrims and poets will want to stop in to see the costumed statue of **Infant Jesus of Prague** (Pražské Jezulátko).

## 5-6

Cross Karmelitská and double back to turn west on Harantova, leading to **Maltézské náměstí**. Turn right into Velkopřevorské náměstí, which crosses a bridge onto **Kampa Island** (➤ 107). Turn right on Hroznová, left and right again on Na Kampě to stroll south through the island's riverside park and back north again to climb the stairs from Na Kampě up onto **Charles Bridge** (➤ 54).

**Charming houses on Na Kampé Square, Kampa Island**

## 6-7

You should not miss the **Palace Gardens** (palácové zahrady) either: Continue left to Mostecká and then west through Malá Strana Bridge Gate to Mostecká. Turn right on Josefská, left on Letenská and right on Tomášská to the monumental square of **Valdštejnské náměstí** on which you will find the main entrance of the extended Wallenstein Palace (Valdšteinský palác). On the north side of the square, at Valdštejnské náměstí 3, is the entrance, through Ledeburský Palác, to the three adjacent **Kolovratská**, **Ledeburská** and **Pálffyovská** gardens (➤ 84; April–Oct).

## 7-8

Exit the gardens onto Valdštejnské náměstí and walk east down Valdštejnská road into the courtyard of the Malostranská metro station. Inside the Metro courtyard is the thoroughly renovated **Wallenstein Palace riding school** (Valdštejnská jízdárna), now an art gallery.

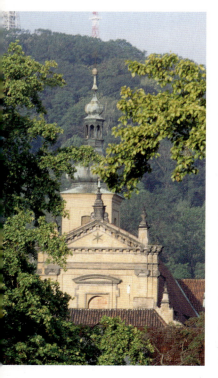

**The tower of the Church of Our Lady of Victory which was rebuilt in 1640**

# Practicalities

| | |
|---|---|
| Before You Go | 194 |
| When You are There | 196 |
| Useful Words and Phrases | 199 |

# Practicalities

## BEFORE YOU GO

### WHAT YOU NEED

- ● Required
- ○ Suggested
- ▲ Not required

Some countries require a passport to remain valid for a minimum period (usually at least six months) beyond the date of entry – check beforehand.

| | UK | USA | Canada | Australia | Ireland | Netherlands |
|---|---|---|---|---|---|---|
| Passport/National Identity Card | ● | ● | ● | ● | ● | ● |
| Visa (regulations can change – check before booking) | ▲ | ▲ | ▲ | ▲ | ▲ | ▲ |
| Onward or Return Ticket | ▲ | ▲ | ▲ | ▲ | ▲ | ▲ |
| Health Inoculations (tetanus and polio) | ▲ | ▲ | ▲ | ▲ | ▲ | ▲ |
| Health Documentation (► 198, Health) | ○ | ○ | ○ | ○ | ○ | ○ |
| Travel Insurance | ○ | ○ | ○ | ○ | ○ | ○ |
| Driving Licence (national) for car hire | ● | ● | ● | ● | ● | ● |
| Car Insurance Certificate | ● | ● | ● | ● | ● | ● |
| Car Registration Document | ● | ● | ● | ● | ● | ● |

### WHEN TO GO

High season    Low season

| JAN | FEB | MAR | APR | MAY | JUN | JUL | AUG | SEP | OCT | NOV | DEC |
|---|---|---|---|---|---|---|---|---|---|---|---|
| 0°C | 1°C | 7°C | 12°C | 18°C | 21°C | 23°C | 22°C | 18°C | 12°C | 5°C | 1°C |
| 32°F | 34°F | 45°F | 54°F | 64°F | 70°F | 73°F | 72°F | 64°F | 54°F | 41°F | 34°F |

☀ Sun   🌤 Sun & Showers   🌧 Wet & Windy   ☁ Cloud

Temperatures are the **average daily maximum** for each month. Prague has a temperamental climate, with some summers sunny and warm, but others rainy and cool. Winters are normally cold with a good deal of snow, but recent winters have been relatively warm and rainy. If **good weather** is the decisive factor, May and June and then September and October are the best times to go – but on the principle that there is no such thing as bad weather, just bad clothing. If you go prepared, Prague's winter snow can be great, with the concert and opera seasons at their height.

If you want to **avoid the crowds** that can make life in the city centre really uncomfortable, mid-March to mid-April, with the exception of Easter weekend, and October are the best times to go.

### GETTING ADVANCE INFORMATION

**Websites**
- ■ PIS (► 36)
  www.praguewelcome.cz
- ■ Prague Daily Monitor:
  www.praguemonitor.com

**In Prague**
PIS Staroměstská radnice
(Old Town Hall) Staré Město
☎ 224 373 162, 224 372 423

**In Australia**
Czech Embassy
8 Culgoa Circuit
O'Malley
ACT 2606 Canberra
☎ 02 6290 0006; www.mzv.cz

# Practicalities

## GETTING THERE

**By Air From the UK** Several airlines operate daily flights from London's major airports and gateways across the UK to Prague Airport. Flag carriers **British Airways** (UK: 08 444 930 787; www.britishairways.com) and **CSA** (Prague: 239 007 007; www.csa.cz) offer several departures daily. Budget carriers like **EasyJet** (www.easyjet.com) offer regular departures to Prague from London's Stansted and Gatwick airports. **CSA** (www.csa.cz) and budget carrier **Ryanair** (www.ryanair.com) have regular nonstop service from Dublin to Prague.

**From North America** CSA (www.csa.cz) operates flights from New York's JFK and Newark airports in association with Delta. Delta Airlines (888 750 3284; www.delta.com) offers regular nonstop service from Atlanta to Prague.

**From Australia** There is no nonstop service to Prague from Australia. Travellers are advised to book through a leading European gateway like London, Paris, or Amsterdam.

**Discount Flights** Prague is a leading destination for budget carriers from the United Kingdom and across Europe. Some of the leading budget airlines that serve Prague include Ryanair, EasyJet, Sky Europe, Smart Wings and German Wings.

**By Train** From London's St Pancras International Station, take a 10am or 1pm train through the Channel Tunnel on **Eurostar** (tel: 08 705 186 186; www.eurostar.com) via Brussels, then on to Cologne for the overnight train, arriving in Prague around 8am.

**By Bus** Frequent service from London Victoria, **Eurolines** (tel: 08 705 143 219 – reservation fee applies; www.eurolines.com – no reservation fee) takes about 20 hours to Prague's Florenc bus station

## TIME

The Czech Republic is on Central European Time (CET), one hour ahead of GMT, six hours ahead of New York and nine hours ahead of Los Angeles, with Daylight Savings Time operating generally (but variably) from April to October.

## CURRENCY AND FOREIGN EXCHANGE

**Currency** is the Czech crown, *koruna Česká* (Kč). Coins come in denominations of 1, 2, 5, 10, 20 and 50Kč, notes 50, 100, 200, 500, 1,000 and rarely 2,000 and 5,000Kč. Czech plans to join the eurozone have been shelved until at least 2012.

**Exchanging Money:** It is well worth comparing rates before you change any currency: exchange offices, travel agencies and hotel receptions often charge very high rates.

**Travellers' cheques** are a safe way to carry money. Most shops and hotels will not accept cheques, meaning you will have to cash them in advance at banks. Just about any major branch will cash them with proper ID.

**Credit cards** are accepted at practically all hotels and most restaurants and shops in the main tourist areas.

**Exchange** You'll find ATM (cash-dispenser; Czech.: *bankomat*) machines everywhere.

## CZECH TOURIST OFFICES: WWW.CZECHTOURISM.COM

**In the UK**
Czech Tourism Great Britain
13 Harley Street
London W1G 9QG
☎ 020 7631 0427

**In the USA**
Czech Tourism USA
1109 Madison Avenue
New York, NY 10028
☎ 212/288-0830, ext 101

**In Canada**
Czech Tourism Canada
2 Bloor St West, Suite 1500
Toronto, Ontario M4W 3E2
☎ 416 363 9928;

# Practicalities

## WHEN YOU ARE THERE

### NATIONAL HOLIDAYS

| | |
|---|---|
| 1 Jan | New Year's Day |
| Mar/Apr | Easter Monday |
| 1 May | May Day |
| 8 May | National Liberation Day |
| 5 Jul | Saints Cyril and Methodius |
| 6 Jul | Jan Hus Day |
| 28 Sep | Czech Statehood Day |
| 28 Oct | Foundation of Czechoslovak Republic |
| 17 Nov | Velvet Revolution Day |
| 24/25 Dec | Christmas Eve/Christmas Day |
| 26 Dec | St Stephen's Day |

### ETIQUETTE

You can be fined up to 30,000Kč for dropping litter (cigarette ends, gum, wrappers, drink cans etc). Police levy fines on the spot. Drinking alcohol in public, especially around monuments, metro stations and main squares is prohibited. Smoking is banned at bus and tram stops.

### OPENING HOURS

○ Shops
● Offices
● Banks
● Main Post Offices
● Museums/Monuments
● Pharmacies

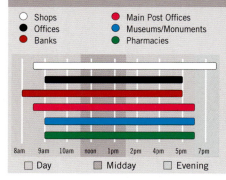

☐ Day  ▨ Midday  ☐ Evening

**Shops** Most open Mon–Fri 9–5, supermarkets and tourist shops close later.
**Offices** Mon–Fri 9–5.
**Banks** Mon–Fri 8–5.
**Post Offices** Mon–Fri 8–6. Stamps are sometimes available at hotel reception and places that sell postcards.
**Museums and Galleries** Tue–Sun 9–5 or 10–6.
**Pharmacies** Usually Mon–Fri 8am–6pm.

### TIPS/GRATUITIES

Tipping is generally expected for all services. As a general guide:

| | |
|---|---|
| Restaurants | Round up to nearest whole (service not included) 10Kč, or 10% |
| Bar service | Round up to nearest 10Kč, or 10% |
| Tour guides | Discretion |
| Taxis | Round up to nearest 10Kč |
| Porters | 50Kč for heavy luggage |
| Chambermaids | 50Kč per night |

### ELECTRICITY

 Power supply is 220 volts AC. UK and North American visitors require an adaptor. North American visitors should bring a voltage transformer for their 110/120-volt appliances.

### TIME DIFFERENCES

**Prague (CET)**
12 noon

**London (GMT)**
11am

**New York (EST)**
6am

**Los Angeles (PST)**
3am

**Sydney (AEST)**
9pm

# Practicalities

## STAYING IN TOUCH

**Post** The main post office is at Jindřišská 14, tel: 221 131 111. Daily 2am–midnight. You'll see orange-coloured letter boxes scattered around town.

**Public Telephones** Almost all public phone boxes in the centre take phone cards only – available from tobacconists, post offices and some newspaper kiosks. Note that there are no area or city codes in the Czech Republic. To dial a local number from within the country, dial the unique 9-digit number. To call a Czech number from outside the country dial the international access code +420 and the nine digit number.

**International Dialling Codes. Dial 00 followed by**
| | | | |
|---|---|---|---|
| UK: | 44 | Republic of Ireland: | 353 |
| USA/Canada: | 1 | Australia: | 61 |

**Mobile providers and services** Eurotel, O₂, T-mobile and Vodaphone are the main service providers. You can buy prepaid SIM cards for all of these providers with credit amounts ranging from 300Kč to 2000Kč; a contract is not necessary. Using a mobile phone in a call shop is far more economical – you'll pay around 2Kč per minute for an international call to the US and EU.

**WiFi and Internet** Average-to-high speed broadband is widely available in cybercafés, bars, restaurants and hotels, with charges ranging from 60–150Kč an hour (sometimes less if you buy a subscription card). Free WiFi connection is increasingly offered in hotels or in cafes and restaurants. You can bring your own laptop with you but if you live in the UK, US or Australia you'll need a European plug adaptor.

## PERSONAL SAFETY

Prague is a safe city by and large with a low level of violent crime. However, theft is commonplace and it's worth taking precautions:

- Leave valuables and important papers in the hotel safe. Carry a photocopy of your passport with you.
- When parking a car, don't leave anything visible. If possible use an underground or guarded car park.
- Pickpockets are especially active on the metro, the 22 tram route, at main railway stations and on crowded streets.
- If you need to report a theft, go to the police station at Jungmannovo náměstí 9 (near Wenceslas Square) where interpreters are available.
- Avoid money changers. Use a bank or ATM.
- Women should avoid Wenceslas Square late at night, because that is where the ladies of the night do their rounds.
- Many streets, especially in the New Town, are poorly lit. If you need to stop or to consult a map, find somewhere conspicuous.

**Police assistance:**
☎ 112 from any phone

| | | |
|---|---|---|
| | EMERGENCY | 112 |
| | POLICE | 112 |
| | FIRE | 112 |
| | AMBULANCE | 112 |

# Practicalities

## HEALTH

**Insurance** Citizens of EU countries receive reciprocal emergency health care with relevant documentation (European Health Insurance Card), but private medical insurance is still advised and essential for all other visitors.

**Dental services** Make sure your health insurance covers dental treatment. Emergency care is at Palackého 5, tel: 224 946 981.

**Weather** Prague is hottest from April to August, although the temperature rarely goes above 23°C (73°F). However, it is worth taking the precaution of applying a good sunscreen if you are out sightseeing, covering up and drinking plenty of fluids.

**Drugs** Take a supply of your own prescription medicines, as you may not be able to find exactly the same in Prague. For general requirements, there is a 24-hour chemist in Na Příkopě 7. A emergency service plan can usually be found in most pharmacies.

**Safe Water** Drinking unboiled tap water is safe. Mineral water is cheap and readily available

## CONCESSIONS

**Students** Holders of an International Student Identification Card (ISIC) are entitled to discounts for public transport, museums, galleries and -theatres.
**Senior Citizens** Senior citizens must produce identity cards proving they are over 70 to obtain discounts on public transport and other facilities.
**Prague Card** The Prague Card (www.praguecard.com; ► 38) provides you with free admission to around 40 sights and enables you to use public transport free of any additional charge (2/3/4 days 880Kč/990Kč/1200Kč). If you buy online at www.praguecitycard.com the card will be delivered to your hotel free of charge.

## TRAVELLING WITH A DISABILITY

Only the newest trams, some Metro stations and two main railway stations (Hlavní nádraží and Nádraží Holešovice) are equipped for wheelchairs. Only since 1994 has there been a law improving access for those with disabilities to all new buildings. Additional information is available at the Prague Wheelchair Association: Benediktská 688/6, Prague; tel: +420 224 826 078, +420 224 827 210 www.pov.cz/en;

## CHILDREN

Some hotels may have a baby-sitting service. Children are generally welcome in restaurants. Special kids' attractions are marked out in this book with the logo shown above.

## RESTROOMS

The cleanest ones are in the major hotels and big cafés.

## CUSTOMS

The import of wildlife souvenirs from rare or endangered species may be illegal or require a special permit.

## EMBASSIES AND HIGH COMMISSIONS

**UK**
☎ 257 402 111

**USA**
☎ 257 022 000

**Canada**
☎ 272 101 800

**Ireland**
☎ 257 011 280

**Australia**
☎ 221 729 260

# Useful Words and Phrases

**Pronunciation:** The Czech language has more accents, especially on consonants, than you may be used to. While you may not get around to learning the language, you may want to know how to pronounce the place names you'll see on signposts and maps.

| | | | | |
|---|---|---|---|---|
| a | as in cat | | q | is pronounced **kv** |
| á | as in bar | | r | is rolled |
| c | as **ts** in **its** | | ř | combines **rolled r** and **zh sound** in **measure** (as in Dvořák) |
| č | as **ch** in **cheap** | | | |
| ch | as **ch** in **loch** | | | |
| d' | as in **duration** | | š | as **ss** in **mission** |
| e | as in **elf** | | t' | as **t** in **overture** |
| é | as **ea** in **wear** | | u | as **ou** in **could** |
| ě | as **ye** in **yell** | | ú and ů | as **oo** in **soon** |
| i | as in **kit** | | w | is pronounced **v** |
| í | as **ie** in **belief** | | y | as **i** in **kit** |
| j | as **y** in **yellow** | | ý | as **ie** in **belief** |
| ň | as **ni** in **opinion** | | ž | as **zh sound** in **measure** |

## SURVIVAL WORDS AND PHRASES

yes / no **ano / ne**
please **prosím**
thank you **děkuji**
sorry **pardon**
hello **ahoj (formal: dobrý den)**
goodbye **na shledanou**
good morning **dobré ráno**
goodnight **dobrou noc**
good evening d **obrý večer**
excuse me **promiňte**
help! **pomoc!**
open **otevřeno**
closed **zavřeno**
today **dnes**
tomorrow **zítra**
yesterday **včera**
day **den**
week **týden**
month **měsíc**
year **rok**
Monday **pondělí**
Tuesday **úterý**
Wednesday **středa**
Thursday **čtvrtek**
Friday **pátek**
Saturday **sobota**
Sunday **neděle**
small / large **malý / velký**

quickly **rychle**
slowly **pomalu**
hot / cold **horký / studený**
left / right **nalevo / napravo**
straight ahead **přímo**
entrance **vchod**
exit **východ**
where? **kde?**
when? **kdy?**
why? **proč?**
here / there **tady / tam**
near / far **blízko / daleko**
bank **banka**
post office **pošta**
art gallery **galerie**
church **kostel**
garden **zahrada**
library **knihovna**
museum **muzeum**
tourist information **turistické informace**
foreign exchange **směnárna**
credit card **kreditní karta**
how much? **kolik?**
cheap **levný**
expensive **drahý**
free (no charge) **zdarma**
more / less **více / méně**
Do you speak English? **Mluvíte anglicky?**

## NUMBERS

| | | | | | |
|---|---|---|---|---|---|
| 1 | **jeden** | 11 **jedenáct** | 21 **dvacet jedna** | 80 | **osmdesát** |
| 2 | **dva** | 12 **dvanáct** | 22 **dvacet dva** | 90 | **devadesát** |
| 3 | **tří** | 13 **třináct** | 23 **dvacet tři** | 100 | **sto** |
| 4 | **čtyři** | 14 **čtrnáct** | 24 **dvacet čtyři** | 1,000 | **tisíc** |
| 5 | **pět** | 15 **patnáct** | 25 **dvacet pět** | 2,000 | **dva tisíce** |
| 6 | **šest** | 16 **šestnáct** | 30 **třicet** | 5,000 | **pět tisíc** |
| 7 | **sedm** | 17 **sedmnáct** | 40 **čtyřicet** | 1,000,000 | **milión** |
| 8 | **osm** | 18 **osmnáct** | 50 **padesát** | | |
| 9 | **devět** | 19 **devatenáct** | 60 **šedesát** | | |
| 10 | **deset** | 20 **dvacet** | 70 **sedmdesát** | | |

# Useful Words and Phrases

## GETTING AROUND

aeroplane **letadlo**
airport **letiště**
train **vlak**
train station **nádraží**
Metro station **stanice**
bus **autobus**
bus station **autobusové nádraží**
tram **tramvaj**
bus/tram stop **zastávka**
pleasure steamer **parník**
ticket **lístek**
single / return **jednosměrná / zpáteční**
first / second class **první / druhá třída**
ticket office **pokladna**
seat reservation **místenka**

## ACCOMMODATION

hotel **7hotel**
room **pokoj**
I would like a room **potřebuji pokoj**
single / double **jednolůžkový / dvoulůžkový**
for one night **na jednu noc**
How much per night? **kolik stojí jedna noc?**
reservation **rezervace**
breakfast **snídaně**
toilet **záchod/WC**
bath **koupelna**
shower **sprcha**
cold / hot water **studená / teplá voda**
towel **ručník**
soap **mýdlo**
room number **číslo pokoje**
key **klíč**

## SHOPPING

bakery **pekárna**
bookstore **knihkupectví**
butcher **řeznictví**
pharmacy **lékárna**
grocery **potraviny**
supermarket **samoobsluha**

## EATING

restaurant **restaurace**
coffee house **kavárna**
pub **hospoda**
wine bar **vinárna**
table **stůl**
menu **jídelní lístek**
fixed-price menu **standardní menu**
the bill **účet**
wine list **nápojový lístek**
lunch **oběd**
dinner **večeře**
starter **předkrm**

main course **hlavní jídlo**
dish of the day **nabídka dne**
dessert **moučník/dezert**
waiter / waitress **číšník / servírka**
bon appetit **dobrou chuť**

## MENU READER

**bílé víno** white wine
**bamborovéknedlíky** potato dumplings
**brambory** potatoes
**brokolice** broccoli
**chléb** bread
**cibule** onion
**cukr** sugar
**čaj** tea
**červené víno** red wine
**dort** cake
**grilované** grilled
**houby** mushrooms
**houskové knedlíky** bread dumplings
**hovězí** beef
**hranolky** chips/French fries
**hrašek** peas
**jablko** apple
**jahody** strawberries
**jehněčí** lamb
**kachna** duck
**káva** coffee
**kuře** chicken
**losos** salmon
**maso** meat
**máslo** butter
**minerálka** mineral water
**šumivá** fizzy
**nešumivá** still
**mléko** milk
**mrkvový** carrot
**okurka** cucumber
**párek** sausage/frankfurter
**pečené** roasted
**pepř** pepper
**polévka** soup
**pomeranč** orange
**pomerančový džús** orange juice
**pivo** beer
**světle pivo** lager
**černé pivo** dark beer
**rajské** tomato
**ryba** fish
**rýže** rice
**salát** salad
**smetana** cream
**sůl** salt
**sýr** cheese
**šunka** ham
**vajíčko** egg
**vepřové** pork
**voda** water
**zelenina** vegetables

# Street Atlas

For chapters: See inside front cover

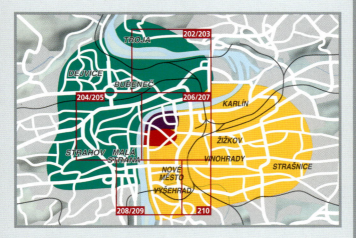

## Key to Street Atlas

| | | | |
|---|---|---|---|
| ℹ | Information | 🚌 | Bus station |
| M̂ | Museum | ✡ | Police |
| 🎭 | Theatre, Opera | ⊕ | Hospital |
| ♟ | Monument, statue | ✉ | Post office |
| ✝ | Church, chapel | 📡 | Television tower |
| ✡ | Synagogue | Ⓜ | Underground with station |
| 📖 | Library | —●— | Tram with stop |
| 🅿 | Car park | —┼— | Rack railway |
| ⚠ | Youth hostel | ★ | TOP 10 |
| ⌇ | Open-air swimming pool | ㉖ | Don't Miss |
| ⌂ | Indoor swimming pool | ㉒ | At Your Leisure |

1 : 11 750

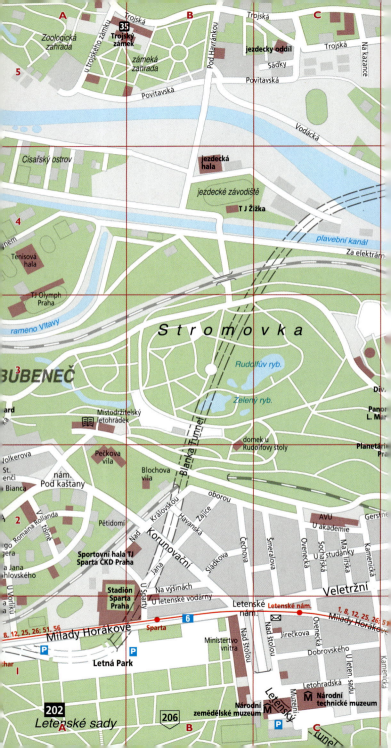

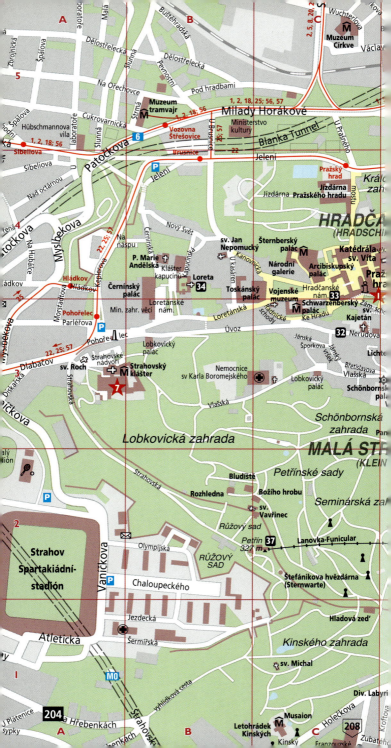

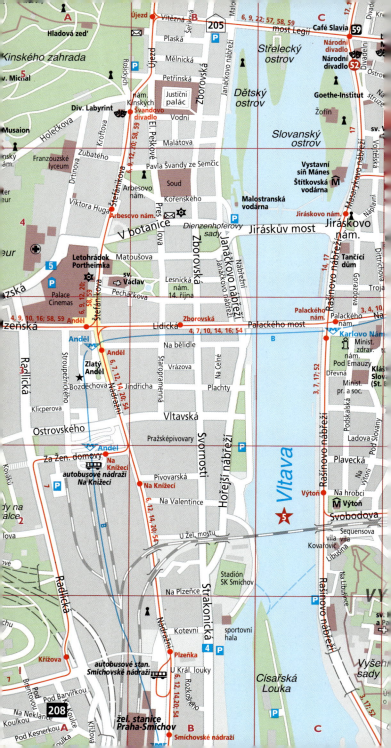

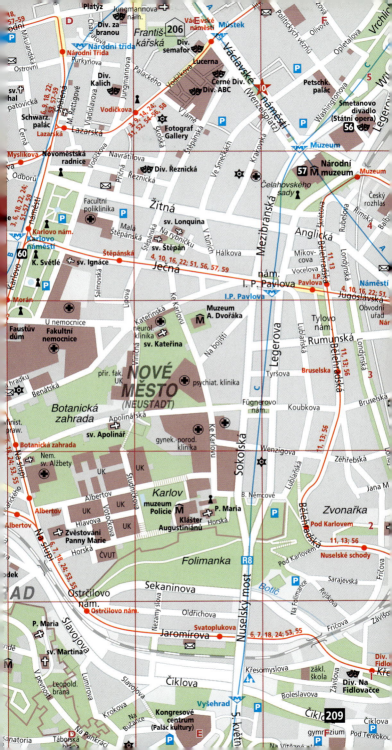

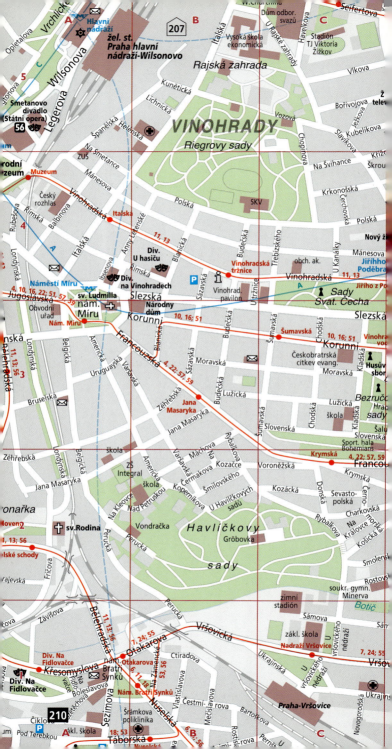

# Street Index

| | | | | | |
|---|---|---|---|---|---|
| 17. listopadu | 206 A3 | Cihelná | 205 E3 | Hradební | 206 C3 |
| 28. října | 206 B2 | Čiklova | 209 E1 | Hroznová | 205 E2 |
| 5. května | 209 E1 | Ctiradova | 210 B1 | Husinecká | 207 F2 |
| | | Cukrovarnická | 204 A5 | Husitská | 207 E2 |
| **A** | | | | Husova | 206 A2 |
| Alšovo nábřeží | 205 F3 | **D** | | Hybernská | 207 D2 |
| Albertov | 209 D2 | Dělostřelecká | 204 B5 | | |
| Americká | 210 A3 | Dittrichova | 208 C4 | **I** | |
| Anenská | 205 F2 | Divadelni | 205 F1 | Ibsenova | 210 A4 |
| Anezská | 206 B4 | Dlážděná | 207 D2 | Italská | 207 E1 |
| Anglická | 209 F4 | Dlabačov | 204 A3 | | |
| Anny Letenské | 210 B4 | Dlouhá | 206 B3 | **J** | |
| Antonínská | 203 E1 | Dobrovského | 202 C1 | Jáchymova | 206 A3 |
| Apolinářská | 209 D3 | Donská | 210 C2 | Jakubská | 206 B3 |
| Arbesovo nám. | 208 B4 | Dražického nám. | 205 E3 | Jalovcová | 206 A2 |
| Argentinská | 203 F2 | Drtinova | 208 A4 | Jana Masaryka | 210 B3 |
| Atletická | 204 A1 | Dušní | 206 B3 | Jana Zajíce | 202 B2 |
| | | Dukelských hrdinů | 203 D2 | Janáčkovo nábř. | 205 E1 |
| **B** | | Dvořákovo nábř. | 206 A4 | Jankovcova | 203 F3 |
| Badeniho | 205 E5 | | | Janovského | 203 E1 |
| Balbínova | 210 A4 | **E** | | Jánský vršek | 204 C3 |
| Bartoškova | 210 B1 | Elišky | | Jaromírova | 209 E1 |
| Bartolomějská | 205 F2 | Krásnohorské | 206 A3 | Ječná | 209 E4 |
| Barvířská | 207 D3 | Elišky Peškové | 205 D1 | Jelení | 204 C4 |
| Bělehradská | 209 F2 | | | Jeruzalémská | 207 D2 |
| Belgická | 210 A3 | **F** | | Jezdecká | 204 B1 |
| Benátská | 209 D3 | Farského | 203 E1 | Jilská | 206 A2 |
| Benediktská | 206 C3 | Francouzská | 210 B3 | Jindřišská | 206 C2 |
| Betlémská | 205 F2 | Franti'ka Křížka | 203 D1 | Jindřicha | 208 B3 |
| Betlémské nám. | 206 A2 | Fričova | 209 F1 | Jiráskův most | 208 C4 |
| Bílkova | 206 B3 | Fügnerovo nám. | 209 E3 | Jiráskovo nám. | 208 C4 |
| Biskupská | 207 D3 | | | Jirečkova | 202 C1 |
| Blanická | 210 B4 | **G** | | Jiřská | 205 D4 |
| Boleslavova | 209 F1 | Gerstnerova | 203 D2 | Jiřské nám. | 205 D4 |
| Bolzanova | 207 D2 | Gogolova | 205 E5 | Jízdárna | 204 C4 |
| Bořivojova | 207 F1 | Gorazdova | 208 C4 | Josefská | 205 D3 |
| Botičská | 209 D2 | | | Jugoslávská | 209 F4 |
| Bozděchova | 208 A3 | **H** | | Jungmannova nám. | 206 B2 |
| Boženy Němcové | 209 E2 | Hálkova | 209 F4 | Jungmannova | 206 B1 |
| Břetislavova | 204 C3 | Harantova | 205 D2 | | |
| Bruselská | 209 F3 | Haškova | 203 D1 | **K** | |
| Bubenská | 203 E1 | Haštalska | 206 B3 | Kamenická | 202 C2 |
| Bubenské nábř. | 207 F5 | Haštalské nám. | 206 B3 | Kamzíková | 206 B2 |
| Budečská | 210 B4 | Havanská | 202 B2 | Kanovnická | 204 B4 |
| Buštěhradská | 204 B5 | Havelkova | 207 F1 | Kaprova | 205 F3 |
| | | Havelská ulička | 206 B2 | Kapucínská | 204 B4 |
| **C** | | Havelská | 206 A2 | Karlův most | 205 E3 |
| Čechův most | 206 A4 | Havířská | 206 B2 | Karlinské nám. | 207 F3 |
| Čechova | 202 B2 | Havlíčkova | 207 D2 | Karlova | 205 F2 |
| Celetná | 206 B2 | Helénská | 210 A5 | Karlovo nám. | 209 D4 |
| Čermakova | 210 B2 | Hellichova | 205 D2 | Karmelitská | 205 D3 |
| Černá | 209 D5 | Heřmanova | 203 D1 | Karoliny Světlé | 205 F2 |
| Černinská | 204 B4 | Hládkov | 204 A4 | Kateřinská | 209 E3 |
| Černomořská | 210 C2 | Hlávkův most | 207 E4 | Ke Hradu | 204 C3 |
| Čestmírova | 210 B1 | Hlavova | 209 D2 | Ke Ítvanici | 207 E3 |
| Chaloupeckého | 204 B2 | Hořejší nábř. | 208 B2 | Ke Karlovu | 209 E3 |
| Charkovská | 210 C2 | Holešovické nábř. | 203 D4 | Keplerova | 204 A4 |
| Charvátova | 206 A1 | Holečkova | 204 C1 | Kinský nám. | 204 C1 |
| Chodská | 210 C3 | Hořejší nábř. | 208 B2 | Klášterská | 206 B4 |
| Chopinova | 210 C5 | Horská | 209 E2 | Kladská | 210 C3 |
| Chotkova | 205 E4 | Hradčanské nám. | 204 C4 | Klárov | 205 E3 |

# Street Index

| | | | | | | |
|---|---|---|---|---|---|---|
| Klimentská | 206 C3 | Ma líř́ska | 202 C2 | Nad diáždénce | 203 F5 | |
| Konviktská | 205 F2 | Malostr. nábř. | 205 E2 | Nad Královskou oborou | 202 B2 | |
| Koperníkova | 210 B2 | Malostranské nám. | 205 D3 | Nad Petruskou | 210 B2 | |
| Korunni | 210 B3 | Maltézské nám. | 205 D3 | Nad štolou | 202 C1 | |
| Korunovační | 202 B2 | Mánesův most | 205 F3 | Nádražní | 208 A3 | |
| Kořenského | 208 B4 | Mánesova | 210 A4 | nám. 14. října | 208 B4 | |
| Kosárkovo nábř. | 205 F4 | Mariánské hradby | 205 D4 | nám. Bratří Synků | 210 A1 | |
| Kostečna | 206 B3 | Mariánské nám. | 205 F3 | nám. Curieových | 206 A4 | |
| Kostelní | 203 D1 | Masarykovo nábř. | 208 C4 | nám. I. P. Pavlova | 209 F4 | |
| Kostnické nám. | 207 F2 | Masná | 206 B3 | nám. Jana Palacha | 205 F3 | |
| Koubkova | 209 F3 | Matoušova | 208 B4 | nám. Kinských | 205 D1 | |
| Kozácká | 210 C2 | Mečislavova | 210 B1 | nám. Míru | 210 A3 | |
| Kožná | 206 B2 | Melantrichova | 206 A2 | nám. Pod Emauzy | 208 C3 | |
| Kozí | 206 B3 | Mělnická | 205 D1 | nám. Pod kaštany | 202 A2 | |
| Krakovská | 209 F4 | Mezibranská | 209 F4 | nám. Republiky | 206 C3 | |
| Králodvorská | 206 C3 | Michalská | 206 A2 | nám. W. Churchilla | 207 E2 | |
| Krásova | 207 F1 | Mickiewiczova | 205 E5 | Náplavní | 208 C4 | |
| Křesomyslova | 209 F1 | Mikulandská | 205 F1 | Náprstkova | 205 F2 | |
| Křižíkova | 207 E3 | Milady Horákové | 202 A1 | Národní | 205 F1 | |
| Křižovnická | 205 F2 | Míšenská | 205 E3 | Navrátilova | 209 D4 | |
| Křižovnické nám. | 205 F2 | Moravská | 210 C3 | Nebovidská | 205 D2 | |
| Krkonošská | 210 C4 | Morstadtova | 204 A3 | Nekázanka | 206 C2 | |
| Krocínova | 205 F2 | most elektr. drány | 203 E4 | Neklanova | 209 D2 | |
| Kroftova | 205 D1 | most Legií | 205 E1 | Nerudova | 204 C3 | |
| Krokova | 209 E1 | Mostecká | 205 D3 | Nezamy slova | 209 E1 | |
| K rotundě | 209 D1 | Muzejní | 206 B5 | Nosticova | 205 D2 | |
| Krymská | 210 C2 | Myslbekova | 204 A4 | Nov. lávka | 205 F2 | |
| Kubelíkova | 210 C5 | Myslíkova | 209 D4 | Nový Svět | 204 B4 | |
| Kunětická | 207 E1 | | | Nuselský most | 209 E1 | |
| | | **N** | | Nuselská | 210 B1 | |
| **L** | | Na baště | 205 E5 | | | |
| Lannova | 207 D4 | Na bělidle | 208 B3 | **O** | | |
| Lazarská | 206 A1 | Na bojišti | 209 F3 | Odborů | 209 D4 | |
| Lázeňská | 205 D3 | Na Florenci | 207 D3 | Oldřichova | 209 E1 | |
| Legerova | 207 D1 | Na Folimance | 209 F2 | Olympijská | 204 B2 | |
| Lesnická | 208 B4 | Na Františku | 206 B4 | Opatovická | 205 F1 | |
| Letenský tunel | 206 B5 | Na hrobci | 208 C2 | Opletalova | 206 C1 | |
| Letenská | 205 E3 | Na Kampě | 205 E2 | Orebitská | 207 F2 | |
| Letenské nám. | 202 B1 | Na Kleovce | 210 A2 | Ostrčilovo nám. | 209 E2 | |
| Letohradská | 202 C1 | Na Kozačce | 210 B2 | Ostrovní | 205 F1 | |
| Libušina | 208 C2 | Na můstku | 206 B2 | Ostrovského | 208 A3 | |
| Lichnická | 207 D1 | Na Moráni | 208 C3 | Otakarova | 210 B1 | |
| Lidická | 208 B3 | Na Ořechovce | 204 A5 | Ovenecká | 202 C2 | |
| Liliová | 205 F2 | Na Opyši | 205 E4 | Ovocný trh | 206 B2 | |
| Lipová | 209 E4 | Na Pankráci | 209 E1 | | | |
| Lodní mlýny | 207 D4 | Na Perštýně | 206 A2 | **P** | | |
| Londýnská | 209 F4 | Na Poříčí | 206 C3 | Palackého most | 208 C3 | |
| Loretánská | 204 B3 | Na příkopě | 206 B2 | Palackého nám. | 208 C3 | |
| Loretánské nám. | 204 B3 | Na rejdišti | 206 A3 | Palackého | 206 B1 | |
| Lublaňská | 209 F2 | Na rybničku | 209 E4 | Panská | 206 B2 | |
| Lumírova | 209 D1 | Na slupi | 209 D2 | Parléřova | 204 A3 | |
| Lužická | 210 C3 | Na Smetance | 210 A4 | Pařížská | 206 A4 | |
| | | Na struze | 205 F1 | Patočkova | 204 A4 | |
| **M** | | Na Ívihance | 210 C4 | Pavla Ívandy ze Semčic | 205 D1 | |
| Máchova | 210 B2 | Na výšinách | 202 B2 | Pecháčkova | 208 A4 | |
| Maiselova | 206 A3 | na valech | 205 D5 | Peckova | 207 F3 | |
| Malá Ítěpánská | 209 D4 | Na Valentince | 208 B2 | Perlová | 206 A2 | |
| Malá Ítupartská | 206 B3 | Na Zámenćké | 210 B1 | Pernerova | 207 F3 | |
| Malátova | 205 D1 | nábř. Edvarda Beneše | 205 F4 | Perucká | 210 A2 | |
| Malé nám. | 206 A2 | nábř. kapitána Jaroše | 206 C4 | Petřinská | 205 D1 | |
| Malého | 207 F3 | nábř. Ludvíka Svobody | 206 C4 | Petrská | 207 D3 | |

# Street Index

| | | | | | |
|---|---|---|---|---|---|
| Petrské nám. | 207 D3 | Sekaninova | 209 E2 | Třebízského | 210 C4 |
| Pevnostní | 204 B5 | Senovážná | 206 C2 | Trocnovská | 207 F2 |
| Pivovarská | 208 B2 | Senovážné nám. | 206 C2 | Trojská | 202 B5 |
| Plachty | 208 B3 | Šeříková | 205 D1 | Truhlářská | 206 C3 |
| Plaská | 205 D1 | Šermířská | 204 B1 | Tržiště | 205 D3 |
| Platnéřská | 205 F3 | Sevastopolská | 210 C2 | Tychonova | 205 D5 |
| Plavecká | 208 C2 | Sezimova | 210 A1 | Tylovo nám. | 209 F3 |
| Plynární | 203 F3 | Šimáčkova | 203 E2 | Týnská | 206 B3 |
| Plzeňská | 208 A3 | Široká | 206 A3 | Tyršova | 209 F3 |
| Pobřežní | 207 E3 | Skořepka | 206 A2 | | |
| Pod Bruskou | 205 E4 | Školská | 206 B1 | **U** | |
| Pod Havránkou | 202 B5 | Škrétova | 209 F4 | U akademie | 202 C2 |
| Pod hradbami | 204 B5 | Škroupovo nám. | 210 C4 | U Bruských kasáren | 205 E4 |
| Pod lisem | 203 E5 | Sládkova | 202 B2 | U Brusnice | 204 B5 |
| Pod Karlovem | 209 F2 | Slavíkova | 207 F1 | U Havíčkových sadů | 210 B2 |
| Pod Slovany | 208 C3 | Slavojova | 209 D1 | Uhelný trh | 206 A2 |
| Pod Vytobnou | 207 F3 | Slezská | 210 B4 | Újezd | 205 D2 |
| Podskalská | 208 C3 | Slovenská | 210 C3 | U Kanálky | 210 C4 |
| Pohořelec | 204 A3 | Slunná | 204 A5 | U kasáren | 204 B4 |
| Politických vězňů | 206 C1 | Šmeralova | 202 C2 | U Král. louky | 208 B1 |
| Polská | 210 B4 | Šmilovského | 210 B2 | Ukrajinská | 210 C1 |
| Povltavská | 202 B5 | Smetanovo nábř. | 205 F2 | U laboratoře | 204 A5 |
| pplk. Sochora | 203 D1 | Smolenská | 210 C2 | U Lanové dráhy | 205 D2 |
| Pres lova | 208 B4 | Sněmovní | 205 D3 | U letenské sadu | 202 C1 |
| Příčná | 209 D4 | Soběslavova | 209 D1 | U letenské vodárny | 202 B1 |
| Prokopská | 205 D3 | Sochařská | 202 C2 | U lužického semináře | 205 E3 |
| Provaznická | 206 B2 | Sokolovská | 207 E3 | Umělecká | 203 D2 |
| Prvního pluku | 207 F3 | Sokolská | 209 E2 | U milosrdných | 206 B4 |
| Purkyňova | 206 A1 | Soukenická | 206 C3 | U nádražní lávky | 207 F3 |
| | | Spálená | 206 A1 | U nemocnice | 209 D3 |
| **R** | | Španělská | 207 D1 | U obecního dvora | 206 B3 |
| Radlická | 208 A3 | Štefánikův most | | U památníku | 207 F2 |
| Radnické schody | 204 C3 | (byv. Švermův most) | 206 C4 | U papírny | 203 E3 |
| Rámova | 206 B3 | Štefánikova | 208 A4 | U Písecké brány | 205 D5 |
| Rašínovo nábřeží | 208 C1 | Šternberkova | 203 E2 | U Prašného | 204 C5 |
| Řásnovka | 206 B4 | Štěpánská | 206 B1 | U Rajské zahrady | 207 E1 |
| Řehořova | 207 E2 | Štupartská | 206 B3 | Uruguayská | 210 A3 |
| Rejskova | 209 F2 | Stříbrná | 205 F2 | U smaltovny | 203 E2 |
| Resslova | 209 D4 | Staré zám. schody | 205 E4 | U Sovových mlýnů | 205 E2 |
| Řetězová | 206 A2 | Staroměstské nám. | 206 B3 | U Sparty | 202 B2 |
| Revoluční | 206 C3 | Staropramenná | 208 B3 | U studánky | 202 C2 |
| Řezáčovo nám. | 203 E1 | Strahovský tunel | 204 B1 | U trojského zámku | 202 A5 |
| Řeznická | 209 E4 | Strahovská | 204 B2 | U výstaviště | |
| Říční | 205 D2 | Strahovské nádvoří | 204 A3 | Partyzánská | 203 E3 |
| Římská | 210 A4 | Strakonická | 208 B1 | U Vltavy | 203 E5 |
| Rostovská | 210 C2 | Strmá | 204 B5 | Úvoz | 204 B3 |
| Rubešova | 209 F4 | Strojnická | 203 D2 | U vršovického nédr. | 210 C1 |
| Rumunská | 209 F3 | Strossmayerovo nám. | 203 E1 | U Žel. mostu | 208 B2 |
| Růžová | 206 C2 | Stroupežnického | 208 A3 | | |
| Rybalkova | 210 C2 | Studničkova | 209 D2 | **V** | |
| Rybná | 206 C3 | Šumavská | 210 C3 | V botanice | 208 B4 |
| Rytířská | 206 B2 | Svobodova | 208 C2 | V celnici | 206 C3 |
| | | Svornosti | 208 B2 | V jámě | 206 B1 |
| **S** | | | | V jirchářích | 205 F1 |
| Salmovská | 209 D4 | **T** | | V kolkovně | 206 B3 |
| Samcova | 207 D3 | Táborská | 210 A1 | V pevnosti | 209 D1 |
| Sámova | 210 C1 | Templová | 206 B3 | V tůních | 209 F4 |
| Sarajevská | 209 F2 | Těšnov | 207 D3 | Václavské nám. | 206 C1 |
| Sázavská | 210 B3 | Těšnovský tunel | 207 D4 | Valdštejnská | 205 E4 |
| Schnirchova | 203 E2 | Thunovská | 205 D3 | Valdštejnské nám. | 205 D3 |
| Seifertova | 207 E2 | Tomášská | 205 D3 | Valentinská | 205 F3 |

213

# Street Index / Index

| | | | | | |
|---|---|---|---|---|---|
| Vaníčkova | 204 A2 | Vnislavova | 209 D2 | **Z** | |
| Varšavská | 210 B3 | Vodácká | 202 C5 | Za elektrárnou | 202 C4 |
| Vejvodova | 206 A2 | Vodičkova | 206 B1 | Zám. schody | 204 C3 |
| Veleslavínova | 206 A3 | Vodní | 205 D1 | Za Poříčskou bránou | 207 E3 |
| Veletržní | 202 C2 | Vojtěšská | 208 C4 | Žatecká | 206 A3 |
| Ve Smečkách | 209 F4 | Voršilská | 205 F1 | Závišova | 209 F1 |
| Velkopřevor. nám. | 205 D3 | Voroněžská | 210 C2 | Za viaduktem | 203 F1 |
| Veverkova | 203 D1 | Votočkova | 209 D2 | Za Žen. domovy | 208 A2 |
| Vězeňská | 206 B3 | Vozová | 207 E1 | Zborovská | 205 D1 |
| Vikářská | 205 D4 | Vršovická | 210 B1 | Zéhřebská | 209 F2 |
| Viktora Huga | 208 A4 | Vratislavova | 209 D2 | Železná | 206 B2 |
| Vinařického | 209 D2 | Vrbenského | 203 F3 | Železničářů | 203 F3 |
| Viničná | 209 E3 | Všehrdova | 205 D2 | Žitná | 209 E4 |
| Vinohradská | 210 A4 | Vyšehradská | 209 D3 | Zlatá ulička | |
| Vítkova | 207 F3 | vyhlídková cesta | 204 B1 | u Daliborky | 205 D4 |
| Vítězná | 205 D1 | | | Zlatnická | 207 D3 |
| Vlašská | 204 B3 | **W** | | Zubatého | 208 A4 |
| Vladislavova | 206 A1 | Washingtonova | 206 C1 | | |
| Vlkova | 207 F1 | Wenzigova | 209 F3 | | |
| Vltavská | 208 B3 | Wilsonova | 207 D1 | | |

# Index

**A**
accommodation 40–44
airports, airport services 36, 195
Anežský klášter 134
apartments 40
architecture 18
Art Nouveau 18–20
Astronomical Clock 60

**B**
Balustrade Theatre 185
Bashevi, Hendel 124
Bazilika sv Jiří 106
beer 30–31
Belvedér 186
Bethlehem Chapel 67
Betlémská kaple 67
Bílá Hora 59, 64
Bílá věž 99
blacklight theatres 78, 168
boat rides 138, 177
Brahe, Tycho 11, 63
Bruno, Giordano 11
Budweiser 30
bus services 36, 38, 195

**C**
cafés 45, 75, 114, 137, 166
Café Slavia 162, 184
car rental 39
Castle Gardens 101–103
Castle Hill 186–189
Castle Square 108, 188
Celetná ulica 70
Ceremonial Hall 130
Čertovka 107
Chamberlain, Neville 15
Changing of the Guard 84, 87, 187
Chapel of Corpus Christi, Kutná Hora 171
Chapel of sv Václav 91
Charles Bridge 54–57, 77, 189
Charles Square 162
children's activities 198
 boat trip on the Elbe 177
 Castle Game, Prague Castle 86
 mineshafts and tunnels, Kutná Hora 172
 Mining museum, Kutná Hora 172
 National Marionette Theatre 78
Petřín park 110
picture puzzle, Jewish cemetery 117
Výstaviště fairgrounds 116
Wax museum 161
Žižkov TV Tower 164
Children's Drawings From Terezín (1942–1944) 126
chrám Matky Boží před Týnem 184
Chrám sv Barbora, Kutná Hora 171
Chrám sv Petra a Pavla, Mělník 176
Church of SS Simon and Jude 138
Church of St Giles 67
cinemas 168
climate and seasons 194
concentration camp, Theresienstadt 178–180

# Index

concessions 38, 87, 198
Convent of St Agnes 134
credit cards 195
Cubist architecture 18
currency exchange 195
custom regulations 198
czech cuisine 44
Czech National Gallery 134

## D
Daliborka 99
Dancing House 145
Decorative Arts Museum 130
Dee, John 12
Defenestration 24–25
dental services 198
Devětsil 162
Devil's Channel 107
disability, travelling with a 198
Divadlo na zábradlí 185
drinking water 198
driving 39
drugs and medicines 198
Dubček, Alexander 17
Dům Pánů z Kunštátu a Poděbrad 67, 184
Dům U bílého jednorožce 184
Dům U černé Matky boží 70, 182
Dům U Dvou slunců 108
Dům U kamenného zvonu 61
Dům U minuty 60
Dům U petržílka 105
Dům U zlatého jednorožce 60
Dům U zlatého prstenu 69, 184
Dvořák, Antonín 27, 158

## E
eating out 72–76, 111–115, 135–137, 165–166
electricity 196
embassies & high commissions 198
emergency numbers 197
entertainment 47, 78, 116, 138
Estates Theatre 65, 183
etiquette 124, 129, 196
Expozice Franze Kafky 133

## F
Faust House 163
Faustův dům 163

FebioFest (film festival) 48
festivals and events 48, 177
food and drink 44–46
  *see also* eating out
  Budweiser 30
  drinking water 198
  Pilsner Urquell 30
Franz Kafka Exhibition 133
Franz Kafka Museum 107

## G
Galerie u Křižovniku 66
Gehry, Frank 145
German Embassy 108, 189
Ginger and Fred 145
Golden Gate 91, 92
Golden Lane 98–100
golem 12
Goltz-Kinský Palace 60
Grand Café Orient 70
Grand Hotel Evropa 149
Granovský palác 63

## H
Havel, Václav 29
health 198
Hebrew clock 132
high commissions & embassies 198
High Synagogue 131
history 14–17, 150
Hitler, Adolf 15
Hodek Apartment House 159
hotels 40
House at the White Unicorn 184
House of the Black Madonna 70, 182
House of the Golden Ring 69, 184
House of the Golden Unicorn 60
House of the Stone Bell 61
House of the Two Suns 108
Hradčanské náměstí 108, 188
Hradčany 116
Hrádek, Kutná Hora 172
Hus, Jan 58, 60, 61, 183

## I
inoculations 194
insurance, health 194
Italian court, Kutná Hora 172

## J
Jalta Hotel 149
Jan Hus Monument 60
Jelení příkop 101
Jesuit College, Kutná Hora 172
Jeu de Paume 102, 187
Jewish community 21–23, 117–200
  *see also* Josefov
Jewish Museum 119
Jewish Town Hall 132
Jezuitská kolej, Kutná Hora 172
Josefov 21, 117–200
Joseph II 22

## K
Kafka, Franz 32–33, 98, 124, 163
Kampa Island 107, 192
Kaple Božího těla, Kutná Hora 171
Karlovo náměstí 162
Karlův most 54–57, 77, 189
Karl von Liechtenstein 104
Karolinum 70, 183
Katedrála sv Víta 90–94
Kelley, Edward 12
Kepler, Johannes 11
King's Garden 101
Klášter sv Anežký České 138
Klášter sv Jiří 106
Klausen Synagogue 131
Klausová synagoga 131
Klementinum 67, 78
Knights of the Cross Square 67
Kostel Panny Marie Před Týnem 62–64
Kostel sv Ignác 162
Kostel sv Šimona a Judy 138
Kostel sv Vavřinec 190
Královská zahrada 101, 186
*králova cesta* 160, 182–185
Křižovnické náměstí 67
Kutná Hora 170–174
  Chapel of Corpus Christi 171
  Chrám sv Barbora 171
  Hrádek 172
  Italian court 172
  Jesuit College 172
  Jezuitská kolej 172

# Index

Kaple Božího těla 171
Mining Museum 172
Old fortress 172
squares 173
St Barbara 171
Vlašský dvůr 172

## L
Libuše 158
Lichtenštejnský palác 104, 116
Liechtenstein Palace 104, 116
Lobkovický palác (Prague Castle) 106
Lobkovický palác (Vlašská ulice) 108
Loreta pilgrimage sanctuary 109, 189

## M
Main Station 36, 163
Maisel, Mordechai 22, 122
Maiselova synagoga 132
Maisel Synagogue 132
Malá Strana 115, 190–192
Malá Strana Bridge Towers 106
Malá Strana Gardens 86
Malá Strana Square 104–105
Malostranské náměstí 104–105
Malostranské věž 106
Maltézské náměstí 192
Mánes Art Gallery 144
markets 47
Martinický palác 109
Masaryk Embankment 144
Masarykovo nábřeží 144
medical treatment 198
Melantrich publishing house 149
Mělník 175–177
 Castle 175
 Chrám sv Petra a Pavla 176
 Prague Tower 176
 Pražská brána 176
 Regional Museum 177
 St Peter and St Paul 176
 wine cellars 175
 Zámek 175
Memorial 77,297 125
Metro 37–38
Mičovna 102
Mining Museum, Kutná Hora 172
Minute House 60

Mirror 110
Morzinský palác 108
Most Legií bridge 145
Mozart, Wolfgang Amadeus 26
Mucha, Alphonse 91, 146, 152, 158
Mucha Museum 152
Muchově muzeu 152
Municipal House 146–147, 182
Museum of Communism 160
Museum of Contemporary Art 110
Museum of Medieval Art in Bohemia and Central Europe 134
music venues 29, 48, 78, 116, 168
Muzeum Bedřicha Smetany 66, 185
Muzeum hlavního města Prahy 164
Muzeum loutkářských kultur 67
Muzeum voskových figurín 161

## N
Nanebezvetí Panny Marie 95
Na Příkopě 160, 167
Národní divadlo 153–156, 168
Národní divadlo marionet 78
Národní muzeum 161
Národní Třída 167
national holidays 196
National Marionette Theatre 78
National Museum 161
National Theatre 153–156, 168
Nazi occupation 15
Nerudova 108
New Castle Staircase 87
Nové Město's town hall 162

## O
Obecní dům 146–147, 182
Obřadní síň 130
Obrazárna Pražského hradu 86
observatory 110
Okresní muzeum Mělník 177
Old Castle Staircase 87

Old fortress, Kutná Hora 172
Old Jewish Cemetery 122–124
Old-New Synagogue 127–129
Old Royal Palace 86, 88
Old Town Hall 59
Old Town Square 58–61, 76
opening hours 47, 196
Our Lady Before the Týn 184
Our Lady of Victory Church 107

## P
Palace Gardens 192
Palace of the Lords of Kunstat und Poděbrady 184
Palác Goltz-Kinských 60
Palác Koruna 151
Palacký Monument 145
palácové zahrady 192
Palais Lobkowitz 106
Panny Marie Vítězné 107, 192
Paradise Garden 103
Paris Boulevard 133, 137
Pařížská třída 133, 137
Parléř, Petr (Parler Peter) 55, 90
Parsley House 105
passports and visas 194
pensions 40
personal safety 197
Peterka House 150
Petřín Hill 110, 190
Pilsner Urquell 30
Pinkasova synagoga 125–126
Pinkas Synagogue 125–126
Platjas
 *see also* beaches
post offices 197
Powder Bridge 101
Powder Tower 160, 182
Prague Autumn Festival 48
Prague Card 38
Prague Castle 84–87
Prague Castle Picture Gallery 86
Prague Municipal Museum 164
Prague Spring 17
Prague Spring Music Festival 48
Prague Symphony Orchestra 147
Prague Tower, Mělník 176

# Index

Prague Writers' Festival 48
Praha hlavní nádraží 36, 163
Prašná brána 160, 182
Pražný most 101
Pražská brána, Mělník 176
Pražský hrad 84–87, 116
Přemysl 158
Presidential Palace 84
public transportation 37–38
pubs and bars 30–31, 74, 113, 136, 166
Puppet Museum 67

**R**
Rabbi Loew (Yehuda Loew ben Bezalel) 13, 22, 122
Rajská zahrada 103
ramparts 102
Regional Museum, Mělník 177
restrooms 198
riding school, Wallenstein Palace 192
Royal Gardens 186
Royal Route 160, 182–185
Rozhledna 110
Rudolf Gallery 84
Rudolf II 10
Rudolfinum 126, 130, 138
Rudolfova galerie 84

**S**
Santa Casa 109
Schörnbornský palác 189
Schwarzenberský palác 108, 188
Sedlec 172
shopping 46–47, 76–77
Slavonic Island 144
Slovanský ostrov 144
Smetana, Bedřich 27, 158
Smetana Hall 147, 168
Smetana Museum 66, 185
Smetanova síň 147, 168
smoking laws 196
Sophie Island 144
souvenirs 138
Španělská synagoga 133
Spanish Synagogue 133
spectator sports 116
Stag Moat 101
St Agnes Convent 138
Staré Město (Old Town) Bridge Tower 55, 57
Staré zámecké schody 87
Staroměstské náměstí 58–61, 76

Staroměstské radnice 59
Staronová synagoga 127–129
Starý královský palác 86
Starý židovský hřbitov 122–124
State Opera House 160, 168
Státní opera Praha 160, 168
Stavovské divadlo 65, 183
St Barbara, Kutná Hora 171
Šternberský palác 109
St George Basilica 106
St George Convent 106
St Havel 183
St Ignatius 162
St James 69
St Lawrence 190
St Nicholas Malá Strana 105
St Nicholas Staré Město 68
St Peter and St Paul, Mělník 176
Strahov Monastery 95–96, 190
Strahovský klášter 95–96, 190
St Roch 95
St Vitus Cathedral 90–94
St Wenceslas Chapel 92
Svatého Jakub 69
Svatého Mikuláš 68

**T**
Tančicí dům 145
Tanec Praha 48
taxis 36, 39
tearooms 45, 75, 114, 166
telephones 197
Terezín 23, 178–180
theatre venues 78, 168
Theresienstadt concentration camp 178–180
Thirty Years War 24–25, 59, 64
Thun-Hohenšteinský palác 108
time differences 195, 196
tipping 196
toilets 198
Toskánský palác 188
tourist information 36, 194
Trade Fair Palace 110
train services 36, 195
trams 38
Trojský zámek 109
Tuscany Palace 188

Týn Church 62–63
Týn Courtyard 63

**U**
Uměleckoprůmyslové muzeum 130
Ungelt 63, 185
United Islands of Prague 48
useful words and phrases 199–200

**V**
Václavské náměstí 148–151
Valdštejnská jízdárna 192
Veletržní palác 110
Velvet Revolution 17, 29
Villa Kovařovic 159
Villa Troja 109
Virgin Mary of the Assumption 95
Vítkov Hill 164
Vladislav Hall 86, 88
Vladislavský sál 86, 88
Vlašský dvůr, Kutná Hora 172
Vltava Embankment 144–145
Vyšehrad Castle 157–159
Vyšehrad Cemetery 157
Vyšehradský hřbitov 157
Vysoká synagoga 131

**W**
Wax Museum 161
Wenceslas 148
Wenceslas Monument 148
Wenceslas Square 148–151, 167
White Mountain 59, 64
White Tower 99
WiFi 197
wine 45
wine cellars, Mělník 175
World War I 14
World War II 15

**Z**
Zahrada na valech 102
Zahrady 101–103
Zámecké schody 87
Zámek Mělník 175
Zappa, Frank 26, 29
Židovská radnice 132
Žižkovský vysílač 164
Žižkov TV Tower 164
Zlatá ulička 98–100
Žofín ostrov 144

# Picture Credits

**AA/C Sawyer:** 10/11, 19, 56, 71, 108, 110, 120, 142, 153, 185, 192

**AA/J Smith:** 63, 68, 118, 130, 133, 144, 145, 149, 152, 159, 163, 164, 187, 188 (bottom), 197 (top)

**AA/T Souter:** 59

**AA/J Wyand:** 23, 27, 34 (left), 52, 70, 85, 91, 97, 121, 127, 132, 162, 172, 175, 178, 180, 191, 197 (bottom)

**akg-images:** 24, Archiv Klaus Wagenbach 33, Manuel Cohen 123

**Bildagentur Huber:** Mirau 4, R. Schmid 101, PictureFinders 171

**DuMont Bildarchiv/Peter Hirth:** 7, 8, 20, 32, 55, 58, 61, 98/99, 126, 131, 148, 155

**DuMont Bildarchiv/Rainer Martini:** 13

**DuMont Bildarchiv/Martin Specht:** 22, 28, 31, 184

**Getty Images:** Elan Fleisher 12, Hulton Archive 15, AFP 16, Michael Ochs Archives 150, Maremagnum 173

**laif:** Peter Hirth 30, 93

**mauritius images:** Rene Mattes 89, ib/Matthias Hauser 105

**picture-alliance:** Arco Images 65, Christoph Mohr 176

**all other photos:** AA/S McBride

**On the cover:** huber-images: P.Canali (top), Ronald Schlager/The New York Tim/NYT/Redux/laif (bottom), Getty Images (background)

# Credits

1st Edition 2016

Worldwide Distribution: Marco Polo Travel Publishing Ltd
Pinewood, Chineham Business Park
Crockford Lane, Chineham
Basingstoke, Hampshire RG24 8AL, United Kingdom.
© MAIRDUMONT GmbH & Co. KG, Ostfildern

**Authors:** Jack Altman, Ky Krauthamer, Christopher Rice, Melanie Rice, Jochen Müssig
**Editor:** Frank Müller, Anja Schlatterer, Anette Vogt (red.sign, Stuttgart)
**Revised editing and translation:** Sarah Trenker, Munich
**Program supervisor:** Birgit Borowski
**Chief editor:** Rainer Eisenschmid

**Cartography:** © MAIRDUMONT GmbH & Co. KG, Ostfildern
**3D-illustrations:** jangled nerves, Stuttgart

All rights reserved. No part of this book may be reproduced, stored in a retrieval system or transmitted in any form or by any means (electronic, mechanical, photocopying, recording or otherwise) without prior written permission from the publisher.

Printed in China

Despite all of our authors' thorough research, errors can creep in. The publishers do not accept any liability for this. Whether you want to praise us, alert us to errors or give us a personal tip – please don't hesitate to email or post to:

MARCO POLO Travel Publishing Ltd
Pinewood, Chineham Business Park
Crockford Lane, Chineham
Basingstoke, Hampshire RG24 8AL
United Kingdom
Email: sales@marcopolouk.com

# 10 REASONS
## TO COME BACK AGAIN

1. In comparison with other leading cities, Prague is still very **good value for money**.

2. The **architecture** of the town is spectacular and is definitely worth a second visit.

3. The **beer** is far too good for one trip to be sufficient to give it the attention it deserves.

4. The **coffee house scene** is so dynamic that there is always something new happening.

5. Last time, there probably wasn't time to enjoy at length the sun on the **Vltava Embankment**.

6. Next summer it would also be fun to rent a **paddle boat** on the Vltava.

7. You need to follow the **Kafka Museum** with the Kafka Tour.

8. **David Černy's** tongue-in-cheek works alone take up one whole day…

9. **Taking a taxi** is so inexpensive that you could leave your car at home next time.

10. In winter, the **Christmas markets** in Prague are also well worth a visit.